POLITICAL SCIENCE AND HISTORY

A BLOOD BORDER

TRIESTE BETWEEN MUSSOLINI AND TITO

POLITICAL SCIENCE AND HISTORY

Additional books and e-books in this series can be found
on Nova's website under the Series tab.

POLITICAL SCIENCE AND HISTORY

A BLOOD BORDER

TRIESTE BETWEEN MUSSOLINI AND TITO

LUISA MORETTIN

nova science publishers
New York

Copyright © 2019 by Nova Science Publishers, Inc.

All rights reserved. No part of this book may be reproduced, stored in a retrieval system or transmitted in any form or by any means: electronic, electrostatic, magnetic, tape, mechanical photocopying, recording or otherwise without the written permission of the Publisher.

We have partnered with Copyright Clearance Center to make it easy for you to obtain permissions to reuse content from this publication. Simply navigate to this publication's page on Nova's website and locate the "Get Permission" button below the title description. This button is linked directly to the title's permission page on copyright.com. Alternatively, you can visit copyright.com and search by title, ISBN, or ISSN.

For further questions about using the service on copyright.com, please contact:
Copyright Clearance Center
Phone: +1-(978) 750-8400   Fax: +1-(978) 750-4470   E-mail: info@copyright.com.

NOTICE TO THE READER

The Publisher has taken reasonable care in the preparation of this book, but makes no expressed or implied warranty of any kind and assumes no responsibility for any errors or omissions. No liability is assumed for incidental or consequential damages in connection with or arising out of information contained in this book. The Publisher shall not be liable for any special, consequential, or exemplary damages resulting, in whole or in part, from the readers' use of, or reliance upon, this material. Any parts of this book based on government reports are so indicated and copyright is claimed for those parts to the extent applicable to compilations of such works.

Independent verification should be sought for any data, advice or recommendations contained in this book. In addition, no responsibility is assumed by the Publisher for any injury and/or damage to persons or property arising from any methods, products, instructions, ideas or otherwise contained in this publication.

This publication is designed to provide accurate and authoritative information with regard to the subject matter covered herein. It is sold with the clear understanding that the Publisher is not engaged in rendering legal or any other professional services. If legal or any other expert assistance is required, the services of a competent person should be sought. FROM A DECLARATION OF PARTICIPANTS JOINTLY ADOPTED BY A COMMITTEE OF THE AMERICAN BAR ASSOCIATION AND A COMMITTEE OF PUBLISHERS.

Additional color graphics may be available in the e-book version of this book.

Library of Congress Cataloging-in-Publication Data

Names: Morettin, Luisa, author.
Title: A blood border : Trieste between Mussolini and Tito / Luisa
  Morettin.
Other titles: Trieste between Mussolini and Tito
Description: New York : Nova Science Publishers, [2019] | Series: Political
  science and history | Includes bibliographical references and index. |
Identifiers: LCCN 2019024810 (print) | LCCN 2019024811 (ebook) | ISBN
  9781536157567 (Hardcover) | ISBN 9781536157574 (Adobe PDF)
Subjects: LCSH: World War, 1939-1945--Territorial
  questions--Italy--Trieste. | Italy--Foreign relations--Yugoslavia. |
  Yugoslavia--Foreign relations--Italy. | Italy--Boundaries--Yugoslavia. |
  Yugoslavia--Boundaries--Italy. | Trieste (Italy)--Politics and
  government--20th century.
Classification: LCC DG499.Y8 M67 2019 (print) | LCC DG499.Y8 (ebook) |
  DDC 940.53/112--dc23
LC record available at https://lccn.loc.gov/2019024810
LC ebook record available at https://lccn.loc.gov/2019024811

Published by Nova Science Publishers, Inc. † New York

This book is dedicated to the memory of Professor Christopher Duggan, *guida e maestro*, who taught me so much when I had the immense privilege of being his doctoral student.

CONTENTS

List of Illustrations		ix
List of Maps		xi
Guide to Pronunciation of Slavic Terms		xvii
Acknowledgements		xix
Introduction		xxi
Chapter 1	Contended Spaces	1
Chapter 2	The Interwar Years	33
Chapter 3	Yugoslavia: War and Occupation	57
Chapter 4	A Journey into Darkness	111
Chapter 5	The Boundary Issue	193
Chapter 6	Anatomy of a Reticence	221
Conclusion		249
Bibliography		265
About the Author		291
Index		293
Related Nova Publications		299

LIST OF ILLUSTRATIONS

Figure 1.	The Narodni Dom (National Hall) of the Slavs in Trieste burnt down by Fascists on 13 July 1920	**185**
Figure 2.	The Italian concentration camp at Gonars, near Udine. It was the first proper civilian camp, especially used for Slovenian political prisoners	**185**
Figure 3.	The Italian concentration camp on the island of Arbe	**186**
Figure 4.	A prisoner at the Italian concentration camp on the island of Arbe	**186**
Figure 5.	Bodies of prisoners at Arbe	**187**
Figure 6.	Entrance to the *foiba* Kevina Jama, in Croatia	**187**
Figure 7.	Entrance to the *foiba* Plutone, near Trieste, Italy	**188**
Figure 8.	Survivors from a Yugoslav concentration camp	**188**
Figure 9.	A survivor from a Yugoslav concentration camp	**189**
Figure 10.	A living skeleton	**189**
Figure 11.	An Italian soldier's helmet found on a heap of human bones, stones and rubble at the bottom of the *foiba* Kevina Jama, Croatia	**190**

x   *List of Illustrations*

Figure 12.   In Gropada, near Trieste, a firefighter discovers
bodies at the bottom of the 146 feet deep local *foiba*   **190**

Figure 13.   Victims exhumed from a *foiba* in 1943   **191**

LIST OF MAPS

Map 1. The Unification of Italy.

xii List of Maps

Map 2. Italy since 1919.

List of Maps xiii

Map 3. The partition of Yugoslavia 1941.

xiv   *List of Maps*

Map 4. The Operational Zone of the Adriatic Littoral.

List of Maps   xv

Map 5. The Morgan Line.

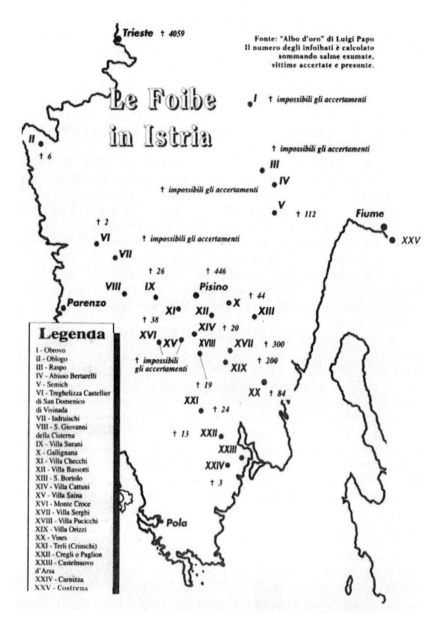

Map 6. *Foibe* in the Istrian peninsula.

GUIDE TO PRONUNCIATION OF SLAVIC TERMS

č - is pronounced as ch in child

ć - is a softly pronounced č

dj - is a softly pronounced dž

dž - is pronounced like a hard j in jungle

j - is pronounced as y in yes

š - is pronounced as sh in shame

ž - is pronounced as zh in measure

To avoid confusion this book uses Italian place names throughout with their Slavic alternative name the first time they are mentioned.

ACKNOWLEDGEMENTS

This book could not have been written without the help of many people. I would like to thank the staff of the *Archivio Centrale dello Stato*; the *Ufficio Storico dello Stato Maggiore dell'Esercito*; the *Archivio Storico del Ministero degli Affari Esteri* in Rome; the *Public Record Office* in Kew and the *Institute of Historical Research* in London for their help. In Rome, I was aided by the *Archivio-Museo Storico di Fiume*, run by Marino Micich and Emiliano Loria. I have benefited enormously from their invaluable knowledge. I was further supported by General Fulvio Capone, who generously provided his expertise on conflicts and shared some of his materials.

Many individuals agreed to speak with me, opening up old wounds and memories. Their painful memories contributed to this research project and helped me to understand the layers of this complex story. This book would not be what it is, without their testimony and reflections.

Whilst at the University of Reading, I taught a course on the Axis Powers during the Second World War. I am profoundly grateful to my colleague, Professor Patrick Major, and students alike for their provocative thoughts on the subject.

My book has been enriched by a number of academic historians, including Professor Guillaume Picketty at Science Po in Paris and Dr Mara Oliva at the University of Reading.

I thank my family for their unconditional love and encouragement throughout the project. In particular my mother and my late father, who always taught me to work hard and stay true to my values. I am indebted to Edson and Alessandro for their continued support and love during the writing of this book. I would also like to thank friends and former colleagues, in particular Lena Montalbano, Jolanta and Colin Watson, Olga Helly, Sabrina Dal Pozzo, and Linda Melaniphy-White.

Finally, I of course take full responsibility for my views and opinions expressed in this book together with any errors, omissions, and infelicities.

INTRODUCTION

Death is not when you cannot communicate,
but when you can no longer be understood.

Pier Paolo Pasolini
Lettere (1940–1954)

Since the end of the Cold War few topics in Italy have had the power to attract more attention, or evoke more emotion for Italians than the *foibe*. The singular form of the word *foiba* comes from the Latin *fovea*, meaning ditch or cave. These are deep natural cavities in the shape of upside-down funnels with narrow openings in the surface, often connected with other caves by corridors, with lakes and rivers sometimes found on the floor of the pits.

The Carso limestone plateau in Venezia Gulia, a geographical area shared by Italy, Slovenia, and Croatia, is scattered with dozens of pits. The first research on the formation of such a landscape was carried out there, hence the definition of the geological phenomenon, *carsismo*, which took the name from this region and was later adopted by other languages.

Over the centuries, *foibe* had been used as dumping sites for many unwanted items, and as hiding places for weapons during wars in this region. Occasionally, they were used as open-air cemeteries to dispose of enemies, and became the final resting place of suicides. Unsurprisingly, people came to consider the pits as synonymous with sinning and evil deeds.

In the past, the presence of these ominous pits became the narrative for folk ballads and legends. In Italian folklore, it was once said that near Trieste, a hideous feudal landowner was flung into a pit because the stab wounds inflicted upon him by a sword had not been sufficient to kill him. His then devilish bones continued to generate misfortune for the people inhabiting the Istrian peninsula, which is part of Venezia Giulia. This became the reason why it was believed that a strange vapour, an evil mist, or a foreboding tragedy emanated from all *foibe*.[1]

People living along the border between Italy and Yugoslavia, interiorised this blood-drenched legend, with one of its most prominent features arising from a Slav superstition. According to Slav folklore, the killing of a black dog could liberate sin from the soul of the assassins. The fact that carcasses of dogs, together with the debris of objects and body parts, were retrieved from the deep graves may be linked to the Slav folk tale.

However, the reason why these chasms received, and are still receiving, much attention is because the *foibe* are a historical fact and a political symbol linked to the irreconcilable forces of the twentieth century: Fascism and Communism. Allegedly, in 1943 and 1945, (and 1944 in order to explain the deaths in Dalmatia, and especially Zara) Communist Yugoslav partisans threw hundreds or possibly thousands of Italians into the pits. Some of them were killed beforehand; others were thrown in alive and left to die slowly in the chasms. The term *foibe* was later extended to include also murders by drowning, and deaths due to illegal deportation, torture, malnutrition, and overwork in forced labour camps across Yugoslavia. More broadly, it has come to mean the gruesome end met by Italians at the hands of Marshal Tito's troops during the Second World War.

---

[1] Carlo Sgorlon, *La foiba grande*, (Milano: Mondadori, 1992), p. 237.

Introduction xxiii

There was awareness of the acts perpetrated, but not at a national level, instead it was limited within a local context, as the contentious issue fuelled political debate during regional political campaigns ahead of elections in Venezia Giulia. In addition, the paucity of academic work on the subject is symbolic of Italy's collective amnesia.

It was the collapse of Communism, made fragile by ideological weariness and economic weakness, and the dissolution of the Eastern Bloc, which brought the *foibe* atrocities to the fore of the Italian political stage after fifty years of neglect. The break-up of Yugoslavia in the 1990s meant the country began reviewing its own communist past and the ideology of Communism in general. As a result, since the mid-1990s the volume of novels and memoirs increased, revealing powerful personal stories, as well as academic literature on the topic.

After the silence of the *foibe* story was broken, an alternative view of the Second World War emerged and with it a whole range of claims and counterclaims on the veracity of the emerging accounts. In Italy, as elsewhere, the post-war period became a time of hope and justice and thanks to the partisans' contribution to the demise of fascism, the new Italy would be built upon the 'values of the Resistance:' the shared ideals of democracy, freedom, and accountability. As a result, the existence of a 'Resistance vulgate' imposed a historiography based on myth, which in turn censored any debate and resulted in a stereotypical version of historical events. For example, it was stated that in the period 1943-1945 there was a 'mass' popular rising against fascism, which however never took place, as the missing Italian Nuremberg demonstrates. In addition, the depiction of the partisans' perfection and bravery was compounded by the claim that in 1945, 'Italians in Venezia Giulia were Fascists who deserved to die.'

The *foibe* killings in Venezia Giulia raised many questions. No matter how barbaric the Fascist's acts were, did they form a basis to indict the whole of Italian civilian population in the region? Perhaps a distinction should be made between whom it was meritorious to kill and whom it was murderous to kill. Does the claim take into account demonstrable individual guilt? Moreover, it should be considered that at the time it was difficult to hold a public position or even get a job without party standing. Should those people considered to be Fascists?

Soon the realm of the public use of history became muddled with ideological interpretations, the emotional resonance linked to the extreme brutality of the *foibe* executions on one side, and the memory of fascist crimes on the other. History was being manipulated by ideology and politics, contributing to heated debates and propagandistic discourses. In the non-academic, yet highly ideological and politicised field of Italian public history, the still sensitive discussion of the 1943-1945 period is portrayed in television programmes and letters to newspaper editors. In such an arena, society tends to make serious, unacknowledged assumptions about events with the inevitable result of a cacophony of voices competing for recognition of the righteousness of their cause. Fact, fiction, myth, emotion, ideological axioms, and unquestioned norms, all coincide to create an unpleasant atmosphere of blame and an outpouring of clichés. It is as if the old power of party propaganda was still altering perceptions of reality and magnifying existing prejudices between the Right and the Left. Sensitivities were hurt and the debate was exacerbated in certain occasions such as, in 2002, when Antonio Baldassarre, the head of the board of directors of the state broadcasting company RAI, advocated that time had come to 'rewrite history' as it was shown on television. 'The old RAI represented only one culture and not others,' he stated, 'Often, they didn't tell real history, but told fables, offered one-sided interpretations.'[2] The fact that the speech was read at the national congress of the right-wing party, *Alleanza Nazionale,* sent out an ominous message of revisionism. Furthermore, at around the same time, Italian Prime Minister Silvio Berlusconi claimed that Mussolini had never killed anyone and that internal exile for dissenters was a sort of 'holiday camp.'[3] According to his narrative, the Duce's positive policy had the trains run on time and the marshes drained in the Lazio region. Understandably, Berlusconi's

---

[2] Alexander Stille, 'Kinder, Gentler Fascism,' *New York Times*, 28 September 2002.

[3] Nick Squires, 'Silvio Berlusconi: 10 memorable gaffes,' *The Daily Telegraph*, 7 November 2008.

Introduction xxv

portrayal of the former dictator as an inspirational leader sparked outrage in Italy.

Nevertheless, the most debated issue in recent years was perhaps the institution of a new memorial day. In March 2004, the centre-right government of Berlusconi instituted the *Giorno del Ricordo* (Memorial Day of Foibe Massacres and Istrian-Dalmatian Exodus) to be held annually on 10 February to commemorate the victims of the *foibe,* and the memory of the forced exodus of 250,000-300,000 Italians from Venezia Giulia. The choice of the date of 10 February is linked to the day when the peace treaty was signed in 1947, thus sanctioning Italy's loss of her eastern territories, the so-called 'unredeemed lands,' which were gained after the First World War. However, the *Giorno del Ricordo* commemoration day is ineptly close to 27 January, the *Giorno della Memoria* (Holocaust Memorial Day), remembering the Holocaust. In Italy, the extermination of Jews was executed with ferocious determination, although it did not reach the same level as the Nazi fanatical, obsessive anti-Semitic hatred and industrial extermination methods.

Every year on the *Foibe* Memorial Day exhibitions, testimonies, and discussions are organised in many cities and towns across Italy, new plaques unveiled, and television documentaries and debates aired. But often the commemorations do not sufficiently contextualise the events they portray, as they fail to present the issue in all its complexities such as the legacy of hatred left by Fascist rule amongst the Slav minority in Venezia Giulia, where a more violent form of fascism took root, and the Italian occupation in the Balkans. Such a lack of perspective provokes animosities that are not conducive to a peaceful confrontation with the past. Many Italians questioned whether the institutionalisation of the *Giorno del Ricordo* was a way to manipulate the traditional memory of the conflict in order to serve dubious ends, such as 'wiping the slate clean.' Could this be a case of historical revisionism? A vile attempt to tarnish the bravery of the liberators? Was this a way to knock the Resistance from its well-deserved pedestal and obliterate its merits?

This book takes the position that the extent of fascist Italianisation of the Slav minority in Venezia Giulia and the brutal occupation of

Yugoslavia (1941-1943) need to be emphasized. An urgent critical appraisal of Italy's fascist past in occupied territories needs to be carried out not in the usual narrow circle of historians and academics, but by the media so that non-specialised audiences can really understand what happened in this region. Italian 'exemplary' punishments, massive transfers of Slavs to internment camps and ruthless counter-insurgency tactics make for shameful reading. To minimise the events would be neither morally honest, nor historically accurate. Furthermore, the values, merits, moral and political importance of the Italian Resistance movement are immense. Not only did it represent a victory of freedom, but it also redeemed the honour of Italy; a vital element for the future as it allowed the country to be accepted back into the international community. The price the Resistance paid for its heroic struggle was high: according to official figures, there were 44,720 deaths among the partisans in the period September 1943 – April 1945.[4]

However, whilst bearing in mind that Fascism and Nazism plunged the world into war and caused the death of millions, this narrative aims to show how the *foibe* killings, like the atrocities carried out by Communism in those countries where it imposed its ideology, were the sign of a regime which, in terms of violent accomplishments, was similar to Fascism. A dictatorship by any other name is still a dictatorship, regardless of the mask they use to conceal their true intentions of taking power by promoting terror and silencing their opponents.

As a result, by revisiting the politically intricate history of Venezia Giulia and of Italo-Yugoslav relations, this book aims to reflect on the following elements. First, the institutionalisation of the Memorial Day exposed a more complex and less heroic version of the post-WWII linear construction, epitomised by the myth of the Resistance, and with it a narrative where episodes are characterised by a not so clear-cut distinction of good and evil. Second, it highlights a re-humanisation of the enemy, which contrasts with the traditional war narrative woven into the very fabric of Italy. Thirdly, it challenges the post-war myth, which was defined

---

[4] Romano Battaglia, *Storia della Resistenza*, (Torino: Einaudi, 1964), p. 662.

Introduction

xxvii

for over half a century by the picture of partisans as knights in shining armour. The story of perfection is easier to understand and to embrace, and easily resonates in the current media culture where there is often no subtle version of history, but everything is either right or wrong. The dangerous result is biased writing and broadcasting, and the wrongful belief in fiction.

However unpalatable the story of the *foibe* killings may be, it illustrates how a chosen memory can distort the historical truth. For some governments, history is not a subject to be treated objectively and with its particular nuances, but rather as a political tool to advance the ideology of the prevailing party. The refugees, whom the author interviewed, are ordinary men and women, who welcomed the Memorial Day's institution as a sign that their ordeals were finally being acknowledged. They did not ask for the superimposition of racial stereotypes against Slavs, nor for the neo-fascist Right to portray them as victims, whose legend set them above their persecutors. They lamented only that their tragedy was neglected both by international diplomatic officials, who ignored them, and their fellow countrymen who, in a fit of collective amnesia about their own very recent Fascist past,[5] labelled them as 'Fascists' and often treated them as pariahs.

It is now realised that many of the survivors were too frightened to describe their accounts, lest authorities and their fellow citizens dismissed their complaints. This led to the marginality, invisibility, and misery of their victimhood being compounded by the anguish of disbelief or indifference. If it is undeniable that the Second World War inflicted deep wounds, in the citizens of Venezia Giulia it also left a bitter awareness that not everybody was equal before the law, but rather, some lives were worth mourning and others are not. It could be argued that in some cases history consists of the lies of the victors.

The purpose of this work is to understand and elaborate upon the complex, entangled causes of the violence in Venezia Giulia. It does not

---

[5] Harold Macmillan, *War Diaries. Politics and War in the Mediterranean, January 1943 – May 1945*, (London: Macmillan, 1984), p. xiv. In his diaries, the British politician Harold Macmillan made this hilarious comment: 'Nobody there [in Italy] could be found who had served Mussolini, nobody admitted to having been a Fascist; and yet it was equally difficult to find anyone who was an active anti-Fascist.'

xxviii   *Luisa Morettin*

aim to belittle the immense self-sacrifice and achievements of the resistance movements in occupied Europe and the rightness of their intentions, nor does it intend to create a hierarchy of grief. It is not, and is not intended to be read as a theory of fascist rehabilitation through the expedient of victimisation at the hands of Tito's partisans, nor does it put a favourable gloss over Italy's brutal invasion and occupation of Yugoslavia. Further, it is not about the rights or wrongs of the Italo-Yugoslav conflict, as trying to assess which genocidal policy has priority 'perpetuates an unsettling and dangerous logic of justification and recrimination.'[6] Rather, the following chapters seek to establish what objectively happened when Italian nationalism clashed with Yugoslav revolutionary Communism, the effects on the Anglo-American policy in the region, and to understand the history of Venezia Giulia in the varying shades of grey, rather than in the black-and-white moralising categories of wartime politics.

Within this study, the exploration of the past reduces the story to a modern territorial contest: two nations, one land, and the attempts to redraw borders in blood, first by Mussolini's army and later by Tito's troops. It is not a morality tale, but simply a complex story set at the intersection between the Second World War and the onset of the Cold War, where Venezia Giulia and Yugoslavia become the symbol of pan-European violence.

The account that follows is an attempt to reconstruct the divisive history of Venezia Giulia by piecing together both the political and diplomatic decisions, the stories of ordinary citizens who were drawn into the tumultuous violence, the thousands of victims caught up in the war, and the dead who cannot speak and who did not receive a proper burial. All crimes of war, whether committed by victims or aggressors, are neither of the Right nor of the Left: they are simply crimes against humanity and as such, historians have the moral and ontological duty to research, narrate, and condemn them. The hope is that this volume will contribute to a deeper

---

[6] Pamela Ballinger, 'Who defines and remembers genocide after the Cold War? Contested memories of partisan massacre in Venezia Giulia in 1943-1945,' in *Journal of Genocide Research*, 2 (1), 2000, pp. 11-30.

Introduction xxix

knowledge of historical facts and restore the sense of humanity for the victims. The reader is invited to read this book with an open mind, free from ideological bias that is deep-seated in some interpretive post-war narrative, whilst bearing in mind that understanding the other side of the historical truth is the only way forward, as a better future is only possible when we refuse to be prisoners of the past.

CONTENT

The period investigated falls into three core phases: first, the years of Fascist rise to power, its harsh Italianisation process of minorities, and Italian crimes in the occupied territories from 1941 until 1943; secondly, the years 1943-1945 with the German occupation of Italy and the violent takeover of power by Communism in Yugoslavia; thirdly, the years 1946 and 1947, the years of the so-called 'peace.'

What triggered the social and political Darwinism in Venezia Giulia was a series of specific steps that cannot be understood without explaining previous historical developments. Therefore, the narrative is not arranged topically, but chronologically, and seeks to place the *foibe* atrocities and their subsequent diplomacy from an Allied perspective.

Chapter 1, 'Contended Spaces,' is concerned with the historical background needed to understand how, and why, violence exploded in twentieth century Venezia Giulia. This chapter outlines the centuries of Italo-Slav tensions in a region located at the intersection of Roman, German, and Slav influences and cohabited by different nationalities. Towards the end of centuries of multi-ethnic Habsburg domination, the idea of nation gained ground and with it, the cultural-conscious communities sought the implementation of the concept of sovereignty. Venezia Giulia thus became the sought-after prize of Italy and Yugoslavia, yet exclusively belonged to no one, whilst existing for everyone in their territorial claims. Trieste, in particular, was the melting pot for diverse cultures and nationalities, but, as this narrative will demonstrate, there is nothing, which makes a location more national than another nationality competing for ownership.

Chapter 2, 'The Interwar Years,' covers the period between 1918 and 1940, when rising Italian nationalism longed for the glories of the past and expressed the need for political change, for new leaders to restore greatness to the nation and traditional values to communities. With this, Italy saw racial and civic nationalism dependent upon extra-national enemies. This chapter aims to illustrate how the discriminatory practices of Fascism turned the native Slav minority of Venezia Giulia into a less valuable ethnic group, labelling them as 'barbaric,' on the grounds of their perceived disloyalty, offering an indication of what was to come, namely the violent aggression shown by Italy toward Yugoslavia in 1941.

Chapter 3, 'Yugoslavia: War and Occupation,' takes the reader into the heart of the combined Italo-German invasion of Yugoslavia in 1941. It provides a survey of the main attacks and victories before the final and brutal breakup and occupation of the Balkan state. Space is given to the Italian Army's wave of terror during anti-partisan reprisal actions against the civilian population seen as potential supporters of the resistance movements, which spread across the country from as early as April 1941. This chapter reveals the true face of Italian occupation in Yugoslavia where military repression verged on a disturbing policy of massacre. The atrocities committed by Mussolini's forces in the Balkans represent the 'dark side' of the Italian war. Yugoslavia suffered enormous destruction of human life and uncountable material damage which, with few exceptions, is often ignored by many Italian historical sources and when it is revealed, it tends to be relegated to the narrow circles of academics and professional historians.

Chapter 4, 'A Journey into Darkness,' parts from the general 'history from above' of the previous (and following) chapters, and offers an opposite perspective 'from the bottom up,' combining the vividness of personal narrative with important questions regarding the nature of events in Venezia Giulia. This chapter describes what happened when the Yugoslavs occupied or liberated, (depending on one's political view), Trieste and Venezia Giulia. From the documents examined, it becomes

Introduction

xxxi

apparent that the magnitude of the crimes committed by Tito's troops was not only due to the violence perpetrated toward victims' bodies, but the impossibility of identifying them and giving them a proper burial. Further, it was the wholesale, indiscriminate use of terror, a psychological weapon of immense power, which became a consistent and coherent strategy in pursuing larger geopolitical aims. Descriptive witness testimony brings the atrocities to life; the hunger, thirst, fatigue of soldiers and prisoners, and the smell of the dying and wounded. It is clear that the foibe killings become the crystallisation point of Tito's policy of expansion through murder.

Closely connected is Chapter 5, 'The Boundary Issue,' which by illustrating the Italo-Yugoslav border disputes, the early Yugoslav claims to Venezia Giulia, and the Anglo-Yugoslav diplomacy surrounding the issue, puts the *foibe* atrocities into a wider, international perspective.

Chapter 6, 'Anatomy of a Reticence,' covers the policy adopted by the Allies toward Belgrade concerning the killings and deportations of Italians in Venezia Giulia. Cabinet papers, ambassador's letters, and meeting minutes all recreate the atmosphere of those frantic months when the illusion of a wartime alliance wore off, and the misperception toward Yugoslav authorities gave way to the realisation that there was a well-articulated expansion plan carried out in the name of the Communist brotherhood. An important note is how and why the Allies failed to respond to the violence that was being carried out right under their noses. The bureaucratisation of diplomacy contributed to the ineffective Allied response toward the suffering of Italian civilians and prisoners of war in Yugoslav camps where people died in droves.

The book ends with a concluding chapter, which draws upon the labels of 'Fascist,' 'Communist,' and 'Partisan,' and the images, which up to this day, evoke strong individual and collective memories for Italians, Slovenes and Croatians. The chapter further examines the current landscape of denial and gathers the loose strands of this violent story.

SOURCES

In order to avoid the danger of biased sources this book analyses mainly the Anglo-American official archival records, which took an impartial stand and provided a detached and authoritative treatment of the subject, not least because the Allies had supported Tito.

More specifically, the author has depended heavily upon internal British Government documents. The British archival collections, which have been examined include the Foreign Office (FO), War Office (WO), Cabinet Office (CAB), Prime Minister Office (PREM) and Admiralty Office (ADM). They all are papers from the vast Public Record Office (PRO) in the United Kingdom. It was not possible to check the Yugoslav archival sources, as the border issue files are still classified. However, the reason for choosing almost exclusively unpublished British sources is justified by the following specific factors. First, as mentioned above, British sources are likely to be fair and reasonably objective given the British help to Marshal Tito. Second, it was because the Soviets were effectively excluded from any power sharing in the Italian theatre of operations, thanks to the manoeuvers of Harold Macmillan, the British Resident Minister at the Allied Forces Headquarters (AFHQ) in Caserta. Third, although the liberation of Italy was nominally a joint Anglo-American effort, the documents signed were originally of British origin and it was Churchill who, having detailed plans for Italy, had urged the invasion of the peninsula. Fourth, after the Casablanca Conference the British insisted on being 'senior partners' in the Italian campaign, and although the Americans imposed a 'joint plan,' London still managed to have a British-run administration of Italy's affairs. Fifth, during armistice negotiations with Italy, it was the British who decided upon the conditions to impose on Italy, producing the idea of co-belligerency. Ultimately, the senior staff and soldiers dealing with civil affairs in Italy in general, and in Venezia Giulia in particular, during the period examined, were mainly British.

It is also important to highlight who, within the narrow circle of British officials, were the decision-makers in the controversial issues regarding

Introduction   xxxiii

Venezia Giulia and Yugoslavia. Although it would seem logical to assume that the British government, and hence the British Parliament, was in charge of deliberating matters of policy, it was in fact the diplomats at the Southern Department of the Foreign Office, in consultation with the Foreign Secretary and the Prime Minister, who were in charge of such decisions. Important contributions also came from the military and the Chiefs of Staff, the Cabinet, and the ambassadors stationed in Rome and Belgrade. Finally, yet importantly, it should be mentioned that basic decisions were taken on the recommendation of the Foreign Research and Press Section of the Foreign Office (FRPS), which wrote many reports influencing foreign policy decisions.

Occasionally, documents from the *Archivio Centrale dello Stato*, the Central Italian Archive, the *Archivio Storico del Ministero degli Affari Esteri*, the Italian Archive of the Ministry of Foreign Affairs, and the *Ufficio Storico dello Stato Maggiore dell'Esercito*, the Archive of the Italian Army General Staff, interviews with and memoirs of Italian survivors have also been used as sources for this study. An integrated reading of Allied and Italian sources – written and oral – yields an astonishing portrait of the extreme brutality in Venezia Giulia and Yugoslavia. In the case of oral witness reports, it is true that personal memories may distort the past due to the time between the action and the narration, and due to the interpretation of hindsight. However, they have the undeniable merit of providing a sample of the wide range of experiences in Venezia Giulia and Italian occupied Yugoslavia, after Italy's capitulation, and give insight into what official documents often miss. As historian John Foot noted, stories need to be told as they make up history. Such an approach illuminates the price of war through the daily grind of terror and the pain of individuals. It allows the bringing of history and the subject together, so the 'ordinary man's' story and his sacrifices are remembered. It is a tribute due to those who were left voiceless and forgotten in unmarked mass graves, pits and at sea. The adoption of this methodology has the merit of drawing attention to the historical and political space in which the crimes were committed. Further, it is motivated by the fact that 'the truth of an action can be seen in the details, in the description of the real scene[s]: this is the viewpoint of the ethnographer who tracks down the material conditions, the bodies' posture, the gestures in real time. Actually ... multiple, crosschecked actions are also verified by the historian who is also after the evidence and for whom one cannot alter the truth of the crime.'[7]

---

[7] Véronique Nahoum-Grappe, 'Anthropologie de la violence extreme: le crime de profanation,' in *Revue internationale des sciences sociales*, 2002/4, n° 174, pp. 601-9.

Chapter 1

CONTENDED SPACES

The origins of Europe were hammered out on the anvil of war.

R. A. Brown
The Origins of Modern Europe

VENEZIA GIULIA THROUGH THE CENTURIES

This complex story takes us further into the past than the twentieth century, when the events recounted in this book took place. To understand the reasons behind the *foibe* massacres in Venezia Giulia and to appreciate the complexity of that intense period of killings, we need to first examine the area's geopolitical location.

Regardless of the shift in sovereignty over the centuries, the region always bordered other countries, so culturally speaking it was the meeting and conflict point of three powers. At the end of nineteenth century, the German and Austro-Hungarian power in the north had conquered the south; the Balkan and Danubian power in the east was pushing towards the west, and the Italian power was driving eastwards.[8] This was caused by the region's incomplete geographical elements, which could not clearly define the parameters of the two adjacent nations of Italy and Yugoslavia. Whilst the Alpine barrier offered such distinct borders and protection by the width and height of the mountain range, in the southern part of Venezia Giulia, it proved weak due to its lesser height than other ranges.

Over time, the detailed sequence of clashing interests and foreign rule in Venezia Giulia went beyond what is detailed in this study, yet there exist certain milestones in its history, which forged its identity, outlook and politics, and which are relevant to understanding its future national concerns.

In Roman times the area was known by the name of *Decima Regio Venetia et Histria*, which was included in the Tenth Italian Region, stretching from the Po River to the Oriental Alps, and from the Oglio River to the Arsa. Before the provinces of Pannonia, Moesia and Dalmatia were conquered, Venezia Giulia was the Empire's eastern outpost against barbarians. Its two major cities, Aquileia and Tergesta (now Trieste), became important trading centres linking central Europe with the Mediterranean.[9] However the same mountain passes in the Karst area, which had allowed Rome to conquer the Danube Basin, later became the route through which floods of barbarian tribes invaded the heart of the Roman Empire.

The first invasion of north-eastern Italy was in 161 A.D., when the tribe of the Marcomanni, under the lead of King Maroboduus who had organised the first confederation of German tribes, infiltrated the Italian peninsula. As cogently noted by Moodie:

> The barbarian invasions of this north-eastern part of Italy left a legacy of disunion and destruction from which the area did not recover fully for over a thousand years. Indeed, it was not until the conclusion of the Great War that the Germans were driven out of Italy. [...] As one result

---

[8] A. E. Moodie, *The Italo-Yugoslav Boundary. A Study in Political Geography*, (London: George Philip & Son, 1945), pp. 16-7.

[9] Gustavo Cumin, *Guida della Carsia Giulia*, (Trieste: Società Alpina delle Giulie, 1929).

Contended Spaces

3

of this unhappy position the history of the region for more than five centuries was marred by wars and political intrigue.[10]

Over time the area became strategically important, not only as a transit point but also as a maritime passage, as the battles for regional control amongst German feudal barons clearly demonstrate.

In 1291 the Istrian coast from Capodistria (Koper) to Rovigno (Rovinij), and from 1420 onwards also the majority of Istria (with the exception of Trieste, Gorizia and Carnia) came under Venetian rule. By the fifteenth century Venice controlled the entire northern part of the Adriatic Sea and set about to subdue the Dalmatian coast, yet without the interior of the Balkans.[11] Such a strategic consolidation of its maritime power was sustained by an expanding navy, which was fundamental for the safety of its seaways to the Levant.

Venice could not have reached its splendour and position without safeguarding its sea routes in the Adriatic, which explains the government's liberal ideas that it used towards its subjects of Venezia Giulia and Dalmatia. Unlike the centralist government established by the rival Austro-Hungarian Empire and Ottoman Empire, the Republic of Venice allowed the subjects of its acquired lands the right to continue with their local institutions provided they did not represent a threat to Venetian monopolistic commercial interests. Consequently, the great merchant power of the Venetians left deep imprints on the coastal towns of Istria and its surroundings, through its architecture, language, culture and the inhabitants' characteristics, traces of which can still be found today. It was this nine hundred year old cultural heritage Italians referred to, at the turn of the twentieth century, when they claimed territory from the Austro-Hungarian Empire for the young Italian national state which was created in 1861.

Unlike the Istrian coast, Trieste entrusted itself to the House of Habsburg in 1382, ending its long rivalry and wars with Venice. This was

---

[10] A. E. Moodie, op. cit., p. 50.
[11] Alvise Zorzi, *La Repubblica del leone,* (Milano: Bompiani, 2001), pp. 46, 53-5, 82.

4   *Luisa Morettin*

also the beginning of a close cultural and financial association with Austria that would last until 1918.

Although from the seventh century onwards Slovenes had penetrated into the region, they were driven back from the coast, which together with the Turkish threat probably helped them 'to retain their ethnic unity' and 'develop the first notion of Slav national consciousness'[12] even before Napoleon Bonaparte's campaigns.

On 17 October 1797 at Villa Manin, the country retreat of the last *doge* Ludovico Manin, France and Austria signed the Treaty of Campoformio – a peace settlement following Napoleon's first Italian campaign. Within the treaty, the French conqueror gave Austria the Venetian territory east of the Adige River, including the city of Venice and its Istrian possessions, marking the end of 1,100 years of Venetian independence. As a consequence, Venezia Giulia became part of the Habsburg monarchy until 1918, a period interrupted only by the Napoleonic period between 1806 and 1813, when it was annexed to the autonomous Illyrian province of the French Empire.

Under the French, and particularly under the rule of the illuminated first governor-general, Auguste Viesse de Marmont, the Napoleonic code and a more modern administration were introduced; roads, schools and universities were built; and for the first time Slovene was added as an official language and was learnt in schools. Although Venezia Giulia's experience of French rule was short, Napoleon's foray into the area had contributed to the evolution of progressive ideas of independence and self-awareness. The main beneficiaries of these developments were the Slavs, which would later impact on frontier disputes when ethnicity equated to territorial sovereignty. However, the French rule came to an end with the Restoration of 1814-1815, which re-established the status quo and awarded the Austrian government the Lombardo-Veneto Kingdom and the whole of Venezia Giulia. The area became known as *Küstenland* (Adriatic Littoral). Such a territorial development determined the presence of a powerful Austrian fleet in the Adriatic Sea, and when Venice and its arsenal were

---

[12] A. E. Moodie, op. cit., p. 78.

Contended Spaces 5

abandoned in 1866, it created the establishment of a strong naval base in Pola (Pula), Croatia.

AT THE TURN OF THE TWENTIETH CENTURY

Trieste became a primary example of the situation in Venezia Giulia. Made a free port by Emperor Charles VI of Habsburg in 1719, under the reign of his daughter, Maria Theresa, the city enjoyed a particularly flourishing era: commercial expansion, rapid urbanisation and an excellent network of rail, sea and road lines earned it the status as one of the most important cities in the empire. Despite several imperial attempts to Germanise it, Trieste managed to preserve its multi-cultural and diverse character thanks to its Italian and expatriate merchants, shipping agents and finance experts, who had adopted Italian as lingua franca.

It was not only a commercial hub, but also a religiously composite and culturally dynamic city that attracted foreign writers and intellectuals. Contemporary English travellers in their observations of city life reported the mixture of 'Italians, Germans, English and Americans, with Greeks and Turks in their national dress.'[13] Despite its dominant Italian culture, Trieste was, throughout the nineteenth and early twentieth centuries, very much a city with European bourgeois social habits, customs and traditions. This was evident in the common practice, amongst upper- and upper-middle classes, of travelling extensively and sending children to complete their education in foreign schools and universities, especially German speaking ones. Instead in the western half of the Istrian peninsula, where most Italians continued their Venetian traditions dating back to the Middle Ages, those who wished to be educated attended the Italian University of

---

[13] Cathie Carmichael, *'Locating Trieste in the Eighteenth and Early Nineteenth Centuries'*, in B. Brumer and Z. Smitek (eds.), *Mediterranean Ethnological Summer School*, (Ljubljana: Slovene Ethnological Society, 1995), pp. 2-11.

6   *Luisa Morettin*

Padua.[14] Such experiences gave them a modern vision of the world and of capitalism.

By 1910, Trieste was the third largest city in the Habsburg Empire after Vienna and Prague. The Austrian census that year showed that its population was 20 to 25 per cent Slavs, who had been attracted to the city by its prosperity and expansion.[15] However, the Austrian census based the concept of nationality on the *Umgangssprache* (everyday language): although a term of reference, it was not a parameter that could provide accurate information. What is interesting to note is that census figures revealed how coastal towns of Venezia Giulia were densely populated by Italians, whereas the countryside was inhabited mainly by the Slav population, which was spread thinly over the inner part of the Istrian peninsula.

The multi-ethnic composition in Trieste did not imply much contact with the surrounding countryside in Venezia Giulia. There were two social groupings: middle and upper classes living in Istrian cities and towns, and peasants, mainly the Slav population, in the country and in remote rural centres. City and town dwellers felt superior to, and had different aspirations from the countryside communities; for a long time the two worlds 'proceeded as if in parallel without ever meeting.'[16] Contact between the two were limited to the Slav presence at markets, or if Slovenians and Croats were hired as labourers and domestic service staff by the upper-middle classes. Whether Slavs worked for the Italian bourgeoisie or remained in the countryside, they were considered and represented as *strati subalterni* (subordinate classes), 'unfit for modern life.'[17] Historian Glenda Sluga, reported how, toward the end of the

---

[14] Dennison I. Rusinow, *Italy's Austria Heritage 1919-1946*, (London: Oxford University Press, 1969), p. 23.

[15] Anna Millo, 'La società triestina agli inizi del Novecento,' in A.A.V.V., *Friuli e Venezia Giulia. Storia del '900*, (Gorizia: Libreria Editrice Goriziana, 1997), pp. 47-8.

[16] Tullia Catalan, 'Trieste: ritratto politico e sociale di una città borghese', in A.A.V.V., *Friuli e Venezia Giulia. Storia del '900*, pp. 13-31.

[17] Robin Oakey, 'Austria and the South Slavs,' in E. Robertson and E. Timms (eds.), *The Habsburg Legacy: National Identity in Historical Perspective*, (Edinburgh: Edinburgh University Press, 1994), p. 53. *The Problem of Trieste and the Italo-Yugoslav Border.*

Contended Spaces

eighteenth century, Johannes Herder defined Slavs as an 'oppressed docile farming people' and Francis Gibbon stated they were 'racially inferior to Germans, savage, and lacking political organization.'[18]

As the social gap was so large, it began to contribute toward a rapidly growing awareness of different cultural and national feelings, which in the final decades of the Habsburg rule increased the possibility of a future upsurge of Slavs wishing to claim an improved status. Indeed, from the 1870s onwards, as a result of the growing industrialisation process, a newly educated and ambitious Slav middle-class settled in Trieste to claim a specific identity. Defying one important city policy in Trieste, which did not allow the establishment of Slovenian schools in the city centre, Slavs established the first Slovene primary school,[19] founded an important press service, called *Edinost* (Unity) and established a network of associations with strong national characteristics.[20] Their ethno-national representation, self-definition, and cultural standing in Venezia Giulia had changed and would never be the same again.

As Slavs became more socially aware and as they made their mark as competitors in the job market, they began to be perceived by local Italians as a menace. This tension between Slavs and Italian nationalists made it quite evident that the forcible union of differing nationalities was now a thing of the past.

IRREDENTISM AND NATIONALISM

The *Risorgimento* and events up to the *Presa di Roma* (capture of Rome) in September 1870 allowed Italy to complete her territorial unity, yet the

---

Difference, Identity, and Sovereignty in Twentieth-Century Europe, (New York: SUNY Press, 2001), p. 15.

[18] Glenda Sluga, *The Problem of Trieste and the Italo-Yugoslav Border. Difference, Identity, and Sovereignty in Twentieth-Century Europe*, (New York: SUNY Press, 2001), p. 15.

[19] Adriano Andri, 'La scuola giuliana e friulana tra Austria e Italia,' in A.A. V.V., *Friuli e Venezia Giulia. Storia del '900*, pp. 205-17.

[20] Tullia Catalan, op. cit., pp. 24-8.

costs of unification were high. The final defeat of the Papal States under Pope Pius IX, who saw Italy as a usurper and called himself a 'prisoner in the Vatican,' triggered the resentment of the papacy who did not recognise the legitimacy of the Italian government. For many years after 1870, Church-State relations were embittered by what became known as the Roman question, which risked alienating the wider Catholic electorate.

Later, in 1882, Italy entered into a defensive alliance with Austria and Germany, which became known as the Triple Alliance. Although the agreement gave Italy a sense of prestige, as she was recognised by the great powers, at the same time it limited the aspirations of those politicians and intellectuals that felt Italian unity was not yet complete. They believed there were still other territories, which had to be won. Both Giuseppe Mazzini, the main theorist of European patriotic movements, and Camille de Cavour, the 'maker of modern Italy,' thought the task of the next generation would be to conquer Istria and Trieste, Dalmatia, the South Tyrol – that is, the area called Trentino-Alto Adige by Italians, - the Ticino, the islands of Malta and Corsica, the cities of Marseilles, Nice and Savoy.[21] Although the latter two cities were the birthplace of the legendary national hero Giuseppe Garibaldi and the Italian royal dynasty respectively, Italy's claims to and the seizing of 'national' lands, occupied a different agenda. It was Venezia Giulia and Trentino-Alto Adige and not the other Italian heritage areas, which were important to Italy.

Unlike what historian Luigi Blanch had written a few decades earlier that 'the patriotism of the Italians is like that of the ancient Greeks, and is love of a single town, not a country,'[22] the Austrian held Italian-populated urban areas, as well as Italian nationalists, supported the cause of Trentino-Alto Adige and Venezia Giulia with their capitals, respectively Trento and Trieste, becoming part of Italy. These areas were what the ex-Garibaldian politician Matteo Imbriani called *terre irredente* (unredeemed lands) and

---

[21] Richard J. Bosworth, *Italy and the Wider World, 1860-1960,* (London: Routledge, 1996), pp. 19-24.

[22] Denis Mack Smith, *Modern Italy. A Political History*, (New Haven and London: Yale University Press, 1997), p. 3.

Contended Spaces

the redemption slogan, which later became the epitome of interventionism in the Great War, was indeed 'Trento and Trieste!'

Irredentism was a major element of Italian history and national consciousness during the late nineteenth and early twentieth century, as it forged foreign policies and it became one of the main reasons for the country's entry into the First World War. Venezia Giulia and Trentino-Alto Adige looked at Italy as a way of stating and preserving *italianità* (Italianness) and thus nurtured a visceral link to the motherland. The Italian crisis of the 1890s; the insufficient economic opportunities in the South where the *latifondo* economy was maintained; employers' oppositions to minister Giovanni Giolitti's programmes, and widespread strikes did not undermine the idealised, anachronistic vision of Italian national greatness of the Italian population in Venezia Giulia. Italy and *italianità* became a seductive, intangible idol, and Trieste, a city both Austrian and Italian or, better, an amalgam of nationalities, was not seen as a contradiction.[23] It did not matter that architecturally Trieste did not look Italian and instead its cityscape was reminiscent of European trends. Rather, it was considered as the city of steamers, insurance companies, and industrial nobility living in splendid buildings; it was a city where the literary legacy left by Trieste's acclaimed writer Italo Svevo coexisted with foreign novelists and poets, such as James Joyce and Rainer Maria Rilke, and where the cult of the Habsburgs, especially of Emperor Franz Josef and his wife Elizabeth, or the tragic story of Archduke Maximilian and Charlotte in their dreamlike Miramar castle, lived next to deep feelings of irredentism.

Historian Diego de Castro claims quite appropriately that within the adverb 'simultaneously' lies the essence of Trieste; a theory supported by Angelo Ara and Claudio Magris who specify that the meaning of the adverb is an 'addition of opposing elements.'

---

[23] See Angelo Ara and Claudio Magris, *Trieste. Un'identità di frontiera*, (Torino: Einaudi, 1982), pp. 200-1. Giorgio Negrelli observes how in Trieste the statue of the beloved Hapsburg Empress Elizabeth, familiarly called Sissi, was erected outside the *Museo del Risorgimento*, which houses the body of irredentist hero and martyr Guglielmo Oberdan. Giorgio Negrelli, 'Trieste nel mito', in Roberto Finzi, Claudio Magris, Giovanni Miccoli (a cura di), *Il Friuli e Venezia Giulia*, (Torino: Einaudi, 2002), p. 1338.

When the regions of Trentino-Alto Adige and Venezia-Giulia advanced their claims to its Italianness, the Italian alliance with Austria started wearing thin. In Trento, a tangible sign of devotion to the Italian Motherland came as early as 1876 when the city paid and erected a monument to Dante Alighieri, author of the *Divine Comedy*, and Italy's most celebrated 'national' writer, who was widely considered as the poet who first showed the way to creating a celebrated Italian country. Minority rights were demanded in Trento and Bolzano.

In Trieste, Minister Giovanni Giolitti tried to influence the victory of Italian representatives in the municipal elections. Venezia Giulia, and its two main cities Trieste and Pola, claimed they could demonstrate their history of Italianness thanks to the supremacy within the literary field of Dante Alighieri and Francesco Petrarca. Petrarca, the Italian Renaissance poet, became the *maestro dell'amor di patria* (master of love for the motherland) and the north-eastern border lands were referred to in Dante's ninth *Canto* of '*Inferno*,' in *The Divine Comedy* (verse 114), where he wrote: '*Sì come Pola presso del Carnaro/che Italia chiude, e i suoi termini bagna*' (to Pola by the Quarnero bay/washing the boundary where Italy ends).

The Irredentist movement started from post-*Risorgimento* territorial discontent amongst middle classes towards the end of the nineteenth century, when the second generation of irredentists advocated the redemption of the Italians retained by the Austro-Hungarian Empire after 1866. In doing so, Italy would fight the fourth and last war of the *Risorgimento*. Under the lead of Menotti Garibaldi, the eldest son of Giuseppe Garibaldi, the movement held a congress in Rome in 1878, where it laid claim to the unredeemed lands and advocated the formation of volunteer battalions to conquer Trentino-Alto Adige. It also gave way to the foundation of political and cultural irredentist associations, such as the *Associazione in pro dell'Italia Irredenta* created in Naples in 1877, which soon had over 500 branches; the association *Giovanni Prati* (1884); the *Pro Patria* (1885); the *Lega Nazionale Italiana* (1891); the *Società Trento e Trieste* (1903) and the *Società Dante Alighieri* founded in 1889, which

Contended Spaces

had the purpose of supporting irredentism by spreading Italian culture, linguistic and national awareness amongst Austria's Italian citizens.[24]

The history of Irredentism is populated by national heroes whose sacrifice seemed reminiscent of greater times. The most famous hero was the Triestine republican Guglielmo Oberdan (1858-1882) who, although born Wilhelm Oberdank, Italianised his name. After an abortive attempt to murder Emperor Franz Josef on a visit to Trieste to celebrate the 500th anniversary of the city's submission to Austrian power, Oberdan was executed on 20 December 1882. If he had been successful in his attempt, Oberdan hoped that the Triple Alliance Treaty, which the Italian King had signed in May of the same year, would be ruined. Despite his failed attempt, he became a famous icon of Italian martyrdom at the hand of Austro-Hungarian ruthlessness, and the episode led the irredentist poet Giosuè Carducci to dub the Habsburg ruler 'Emperor of the Hanged.' Further, within five years of his death, in both Italy and Austria there were forty-nine Oberdan societies founded, that tried to make the dream of liberation from Habsburg rule and unification with the motherland come true.[25]

Narratives of patriotic heroism surround other central figures in Irredentism: Austrian-born Nazario Sauro (1880-1916), Istrian Fabio Filzi (1884-1916), and the more famous Socialist deputy and agitator for the Italian cause, Cesare Battisti (1875-1916), were 'all martyrs of the Italian nation in war.'[26] The activities of the Triestine lawyer and politician Salvatore Barzilai (1860-1939) also played a role in fanning the fire of irredentist feelings. In his political speeches he advocated the sense of national duty towards the unredeemed Italian provinces, and published pamphlets on the subject.[27]

---

[24] Gian Francesco Guerrazzi, *Ricordi d'Irredentismo. I primordi della Dante Alighieri (1881-1894)*, (Bologna: Zanichelli, 1922).

[25] Mark Thompson, *The White War. Life and Death on the Italian Front 1915-1919*, (London: Faber and Faber, 2008), pp. 15-6.

[26] Richard J. Bosworth, *Mussolini*, (London: Arnold, 2002), p. 68.

[27] Raffaele Colapietra, 'Salvatore Barzilai', in *Dizionario Biografico degli Italiani – Vol. 7*, (Roma: Treccani, 1970); available online at http://www.treccani.it/enciclopedia/salvatore-barzilai_(Dizionario-Biografico), accessed 16 November 2013.

12 Luisa Morettin

Although Irredentism was a vigorous proponent of patriotism, its early design showed that it was not an organic movement and sometimes lacked a commonly devised political agenda in which to regain possession of Italian lands. For example, in 1866 Istrians separated their cause from the more complex one that existed in Trieste; Italians from Fiume (Rijeka) joined the irredentist fight late, whilst the Dalmatians often felt excluded.[28] During the Giolittian era, the period between 1901 and 1914, Irredentism grew closer to the appeal of militarism and of ANI, the *Associazione Nazionalista Italiana* (Italian Nationalist Association), which was a movement developed under the influence of activists Enrico Corradini, Giovanni Papini, Luigi Federzoni and others from the national rejuvenation.

Italy's first nationalist association emerged as a reaction to socialism and the mishandlings of the liberal ruling class. It filled a vacuum on the Far Right of the political spectrum, and would later become an important force, eventually merging into the Fascist Party in 1923. Its origins stem both from the Italian defeats at Dogali in 1887 and Adowa in 1896, and the Bosnian crisis in 1908. These defeats triggered a sense of national inferiority in a fragile proletarian state, with subsequent revanchist feelings. As mentioned before, they also led to the awareness that Italy's commitment to the Triple Alliance and to expanding Austria went against national interests. The writer and historical essayist Alfredo Oriani (1852-1909) from Faenza, Emilia-Romagna, little known until after his death, had managed to encapsulate within his works the psychology and frustrations behind the nationalist feelings of a country that wanted to be treated as a great power. Oriani preached national revival and the necessity of restoring Trento and Trieste to Italy, labelling the Triple Alliance pact as the last stage of Italy's political inferiority. Such views were published in the 14 March 1915 issue of Benito Mussolini's newspaper *Il Popolo d'Italia* as an

---

[28] Attilio Tamaro, 'Irredentismo,' *Enciclopedia italiana*, (Roma: Treccani, 1933); available online at http://www.treccani.it/enciclopedia/irredentismo_(Enciclopedia-Italiana)/, accessed 16 November 2013.

Contended Spaces

article titled '*Il monito di Oriani*' (Oriani's Warning), where the future Duce urged the Italian Royal House to fulfil the revolution.

Throughout its history, from 1910 to 1923, ANI remained a fairly small party, yet its imperialist and extreme nationalist ideology, together with ideas on protectionism and productivism, caught the spirit of the times and of the current societal feeling, which were formed around the idea of romantic imperialism and violence over restraint.[29] Early nationalists used the magazines *Il Regno* (1903-1904), *La Voce* (1908-1914), and later local weekly papers such as the *Mare Nostrum* of Venice, the *Grande Italia* of Milan and the *Tricolore* of Turin, to propagate their ideas. A further sign of a new self-conscious and outward-turning nationalism was that by 1911 even moderate newspapers employed nationalist journalists.[30]

Support toward the theories of nationalism and colonial expansion came not just from ordinary educated men, but also from well-established writers who ranged from charismatic, bellicose poet and novelist Gabriele D'Annunzio, to quiet scholars, such as the melancholic poet Giovanni Pascoli, whose famous speech *La grande proletaria si è mossa* (The Great Proletarian Has Stirred) urged the Italian conquest of Libya. His public speech, held in November 1911 at the *Teatro Comunale* in Barga (Tuscany), and printed one week later by *La Tribuna,* espoused the theory of 'proletarian colonialism,' which justified armed conquest as a way of spreading Italian proletarian civilisation. This course of action was considered justifiable by Italy's desire to assert herself as a prestigious actor in international politics, as well as by her grinding poverty and backwardness. That compelled many Italians to migrate as colonial expansion was thought as a means to improve economic and social conditions, especially for the inhabitants of the southern provinces, who lived in desperate conditions. By December 1910, the Nationalists had

---

[29] Alexander J. De Grand, *The Italian Nationalist Association and the Rise of Fascism in Italy*, (Lincoln and London: University of Nebraska Press, 1978), p. 11.

[30] Christopher Clark, *The Sleepwalkers. How Europe Went to War in 1914*, (London: Penguin, 2013), p. 226; Richard J. Bosworth, *Italy, the Least of the Great Powers: Italian Foreign Policy before the First World War* (Cambridge: Cambridge University Press, 1979), p. 44.

14 *Luisa Morettin*

such a broad appeal that they organised the first new Nationalist Congress, under the presidency of the distinguished sociologist Scipio Sighele.

That Italy was a state still in search of a nation could be seen by the incongruity between irredentism and new imperialism. If it was true that ANI's main newspaper *L'Idea Nazionale* demanded 'the immediate repatriation of the Italian-populated territories along the Adriatic coast of the Austro-Hungarian Empire,'[31] which was a foreign policy obviously in open contrast with Italy's existing alliance with Austria, it was also evident that Italian imperialists looked well beyond unredeemed areas toward Africa, thus hinting at a foreign policy tied to that of the Central Powers.

The attitude of Rome's government toward Irredentism was ambiguous. Whilst it formally condemned any manifestation by inflamed nationalists who might have jeopardised Italy's relations with Austria, it never really disavowed the movement. Prime Minister Agostino Depretis became known for dismissing irredentist claims as '*des vieux cancans*'[32] and was fiercely attacked by Benedetto Cairoli, a vocal irredentist speaker.[33] However, once Cairoli became Prime Minister, he came to realise that Italian realpolitik required him to officially repudiate irredentists. Likewise, ex-Garibaldian Prime Minister Francesco Crispi, at first, expressed harsh concerns against Irredentism during a speech in Florence in October 1890, but then showed some leniency.[34]

The secret contents of the Triple Alliance agreement, revealed only later in 1920, showed that behind Rome's contradictory attitude in its foreign policy towards Austria-Hungary was the unwritten pact that if Italy kept irredentism at bay, Austria would, in exchange, do the same with the

---

[31] Christopher Clark, op. cit., p. 226.

[32] Denis Mack Smith, *Modern Italy. A Political History*, (New Hale and London: Yale University Press, 1997), p. 132.

[33] Augusto Sandonà, *L'irredentismo nelle lotte politiche e nelle contese diplomatiche italo-austriache, Volume I,* (Bologna: Zanichelli, 1932), pp. 124, 126, 144-5. For further details about Italy's ambiguous foreign policy towards Austria see Christopher Clark, *The Sleepwalkers*, cit., pp. 92-3.

[34] John A. Thayer, *Italy and the Great War. Politics and Culture, 1870-1915*, (Madison and Milwaukee: University of Wisconsin Press, 1964), p. 147.

much feared clericalism.[35] In other words, Italy's entry into the Triple Alliance would guarantee that the catholic Austria would not support the 'subversive' restoration of papal sovereignty in Rome.

Yet Crispi is reported to have politically and financially supported the development of the cultural association *Dante Alighieri*. When the Austrian government suppressed the *Pro Patria,* accusing it of irredentist plans, and when they publicly attacked the *Dante Alighieri,* Crispi vehemently defended both the association and its president, Ruggiero Bonghi. Later, in the summer of 1890, the Italian government started secretly sponsoring it. Further, from 1893 onwards, the Italian Liberal parties in Austria began to receive their funding for their electoral campaigns directly from the *Dante Alighieri,* - hence from Rome. According to historian Luciano Monzali, the work of the association became invaluable for 'gathering military information to pass on to Italian high commands worried by the possibility of a conflict against Austria-Hungary.'[36]

Despite its martyrs and lively following, Irredentism seems to have exaggerated and eulogised the level of support it enjoyed in the unredeemed areas. Nationalist, and theorist of mass psychology, Scipio Sighele, lamented that there was a general lack of Italian interest for the unredeemed lands.[37] Indeed, the notorious Triestine irredentist, Mario Alberti, is reported to have bemoaned that the pre-war movement had only approximately 500 activists and no more than 4,500 sympathisers – mainly amongst intellectuals and the middles classes and it had no supporters in small villages and amongst entrepreneurs and bankers.[38]

---

[35] See Francesco Salata, *Per la storia diplomatica della questione romana*, (Milano: Treves Editore, 1929).

[36] Luciano Monzali, *Italiani di Dalmazia. Dal Risorgimento alla Grande Guerra,* (Firenze: Le Lettere, 2004), pp. 164-68.

[37] Denis Mack Smith, *Italy. A Modern History*, (Ann Harbor: University of Michigan Press, 1959), p. 125.

[38] Mark Thompson, op. cit., p. 102.

16 *Luisa Morettin*

Freedom from the Austrian yoke was not the only feature that set the tone for Irredentism in Trieste. There further existed a need (which did not exist in Trento) to alleviate the growing menace emerging within Socialism[39] and the loathed *marea slava*, the Slav tide, which many feared would consume Italian identity, and the *civiltà* (civilisation) of Italian Trieste. Slavs were perceived as undeveloped, rural, plebeian people whereas Italians enjoyed the eternal values deriving from centuries of Roman civilisation.[40]

The powerful mix of nationalism and irredentism in Trieste was the result of close links with nationalist organisations based in Rome, such as the aforementioned ANI and *Dante Alighieri* Society,[41] rather than a spontaneous sense of national awareness. Such a thesis is corroborated by Triest journalist, Angelo Vivante, whose definitive study, *Irredentismo adriatico* published as early as 1912, claimed that irredentism was not the natural expression of Italian desire for national liberation, but rather an induced temperament that was politically manipulated. He also maintained that if the Italians had the right to oppose Habsburg domination, for the same reason the Slavs could do the same with Italy. Therefore, he wished for ethnic conciliation and cohabitation, which did not sit well with nationalists.[42]

When the universal male suffrage was introduced in 1907, socialists in Trieste won the elections and ousted the liberal-nationals, yet Irredentism had sown the dormant seeds of the Italian national question, which would grow quickly, as interventionism in the Great War would soon demonstrate.

---

[39] See Scipio Sighele, *Pagine nazionaliste*, (Milano: Treves, 1912), pp. 217-22; idem *Il nazionalismo e i partiti politici*, (Milano: Fratelli Treves Editore, 1911), pp. 114-25, 161-79. Sighele's proposed solution to this issue was to encourage intellectuals to write and spread the principles of Italian national awareness. He was very critical of the antidemocratic turn that became associated with nationalism.

[40] Attilio Tamaro, *Trieste: storia di una città e di una fede,* (Milano: Istituto Editoriale Italiano, 1946), p. 129.

[41] Richard J. Bosworth, *Italy the Least of Great Powers*, cit., p. 203.

[42] Angelo Vivante, *Irredentismo Adriatico,* (Firenze: Parenti, 1912), quoted in Glenda Sluga, Op. cit., pp. 20-21. See also Mark Thompson, op. cit., p. 105.

Contended Spaces 17

THE SOUTHERN SLAV AND ADRIATIC QUESTION

Next to the issue of Irredentism, was the complex problem of the Balkans and of the 'Slav question.' On the eve of the Great War, Europe's political situation was very complex and this was especially so for the multinational state of Austria-Hungary, where the surge of national self-determination was challenging its national unity. Even if by the end of 1849 nationalistic insurrections in Milan, Venice, Prague, Bratislava and Vienna were all repressed, their cause, and deep seated discontent on the domestic politics front, were far from dead.

According to Austrian thinker, Otto Bauer, in the Austro-Hungarian Empire there existed eleven recognised national groups, classified into 'historic nations:' Germans, Magyars, Poles, Italians and Croats on the one side, and 'nations without a history,' without an independent political history, hence without a historic state right: Czechs, Slovaks, Serbs, Slovenes, Ruthenians and Rumanians on the other.[43] Even if the Roman technique of *divide et impera,* (divide and conquer) was used by the Habsburgs in order to take advantage of the national frictions and enmities, it still would not succeed as the monarchy had failed to solve the nationality question, and especially what is known as the 'Southern Slav question.'[44] The Southern Slav group included Slovenes, Croats, Serbs, Montenegrins, Macedonians and Bulgarians. As early as 1903, it became apparent that 'Yugoslavia,' literally the Land of Southern Slavs, was a political idea rather than an ethnic one, and in the age of powerful nationalism it would have been wise to allow the South Slav provinces satisfaction in peaceful isolation from one another within the existing dualist structure of the monarchy.

---

[43] John W. Mason, *The Dissolution of the Austro-Hungarian Empire 1867-1918,* (London and New York: Longman, 1985), pp. 9-22. See also Robert Adolf Kann, *The Multinational Empire. Nationalism and National Reform in the Habsburg Monarchy, 1848-1918,* 2 Vols., (New York: Columbia University Press, 1950).

[44] Janko Pleterski, 'The Southern Slav Question' in Mark Cornwall (ed.), *The Last Years of Austria-Hungary. A Multinational Experiment in Early Twentieth-Century Europe,* (Exeter: University of Exeter Press, 1990), pp. 119-48. Illuminating is also an editorial titled 'The Southern Slav Question' published by the Viennese newspaper *Die Zeit* on 30 May 1903.

In Sarajevo, the plot and assassination of Archduke Franz Ferdinand of Habsburg and his wife, by Bosnian Serb student Gavrilo Princip, became the last straw for many. As the hearse and funeral procession passed in the streets of Trieste on 2 July 1914, it was realised that things were about to change. Indeed, Princip was affiliated to a Slav irredentist movement, which sought to end Vienna's rule in Bosnia and Herzegovina. The murder of the Archduke forced the Austrian Government to ultimately seek an answer to the Serbian problem, as it was the seventh time in four years that Bosnians had made assassination attempts of the Habsburg monarchy.[45] Vienna's response was an ultimatum to the Serbian foreign ministry, followed by what was supposed to be a 'local' conflict, yet it was one which would instead escalate into a European conflict and finally develop into the First World War.[46]

At this stage a new war meant that more questions would arise. In view of a potential demise of the Austro-Hungarian Empire at the end of hostilities, in addition to the Southern Slav question there would also be the Adriatic question, that is a quarrel over sovereignty of Venezia Giulia. From a general point of view the region was not especially significant, but, as it had already happened in the past, its value lay in it being an important transit area which also offered sea outlets for all Balkan regions. Further, over time Trieste had become a strong, multicultural centre of finance and a great emporium of commerce.

Italy's territorial demands were defined by foreign scholars as 'extravagant claims for expansion,'[47] as 'Italy's imperial hangover,'[48] and irredentism was labelled as the 'eldest child of *Risorgimento* nationalism and the half-brother of Italian imperialism.'[49] But for Italians, annexing

---

[45] Bruce F. Pauley, *The Habsburg Legacy 1867-1939*, (New York: Holt, Rinehart and Winston, p. 1972), p. 38.

[46] See Joachim Remak, *The Origins of World War I*, (Austin: Holt, Rinehart and Winston, 1967).

[47] Hugh and Christopher Seton-Watson, *The Making of Europe, R. W. Seton-Watson and the Last Years of Austria-Hungary*, (London: Methuen, 1981), p. 121.

[48] Christopher Seton-Watson, 'Italy's Imperial Hangover,' in *Journal of Contemporary History*, 15, (1980), pp. 169-70.

[49] Dennison Rusinow, op. cit., p. 15.

Contended Spaces

Venezia Giulia and Trentino-Alto Adige, became the realisation of a long coveted dream of obtaining the physical and 'appropriate' borders.

Italian territorial claims implied two issues: on the one side it was necessary to define where exactly Italy ended; on the other, such aspirations clashed with the late awakening of Southern Slav nationalism and their territorial demands. As to the first point, the lack of a clearly recognisable definition of 'just frontiers' for Italy acquired an important role in later controversies as it divided politicians, diplomats, and intellectuals, and at the 1919 Peace Conference, the open discord over pledged territories had extensive consequences. As historian Dennison Rusinow clearly stressed:

> In the northern part of the peninsula, this [the *Risorgimento*] meant driving out the Habsburgs: but how far? Out of Lombardy and Venetia, which the disappearance of Venetian power and the defeat of Napoleon had finally left to the House of Austria only in 1815? ... Out of Gorizia and Trieste, Italian cities subject to the House of Austria since the thirteenth or fifteenth centuries? Out of Venetian Istria and Dalmatia, districts predominantly Slav in race, but part of the Italian Republic of Venice before 1797?[50]

Rusinow's factual remarks identify the problem of territorial definition, as well as the continuity between the *Risorgimento* and the *Postrisorgimento*.[51] On the north-eastern border it was difficult to chart Italy's 'fulfilment,' as the area was historically, geographically and linguistically mixed and ethnic groups were scattered in pockets around the territory.[52] Despite these concrete realities, a new generation of irredentists encouraged political extremism. Among them was Virginio Gayda, a future prominent Fascist, who described Trieste as the 'moral centre' of the racial struggle amongst Germans, Slavs and Italians, adding that even

---

[50] Ibid., p. 15.
[51] Luigi Salvatorelli, *Pensiero e azione del Risorgimento*, (Torino: Einaudi, 1950), p. 174.
[52] See Srđa Orbanič and Nataša Musizza Orbanič, 'Regionalismo istriano: finzione da fine millennio', in *La Battana*, 108, (1993), pp. 55-62.

20   *Luisa Morettin*

Dalmatia, where objectively the population was mainly Slav, had an Italian soul and a 'wholly Italian past.'[53]

As to the second point, at the turn of the twentieth century, the Croat anti-clerical politician, Frano Supilo, after relinquishing the traditional ideas of the Croatian right party that were anti-Serb because of historical and religious differences, became the proponent of Slav solidarity and unity. Recognising the potential for gain by means of an alliance of Southern Slavs, along with the mayor of Spalato (Split), Ante Trumbić, and the Dalmatian deputy to the Reichsrat, Josip Smodlaka, Supilo created a Croat-Serb Coalition. The purpose of this was to oppose Italian irredentist ambitions and to challenge the Austro-Hungarian Government. In order to achieve his aim, Supilo tried to reconcile Croatian national interests with the idea of a South Slav alliance, which led him to campaign among the Croat masses, and to influence Croatian politics through *Novi List*, the daily newspaper which he edited. Such a febrile activism earned him the sympathies of Wickam Steed, the correspondent of *The Times* in Austria-Hungary.[54] Other British intellectuals, and in particular the influential Professor Robert Seton-Watson, an advisor at the Foreign Office and founder of the University of London's School of Slavonic and East European Studies, were keen supporters of the principle of nationality as a basis for the democratic reordering of states in Central and Eastern Europe. During a lecture at King's College in 1915, Seton-Watson stated that the main issues were 'the reduction of Germany to her national boundaries, the restoration of Polish and Bohemian independence, the completion of Italian, Romanian, Yugoslav and Greek national unity, the ejection of the Turks from Europe.'[55] Therefore, in Seton-Watson's view,

---

[53] Virginio Gayda, *Modern Austria: Her Racial and Social Problems with a Study of Italia Irredenta,* (London: Fischer Unwin, 1915), p. 28. See also Virginio Gayda, *Gli Slavi della Venezia Giulia,* (Roma: Rava & Co., 1915).

[54] Leo Valiani, *La dissoluzione dell'Austria-Ungheria,* (Milano: Il Saggiatore, 1966), pp. 1-47. Luigi Albertini, *Le origini della guerra del 1914,* (Milano: Fratelli Bocca, 1942). Peter F. Sugar and Ivo John Lederer (eds), *Nationalism in Eastern Europe,* (Seattle and London: University of Washington Press, 1969).

[55] Robert Seton-Watson, Editorial 'Italy and the Southern Slavs' quoted in Glenda Sluga, *The Problem of Trieste and the Italo-Yugoslav Border,* (New York: State University of New York Press, 2001), p. 185.

Contended Spaces

the creation of a new Southern Slav state did not exclude sovereignty to Italy of some areas such as Venezia Giulia, provided that Trieste could be a free port and that the frontier line would be drawn according to the principle of national self-determination.[56]

As early as 6 October 1914, and before Italy's intervention in the war, *The Times* newspaper in London, published articles urging Italy to pursue the policy of national unity advocated by *Risorgimento*, but highlighted that annexing Istrian or Dalmatian areas inhabited by Slavs would be a reckless move. Giovanni Amendola, the political correspondent in Rome for the Milan newspaper, *Corriere della Sera*, replied to his English colleague's criticism, writing:

> The ideas put forward by *The Times* on the relations between Italians and Slavs on the Adriatic coast are the well-known ideas of Mr Steed, a publicist who has studied the problems of the Danubian monarchy with seriousness and acumen, but has come to conclusions with regard to the Southern Slavs which will meet with much disagreement in Italy. ... There would be room for discussion, we admit, about Dalmatia.[57]

It is known that journalist and historian Henry Wickham Steed, together with his eminent friend Robert Seton-Watson, had Slav friends, solid pro-Slav views and believed in the creation of a federation of Slavs against pan-Germanism. Through his books and editorials, Steed energetically encouraged the dissolution of Austria-Hungary, the emergence of Yugoslavia and strongly wished for Italo-Yugoslav relations to be those of permanent tranquillity.

The exchange of views between Steed and Amendola, and the heated debate over the Adriatic question, offered an understanding of two trains of thought: on the one hand, British national liberals supported spreading the principle of national self-determination, and in doing so, were ensuring that

---

[56] David Lloyd George, *War Memoirs*, 2 Vols., (London: Odhams, 1938), p. 515. Alan Sharp, *Consequences of Peace. The Versailles Settlement: Aftermath and Legacy 1919-2010*, (London: Haus Publishing, 2010), of particular interest are pp. 99-132.

[57] Leo Valiani, op. cit., p.88.

22   *Luisa Morettin*

some political powers would not take advantage of the war.[58] On the other hand, the revival of the irredentist discourse in newspapers showed that the topic had become part of the Italian political consciousness.

Objections to securing Dalmatia came also from the domestic front. Amongst the most vocal opponents of expansion in the region was the democrat and ex-socialist politician and historian, Gaetano Salvemini, who called Italian claims to Dalmatia as '*dalmatomania*,'[59] and the socialist interventionist, Austrophobe Minister, Leonida Bissolati, who was a strong supporter of the *delenda Austria* campaign and in a speech had called Austria-Hungary 'that monstrous structure which is a negation and suppression of all nationalities that are not German or Magyar.'[60]

In November 1914, from the pages of the newspaper *Il Secolo*, Leonida Bissolati urged Italy to join the war in order to complete her national territorial unification. Yet, he further, quite reasonably, warned that annexing Dalmatia would trigger Slav irredentism. He foresaw that such a move could weaken Italy in the same way as it had the Austro-Hungarian monarchy. Indeed, although Dalmatia had once belonged to Venice, it had become mainly Slav – with the exception of Zara (Zadar), a city that was compactly Italian. Such a farsighted urging was not welcomed by Bissolati's fellow politicians, let alone taken into account. In order to legitimatise its territorial claims over Dalmatia, the Italian government and many exiles from Venezia Giulia and Dalmatia, engaged in an extensive propaganda agenda to encourage both domestic and international acceptance of Italian sovereignty.[61]

The Italian territorial demands were based on nationality, self-determination and natural borders. However, the difference between the

---

[58] Luciano Monzali, *Italiani di Dalmazia. 1914-1924*, (Firenze: Le Lettere, 2007), pp. 30-31. Hugh and Christopher Seton-Watson, *The Making of a New Europe*, Op. cit., and R. W. Seton-Watson editorial board et al., *R. W. Seton-Watson and the Yugoslavs: Correspondence 1906-1941*, Vol 1, (London : British Academy, 1976).

[59] Gaetano Salvemini, *Dalla guerra mondiale alla dittatura (1916-1925)*, (Milano: Feltrinelli, 1964).

[60] Quoted by Leo Valiani, op. cit., p. 143. See Francesco Lo Parco, *Lo spirito antitedesco e l'irredentismo di Giosuè Carducci*, (Salerno: Spadafora, 1915).

[61] Luciano Monzali, op. cit., pp. 14-21.

Contended Spaces 23

irredentists of the first generation of the *Risorgimento* under Mazzini's influence, and the second generation, that is the new irredentists of *Postrisorgimento*, was evident in that they did not share the formers ideals of 'fraternity of free nations coexisting in friendship.' Thus the old sympathy for the Slavs viewed as 'a fellow-suffering, suppressed nation' gave way to 'a bitter struggle.'[62] The Slavs' development of a national consciousness and improvement in social status at the turn of the century caused much tension between the two nationalities and, prior to the collapse of the Austro-Hungarian Empire, confrontation became unavoidable. Centuries-old Italian cultural domination was taken aback by such 'dramatic' changes, which were considered as a real and immediate menace, especially in Trieste where it was feared that *italianità* could be broken by Slav pressure.[63]

THE CAMPAIGN FOR INTERVENTION

An overview of the Italian events between 1914 and 1915 suggests Italy and Austria were allies more in name than in fact. The already mentioned conflicting territorial interests had made Italy's loyalty to the Triple Alliance ambiguous, which mirrored Italy's long history of contradictory diplomacy towards its powerful neighbour.

After Vienna declared war on Serbia on 28 July 1914, Venezia Giulia, still part of the Austro-Hungarian Empire, was officially at war. Italy instead, nominally allied with the Central Powers, first declared her neutrality (2 August 1914) on the grounds that Austria-Hungary had breached their treaty.[64] As Rome was not informed in time about the

---

[62] Dennison Rusinow, op. cit., pp. 20-21. See also Carlo Schiffrer, 'Il problema nazionale di Trieste nella storiografia austrofila e in quella irredentista', in *Trieste*, No. 40, (Nov.-Dec., 1960).

[63] In this respect a significant example is provided by Rusinow who reports how, in the headquarters of Istrian cultural groups, maps were kept signalling the loss of Italian towns when an Italian mayor was replaced by a Slav one. Dennison Rusinow, op. cit., p. 23.

[64] Leo Valiani, op. cit., p. 50.

24   *Luisa Morettin*

ultimatum given by Vienna to Serbia, Italy did not feel constrained to honour the Treaty of Alliance signed in 1882. For the following ten months, the government in Rome was undecided as to whose side to take – whether to remain neutral or enter into the war – and delayed their stance, enabling them to carefully assess which side they thought would win the war, thus bringing larger profits for Italy.

The country was bitterly divided between *interventisti*, who supported intervention in the hostilities, which included Nationalists, irredentists, university students, the artistic movement of the Futurists, most of the Freemasons, democrats and dissident socialists; and on the other side were the neutralists, opposing the war, which consisted of the Socialist Party, liberal deputies and many Catholics. Several reports, from provincial monitors, showed that only a small minority of Italians favoured intervention, but Giolitti's farsighted vision that Italy would gain enormously by staying neutral was bitterly opposed by vocal radicals and newspapers. Amongst the opposition was Benito Mussolini's interventionist *Il Popolo d'Italia*[65] that used regionalist resentments as a leverage for war, and Luigi Albertini's *Corriere della Sera*, that stated neutrality would 'sabotage the true interests of the country.' Albertini's newspaper, historian Denis Mack Smith noted, 'was more of a political force than the Chamber of Deputies, so irrelevant had representative institutions become.'[66] Interventionists were further emboldened by the inflammatory speeches delivered by the influential writer, hedonist and warmonger Gabriele D'Annunzio, who quickly became the figurehead of intervention against Austria. In his vociferous and extremist speeches D'Annunzio preached how only 'a great conflict of the races' could purge society of their decadence, and spoke about the once-Venetian Adriatic areas as 'our diseased left lung,'[67] all the while hurling offences to attack the peace party. His orations were sensational – imbued with sentiment,

---

[65] Barone Bernardo Quaranta (ed.), *Mussolini as Revealed in His Political Speeches (November 1914 – August 1923),* (London and Toronto: J. M. Dent, 1923), pp. 18-24.

[66] Denis Mack Smith, *Modern Italy*, p. 258.

[67] Lucy Hughes-Hallett, *The Pike. Gabriele d'Annunzio. Poet, Seducer and Preacher of War*, (London: Fourth Estate, 2013), p. 298.

Contended Spaces 25

but void of rational substance; a form of communication which was intended to manipulate.[68]

Italy's pro-interventionist rallies were both an act of foreign and domestic policy. Indeed, Italy's war campaign became one of judgement and animosity toward Giolitti's *Italietta,* 'little Italy,' a label intended for the small minded, and internally divided, Italy of young intellectuals who accused bureaucrats and diplomats of pursuing demeaning policies, and of working in the interest of the enemy. It was felt that by signing and renewing the alliance with Austria and Germany, both in 1891 and 1902, the liberal government had betrayed the ideals of the *Risorgimento.* What was advocated was a new political system and *interventisti* were convinced that for the new political system to be fulfilled, its future lay in conflict.

In Trieste, the Italian socialists asserted their loyalty to proletarian internationalism and fiercely opposed the war, militarism and the line adopted by the Austrian Social Democratic Party.[69] However, the national wing of the socialist party, led by Edmondo Pücher,[70] later cautiously adopted the belief that the Southern Slav outrages, and their aggressive attitude, were a menace to the *italianità* of the region. This was also shared by some public opinion that, horrified by the murder of Franz Ferdinand, thought military intervention was needed to bring an end to Slav threats once and for all.

Despite not being a sizeable movement and failing to win over the majority of Italians, interventionists, headed by shrewd realist Prime Minister Antonio Salandra and Foreign Minister Sidney Sonnino, opted for war. Just as Mussolini believed twenty-five years later during the Second World War, Salandra was convinced the conflict was almost over, so Italy could go to war and survive with minimal damage.

---

[68] Patrizia Piredda, 'Interventionism in 1915 and the Man of Letters: The Ethical Commitments of Serra and the 'Armed Poet' D'Annunzio', in *Bulletin of Italian Politics*, Vol. 3, No. 2, 2011, pp. 303-17.

[69] Ernesto Ragionieri and Leo Valiani, *Il movimento nazionale a Trieste nella prima guerra mondiale*, (Udine: Giulio Cervani editore, 1968).

[70] Angelo Ara and Claudio Magris, op. cit., pp. 102-13.

Italy had the choice to ally herself with the Triple Alliance or with the Triple Entente (France, Russia, and Great Britain), so before entering the conflict, in a rather duplicitous move, Rome held simultaneous negotiations with both. The dream of a greater Italy came true on 26 April 1915 with the secret Treaty of London, (which stopped being secret in November 1917, when Bolshevik revolutionaries made it public), that aligned Italy with the Triple Entente.

Austria-Hungary tried to make some last-minute territorial concessions to Italy, but it did so partially and very slowly. On the contrary the Entente powers managed to offer more, without damaging their own vital interests or territories. Italy would receive, Trentino and Tyrol up to the Brenner pass, the Istrian peninsula and the Quarnero Islands, Trieste ('the lung of the empire' as it was called in Vienna), the county of Gorizia and Gradisca, the province of Dalmatia, sovereignty over Valona, and the island of Saseno. In addition, the Treaty allocated the confirmed possession of the Dodecanese islands, which had been militarily occupied by Italy since 1912, a loan from Great Britain, a share in the indemnity costs to be imposed on the enemy and the exclusion of the Holy Sea from peace conferences and negotiations at the end of the conflict.[71] The last clause, revealed the extent to which the Italian government feared the temporal power of the papacy, the arch-enemy of the new Kingdom of Italy. The long political and secular governmental activity of the popes brought many to believe that the Vatican might claim some form of restoration of its temporal power at the end of the war.

The agreement reached by the Triple Entente promised an attractive reward for Italy's participation in the war, as the territorial acquisitions at the expense of the Austro-Hungarian Empire meant the completion of the glorious *Risorgimento,* which linked the memory of past greatness with dreams of future national power.

On 23 May 1915 Italy joined the conflict. It is significant that war was declared only on Austria-Hungary, and not on Germany who had invaded

---

[71] Richard J. Bosworth, *Italy and the Approach of the First World War*, (London: Macmillan, 1983), pp. 21-2.

Belgium, and by this declaration, the Italian government gave away that for Rome it was indeed an expansionist war at the expense of Vienna. Despite the demagogic campaign spurring Italians to enter a glorious conflict, not everybody was taken by war mysticism, heroism ideals and territorial promises, and, as a *Daily Telegraph* correspondent objectively noted: 'Nowhere in Europe is there a people more averse to war than the subjects of Victor Emmanuel.'[72]

THE FIRST WORLD WAR

How was the intervention in the war taken by Venezia Giulia? One of the historic themes running through the region in those years is the contrast between the Italian pro-war propaganda, arousing strong emotions and maximising the size of noisy interventionist rallies, and the real composition of irredentism and interventionism, which was not so unanimous. According to Alberti, in 1914, only two per cent of Triestines were irredentist.[73] Mussolini himself, had confessed that his interventionist campaign did not have sufficient backing[74] and as Salandra wrote later, 'without the newspapers, Italy's intervention would perhaps have been impossible.'[75]

This disparity is captured in the data available: many Triestines remained loyal to the Habsburg monarchy and, of the estimated 50,000 soldiers from Venezia Giulia, it is claimed that only 1,000 deserted from the Austrian Army to fight on the side of Italy.[76] Historian Lucio Fabi noted that when Austria entered the war in 1914, the public's hopes were mixed: in the streets of Trieste they cried both '*Viva l'Italia!*' (Long live

---

[72] John A. Thayer, op. cit., p. 303.

[73] Ive Mihovilović, *Trieste et son port*, (Susak: Ed. de l'Institut adriatique, 1945), p. 43.

[74] John A. Thayer, op. cit., p. 307.

[75] Richard F. Hamilton and Holger H. Herwing, *Decisions for War, 1914-1917*, (Cambridge: Cambridge University Press, 2004), p. 200.

[76] Lawrence Sondhaus, *In the Service of the Emperor: Italians in the Austrian Armed Forces 1814-1918*, (Scottsdale: Boulder, 1990), p. 105.

Italy!) and '*Viva l'Austria!*' (Long live Austria!).[77] Such an attitude is encapsulated by the motto of the Triestine historian Pietro Kandler, (1804-1872): 'With Austria, but not in Austria.' His perspective was shared by other town dwelling Italians who, aware of their privileged position within the Habsburg Empire, yet not identifying as Germans, could not conceive of the dissolution of Austria-Hungary, and yet hoped for a new order with the creation of a federal monarchy. As early as the beginning of April 1915, riots and street protests in Trieste were portrayed by Italian nationalist propaganda as 'local reaction to Austrian authoritarianism.'[78] Yet, in fact they were caused by general dissatisfaction, shortages and poverty.

From Trieste and its immediate surroundings 32,500 people were called to arms, but instead of a wave of enthusiasm to enlist, the news of Italy's about-face triggered attacks against symbols of Italian identity. The *Società Ginnastica Triestina* (Triestine Sports Club), a social meeting place for irredentists, who considered it related to the *Risorgimento* secret society *La Carboneria*, was attacked. The offices of the pro-Italian liberal newspaper *Il Piccolo* were set on fire; Italian shops and coffee houses were looted and destroyed; the statue of Italian composer, Giuseppe Verdi, soiled and defaced, and the seat of Italian associations destroyed. On the fringes of towns, factory equipment was stolen as were animals and oxcarts deep in the countryside. Italians in Trieste suffered acts of reprisal: prominent and cultivated citizens with declared or suspected pro-irredentist feelings were arrested and sent to internal exile to places such as Göllersdorf, Sitzendorf and Rashalaa. Nearly 10,000 Italians living in Trieste and Venezia Giulia left the city and were repatriated to Italy via Switzerland under the protection of the American Consulate.[79]

---

[77] Lucio Fabi, *Trieste, 1914-1918: una città in guerra*, (Trieste: MGS Press, 1996), pp. 16-8.

[78] Maura Hametz, *Making Trieste Italian. 1918-1954*, (Rochester: The Boydell Press, 2005), p. 15.

[79] Lucio Fabi, *Trieste, 1914-1918*, cit., p. 43 and Angelo Visintin, 'L'assalto a «Il Piccolo»', in A.A.V.V., *Un percorso tra le violenze del Novecento nella provincia di Trieste*, (Trieste: IRSML, 2007), pp. 11-8.

Contended Spaces 29

Many expected the conflict to be short, as in the case of nineteenth century wars, but in fact, Europe and with it Italy had launched themselves into a long tragedy, the consequences of which would be far-reaching. World War I proved to be not just a conflict, but a watershed – a disaster that would wipe out a way and an order of life.[80]

Italy's unpreparedness for war was complete. If the Libyan War had momentarily appeased imperialist appetites, it had also drained the Treasury. Italy's foreign policy was founded on an idea of greatness, rather than military power, whilst old-school military theory turned out to be unsuitable to keep the rhetorical promises of force. There was an exceptional disregard for the realities of warfare, as exemplified by Luigi Cadorna, the austere Chief of General Staff, who 'did not explain his strategic presuppositions to the politicians and they never bothered to explore.'[81] The army lacked modern equipment and supplies and geography on the north-eastern front did not favour Italy.

The alleged quick, glorious war turned out to be interminable and the human face of conflict revealed itself very different to the fanfare of interventionist speeches. There was nothing noble in the battles on the Isonzo River valley, on the slopes of Monte Grappa, in the muddy trench fighting and precipitous escarpment warfare in the Alpine mountains or in the plateau of Carso. The front from Gorizia down to the Adriatic Sea became known as '*l'inferno carsico*' (Carso hell), where trenches had to be made by using explosive to break rocks, while on the Collio area the brittle soil, precious for local farmers and winemakers, transformed trenches into slippery waterlogged holes. Troops' hardships were at the limits of human endurance. [82]

---

[80] Bruce F. Pauley, *The Hapsburg Legacy 1867-1939*, (New York: Holt, Rinehart and Winston, 1972), p. 14. See also Lothar Höbelt, 'Well-tempered Discontent. Austrian Domestic Politics' in Mark Cornwall (ed.), *The Last Years of Austria-Hungary. A Multi-National Experiment in Early Twentieth-Century Europe,* (Exeter: University of Exeter Press, 2002), pp. 47-74; and Leo Valiani, op. cit., pp. 1-47.

[81] Richard F. Hamilton and Holger H. Herwing, op. cit., pp. 200-201.

[82] For a portrait of soldiers' and civilians' living conditions during the Great War see Lucio Fabi, *Gente di trincea. La grande guerra sul Carso e sull'Isonzo*, (Milano: Mursia Editore, 1994).

30   *Luisa Morettin*

Between the end of 1916 and 1917, the Italian Army experienced rebellion and a considerable number of defections from its ranks. This was mainly due to the fear caused by the physical proximity to the enemy, who were entrenched only a few hundred yards away; the sight of senseless deaths, and the fact that front-line soldiers were often poor peasants and illiterate labourers from Southern Italy, who did not have much sense of attachment to, or identity with, the cause of unredeemed lands. Amongst the deserters there were Socialists, Catholics and democratic neutralists, who had opposed the war since the beginning, yet had to fight against their will and ideology. It was a clear sign that the nation had failed its attempt to forge a united war effort. The phenomenon of disobedience and desertion reached such high proportions that it is estimated one in twelve soldiers were strictly punished and 4,028 were sentenced to death for defection, hiding or self-harm.[83]

The province of Udine, on the west side of Trieste, endured most of the logistic war effort until the military disaster at Caporetto (Kobarid), a small alpine town, after the Austro-German offensive drove Italians back fifty miles in November 1917.

The conflict had far reaching implications for civilians. Due to the fact that the front coincided with densely inhabited areas, which were only partially evacuated, it resulted in requisitions, looting, reprisals and a very high mortality rate, especially in the cities of Trieste and Gorizia.[84] Historian Lucio Fabi reports how Gorizia had the sad record of spending thirty months fighting on the front line, first on one side and then on the other of the Austro-Italian front, noting how this would have affected civilians who found themselves in this situation. Hardships, epidemics and unemployment distinguished life during the war in Trieste. Of its 250,000 inhabitants, between 160,000-180,000, remained in town until 1917, during the most difficult period of the conflict. As to small villages and

---

[83] Lucio Fabi, 'La Grande Guerra', in A.A. V.V., *Friuli e Venezia Giulia. Storia del '900*, pp. 100-3. Enzo Forcella e Alberto Monticone, *Plotone di esecuzione*, (Bari: Laterza, 1968). Ernesto Ragionieri, *Storia d'Italia, Vol 4:3, La storia politica e sociale*, (Torino: Einaudi, 1976), p. 2051.

[84] Lucio Fabi, 'La Grande Guerra,' op. cit., pp. 106-9.

Contended Spaces

towns along the Isonzo front and coastal Istria, it is estimated that at least 400,00 Austrians of Italian and Slovenian nationality were dislodged from their homes, and found shelter in improvised refugee camps in Styria, Boemia, Oberösterreich (Upper Austria) and Niederösterreich (Lower Austria).

Despite the infamous reverse at Caporetto in June 1918, Italian forces pushed back the enemy on the River Piave. By 24 October, they crossed it reaching the village of Vittorio Veneto. Trento fell into Italian hands on 3 November and, on the same day, the Italian destroyer *Audace* was the first Italian ship to enter Trieste.

Although military planners had expected the war on the Western front to last longer, Austria-Hungary was in complete dissolution. On 11 November 1918, the guns finally fell silent. The armistice, concluded in a large room at Villa Giusti, near Padua, put an end to the worst bloodshed Italy had ever experienced. The sacrifice of almost 600,000 Italian men who gave their life and of 500,000 who were *mutilati* (incapacitated) secured Italy's victory, allowing her to finally gain the unredeemed lands of Trentino-Alto Adige and Venezia Giulia. The multi-layered horrors of the conflict left deep scars throughout the country, and particularly in Venezia Giulia, where most of the bitterest battles of World War I were fought. With the dissolution of the Austro-Hungarian monarchy, the region shared the insecurity and unsettling challenges of similar areas that, due to the fall of the great empires, had to reinvent their future. It was against this background that the function of Venezia Giulia as a border land stopped being of just local importance and became an essential part of international politics.

Chapter 2

THE INTERWAR YEARS

It is certain, in my view, that without Mussolini, three-quarters of Italian youths who had returned from the trenches would have become Bolsheviks.

Italo Balbo
Diary, 1922

THE POSTWAR CRISIS

As a result of the Great War, much of the pre-1914 world was gone, never to be restored. What George Kennan called '*the* great seminal catastrophe' of the twentieth century[85] not only enabled social and cultural revolutions, but also helped to harden warfare and politics. The vacuum of power, which ensued as a result of the disintegration of the Russian, German, Austro-Hungarian, and Ottoman empires, led to the emergence of new states inspired by President Woodrow Wilson's principles of self-determination and with these new states came territorial disputes. Defeat,

---

[85] Quoted in Roger Chickering, *Imperial Germany and the Great War*, (Cambridge: Cambridge University Press, 1998), p. 192.

or disappointment in victory, resulted in contested territorial losses, gains, and demands. With the Treaty of Brest-Litovsk Soviet Russia, the first vanquished state of World War I, lost almost all of the western non-Russian lands of the Romanovs and saw the creation of three small Baltic Republics: Estonia, Latvia, and Lithuania. Finland became an autonomous region, whilst Poland regained its independence as the Second Polish Republic. From the ruins of the Habsburg Empire Romania was enlarged and there emerged a new Czechoslovakia, as well as a new multi-national Yugoslavia, for which there was no historical precedent. The Treaty of Sèvres in 1920 partitioned the Ottoman Empire into zones of influence. Germany's loss of Alsace-Lorraine to the French, the coal-mining Saar region to the League of Nations, and of her former colonies to Britain, France and Japan, was perhaps not that much compared to the financial liability imposed by the victors – something which every German party saw as unacceptable. What all of the above-mentioned European territorial revisions had in common was that they became contested areas, and as such, the source for new disputes.

If the Great War cost very much in blood and treasure and post-war years were difficult for any country, in Italy they seemed to be aggravated further. The state had a weak political framework and was more split than it had been before 1915: class and political divisions were widened; tensions increased; and the government's failure to lead the country from wartime to a peacetime economy bedevilled the Liberal ruling system. It was also clear that the pre-war animosity between interventionists and neutralists still continued.

The impact and lasting outcome of the war on Italy's politics and society were dramatic as the government struggled to reassert control over the rural and urban working classes. Further, unemployment, devaluation of the lira, uncertainty, and the expectations engendered by the war created tense situations among the returning soldiers, who engaged in violent agitations during the so-called, *biennio rosso,* the red biennium of 1919-1920. The turmoil of these social conflicts and the aggressive campaign of strikes, together with the creation of a Bolshevik Russia and the

The Interwar Years

intensification of trade union efforts in Italy, triggered the fears of conservatives and attitudes on the Nationalist front became hardened.

To make things worse, the Paris Peace Conference, which deliberated throughout 1919, turned out to be not only a congress of victors, but also a national disappointment. Italy's expectation of easy spoils was not realised as the territories mentioned in the Treaty of London had been negotiated with France and Britain and not with America, whose President Wilson set the agenda of the conference. At the start of the conference in January 1919 Italian Prime Minister, Vittorio Emanuele Orlando, and Foreign Minister, Sidney Sonnino, demanded the fulfilment of the terms set out in the Treaty of London. However, their demands clashed with President Wilson's 'principle of nationality,' which equated identity to territorial sovereignty.[86] The President's Fourteen Points did not offer suitable guidance for the 'readjustment of the frontiers of Italy [which] should be accomplished through clearly recognizable lines of nationality.' Indeed, the relationship between identity and sovereignty along the Italian north-eastern border, which had particularly complex ethnic and national make-up, was not as easy as Wilson had envisaged.

Italy's claim of the Adriatic city of Fiume (Rijeka),[87] which had not been an objective of Italian irredentism, strained the already tense diplomacy of territorial demands. Although Wilson conceded Trentino and Venezia Giulia to Italy, he refused to give her Dalmatia, Fiume and the protectorate over Albania.[88] In the eyes of the Rome government, the Peace Conference showed Italy to be the least important of the Great Powers and the war felt like a lost victory or, better, a *vittoria mutilata*.[89] Such a myth of a 'mutilated' victory became a particularly potent sentiment, not only in shaping the Italian post-war political discourse and the takeover of Fiume

---

[86] Woodrow Wilson, *Speech on the Fourteen Points Jan 8, 1918*, available online at http://www.fordham.
edu/halsall/mod/1918wilson.html, accessed 25 January 2014.

[87] René Albrecht-Carrié, *Italy at the Paris Peace Conference*, (New York: Columbia University Press, 1938), p. 100.

[88] Dennison Rusinow, op. cit., p. 45.

[89] Gabriele D'Annunzio, *Versi d'amore e di gloria,* (Milano: Mondadori Meridiani, 2004), vol. II.

by proto-fascist poet D'Annunzio, but also in informing the collective memory of Italian soldiers in the Balkan theatre of operations during World War II.

Allocating not only Trieste, but also Fiume to Italy, would have meant allowing her to control central European trade and this did not sit well with the other Great Powers. In particular, French Prime Minister Georges Clemenceau was opposed to Italy's claims to the city as, out of the complete collapse of the Austro-Hungarian Monarchy, France looked to the new Yugoslavia, Poland and Czechoslovakia as buffer states against Soviet Russia and as future allies in the containment of Germany in the east. Yugoslavia would therefore need Fiume as a main strategic maritime outlet, as it had no other viable port for merchant shipping. Also, due to rivalry and tensions over the years, since 1860 the relationship between France and Italy had been severely strained.

In 1881 the creation of the French protectorate over Tunis helped to drive Italy into the Triple Alliance, and in the late 1880s Francesco Crispi tempted Germany, by then an ally in the military alliance, to wage war against France. Crispi's initiative was motivated by the desire of 'building a nation' and replacing France as an important Mediterranean power. Consequently, in Cleamenceau's view, creating a strong Yugoslavia was a way to stop Italy becoming too powerful and to avoid Yugoslav irredentism. As for Britain, Prime Minister David Lloyd George considered that supporting Wilson with the Adriatic question, (as the debate over the fate of the territories along the eastern coast of the Adriatic Sea became known), and the creation of the League of Nations would ease American pressure on other issues such as freedom of the seas, which ranked high on the British agenda.

Negotiations to define the border of Venezia Giulia became so complex and fraught that they lasted over five years: from the armistice of November 1918 until March 1920, when negotiations were conducted in Paris, and from March 1920 until January 1924, when Italy and Yugoslavia negotiated directly. The suggested compromise, reached in April 1919 and

The Interwar Years 37

later known as the 'Wilson Line,'[90] envisaged the frontier would run very close to that which was promised by the Treaty of London, so the cities of Gorizia and Trieste and the Istrian peninsula would be in the domain of Italy. However, Fiume would be a separate state under the League of Nations, governed by a multinational council; Sebenico (Šibenik) and Zara would become free ports under Italian mandate, whilst the majority of the islands would be granted to Yugoslavia. Orlando's successor, Francesco Saverio Nitti, fearing non-cooperation with the Allies might induce them to halt their financial support for Italy, evacuated Fiume, which at the end of the war had been occupied by Italian troops under the lead of D'Annunzio, handed it over to Allied military control and conceded Dalmatia to Yugoslavia. But the issue was far from solved as it soon became apparent that strong nationalist sentiments had emerged after the war, therefore, making the Fiume question their major theme.

The Adriatic struggle would eventually end with the Treaty of Rapallo, ratified on 22 November 1920. Accordingly, Italy obtained the islands of Cherso (Cres), Lussino (Lošinj), Lagosta (Lastovo), and Pelagosa (Palagruža); Zara became an Italian enclave in Dalmatia, whilst Fiume was declared independent 'in perpetuity,' although territorially linked to Italy. Such an ambiguous state for Fiume would not last long. The 'mutilated victory' theme continued and, after diplomatic pressure from Mussolini's government on Belgrade, Fiume was ceded to Italy by the Yugoslavs under the terms of the Treaty of Rome in January 1924. Later, Marshal Tito bitterly regretted this decision, complaining about Slavs being parcelled out as compensation 'with the aim of preventing the spread of the revolutionary movement.'[91]

---

[90] Hugh Seton-Watson, op. cit., pp. 123-31.
[91] Josip Broz Tito, "Politički izvještaj", V Kongres Komunističke Partije Jugoslavije; *Izvještaji i referati*, (Belgrade: Kultura, 1948), p. 45, quoted by Michael B. Petrovich, 'Russia's Role in the Creation of the Yugoslav State, 1914-1918,' in Dimitrije Djordjevic (ed.), *The Creation of Yugoslavia 1914-1918*, (Oxford: Clio Books, 1980), p. 89.

INTERWAR VENEZIA GIULIA: TOWARDS THE BRINK

We now know that what was the epilogue of the Adriatic question would become the first chapter of Yugoslav irredentism. Like historian Gaetano Salvemini, author Henry Baerlein predicted as early as 1922 that despite the treaties the Adriatic would become an area of unrest, stating: 'The most serious phase of the Adriatic crisis is now ushered in, for a new Alsace has been created.' [92] With the acquisition of the new provinces of Venezia Giulia and Venezia Tridentina, the 'Great Patriotic War' was to reward Italy with nine thousand square miles of new territories. Venezia Giulia comprised the former county of Gorizia and Gradisca, the Tarvisio area, Trieste, and Istria with the Quarnero Islands. Along with the new territories, the Kingdom of Italy also gained 1.5 million new citizens and with them the problems caused by the high number of non-Italians, who held strong nationalist feelings.. It was calculated that in the new province of Venezia Giulia there were 98,000 Croats and 327,000 Slovenes. [93]

Whilst Italy was occupied by the widespread unrest and strikes of the 'red biennium,' the border lands were trying, with difficulty, to adjust to the transition from the Austro-Hungarian Empire to the Kingdom of Italy. Venezia Giulia struggled to recover from massive wartime destruction, as the area had been alongside the front lines of the opposing armies. Social and welfare institutions were overwhelmed and aid programmes were not well co-ordinated. Dealing with the repatriation of thousands of refugees and demobilised soldiers put an enormous strain on the regional administration. In January 1919, 12,000 refugees arrived in Trieste and by June of the same year between 400 and 700 displaced people made their way through the city every day; a number far too high for local officials to deal with. [94]

---

[92] Henry Baerlein, *The Birth of Yugoslavia*, (London: Leonard Parsons, 1922), p. 237.
[93] Martin Clark, op. cit., p. 252.
[94] Maura Hametz, op. cit., pp. 16-17.

The Interwar Years

Likewise, the war destroyed the region's economic structure. The exchange rate of the Austrian currency, the krone, to the Italian lira was previously one krone to one lira, but in April 1919, the rate was just forty percent of its pre-war value, thus condemning Venezia Giulia to a vast loss of assets accrued in the pension and credit sectors, as well as in capital stock.[95] The frontier change hit Istrian agriculture particularly hard, as its Mediterranean products had previously enjoyed an excellent market in Austria-Hungary, but was now hindered by Italian competition. Industry was also immobilised since in view of the Italian invasion pieces of machinery and equipment had been moved to the inner part of the Austrian empire, and now factories could not be rebuilt without a large injection of capital.

Frustrated in its hopes of being reunited to the motherland, Trieste was bound to have other dreams shattered as well as its role decreased in importance, stability and economic power. The trade monopoly, which the city had enjoyed with the Austrian hinterland, as it had been the only maritime outlet, meant that its most powerful interests, insurance, shipping and shipbuilding were badly affected, as major local shipping companies, the Austrian Lloyd, the Navigazione Libera and the Austro-Americana, were sold.[96] Such upheaval and economic crisis in Venezia Giulia worsened, as diplomatic negotiations concerning the delineation of the new frontiers dragged on. Contemporary novelists, such as Scipio Slataper and Giani Stuparich, who had fought and longed for an Italian Trieste, which was seen as a sort of unobtainable object of desire and the Karst area as a dreamscape, now reflected on the impact of annexation to Italy with crude realism. They depicted Trieste as it really was: a city torn apart by social tensions that made her citizens feel more and more uncomfortable with the real situation. Stuparich expressed vividly, in November 1919, how Triestines eventually came to see Italy as 'still small, [...] with its cumbersome apparatus and inertia of its bureaucracy, with the

---

[95] Paolo Ziller, 'La Venezia Giulia dalla dissoluzione dell'Austria-Ungheria al regno d'Italia', in A.A. V.V., *Friuli e Venezia Giulia. Storia del '900*, p. 164.

[96] Dennison Rusinow, op. cit., pp. 86-87, 112-3.

40   *Luisa Morettin*

superficiality and bombast of its character,'[97] whilst historian Attilio
Tamaro lamented that 'a flock of parasites, tenors, violinists, mandolin and
guitar players came up here.'[98] Such contradictory feelings were not
uncommon among promoters of *italianità*, who had great difficulties
reconciling their idealistic, mystic ideas of Italy with the harsh authenticity
of a poor country as was clearly reflected in its inhabitants.

Italian control of Trieste caused the city to almost lose her
multicultural aspect. In 1921, there were only 138,000 inhabitants in
Trieste, a figure well below pre-war levels.[99] Apart from Triestine
casualties, many inhabitants did not return because, as non-Italians, they
now felt they were outsiders in this new national context. At the same time
the newly acquired province became the receiving area of migrants from
the Kingdom of Italy, mainly from its poor southern part, who were
looking for improved living conditions. Germans and Magyars, mainly
those belonging to the highest social classes, left immediately and almost
in their entirety.[100]

Many Slavs preferred to relocate to areas under Yugoslav rule, whilst
others resettled elsewhere. It is reported that 20,000 Slavs emigrated from
the town of Pola alone, corresponding to 22.2 per cent of its population. As
a result, a good part of the intellectual and ruling Slav class was lost; an
element which aggravated tensions already existing since the fin-de-siècle
between the Italian and Slav social communities. The Triestine socialist
reformer, Aldo Oberdorfer commented, 'They left full of hatred,'[101] and
this hatred proved significant twenty years later.

---

[97] Sandra Arosio, *Scrittori di frontiera. Scipio Slataper, Giani e Carlo Stuparich*, (Milano:
    Guerini Editore, 1996), pp. 136-7.
[98] Maura Hametz, op. cit., p. 17.
[99] Lucio Fabi, 'La Grande Guerra,' cit., pp. 116-7.
[100] Ernesto Sestan, *Venezia Giulia. Lineamenti di storia etnica e culturale*, (Roma: Edizioni
    italiane, 1947), pp. 105-6.
[101] Elio Apih, *Italia. Fascismo e antifascismo nella Venezia Giulia (1918-1943)*, (Bari: Laterza,
    1966), pp. 38-9.

The Interwar Years 41

EARLY FASCISM ON THE OUTSKIRTS

After the *Fasci di Combattimento* (Fighting Units) movement, the earliest organisational cells of Fascism, were formed by Mussolini in Milan at a small meeting held on 23 March 1919 in Piazza San Sepolcro, it was mainly in Venezia Giulia that the ultra-nationalist, anti-Bolshevik and anti-Slav dimension of Fascist ideology gained a foothold. On 26 August 1920 Francesco Giunta, the head of the Trieste section of the budding Fascist Party and later the National Secretary of the *Partito Nazionale Fascista*, wrote to Mussolini: 'Let's not forget that here [in Trieste] is the land of Fascism and from here the spark of revolution could catch fire in order to win over the country to our ideas.'[102] Indeed, the unresolved border controversies on the eastern fringes of Italy granted Trieste and the surrounding region the important role of stronghold of *italianità* (Italianness) against any 'antinationals' and 'subversives.' It is therefore not by chance that precisely in Venezia Giulia, with its large Slav populations and strong nationalist tensions, the *fascio* was formed on 3 April 1919, only ten days after the Milan meeting.

As the *Fasci di combattimento* was a movement rather than a party, it allowed early fascism a degree of 'flexibility in tactics and program.'[103] In that respect, in the autumn of 1921, Guido Bergamo, an ex-republican Fascist, described the ideological heterogeneity of fascism in the following terms: 'Every region, every province, possesses its own Fascism.'[104] The possibility to pursue different types of policy, adjusting them to local contexts and needs, meant that in Venezia Giulia the *fascio* was inevitably informed by the sensitive task of defending national identity. As a result, Julian *fasci* soon converted the rhetoric of *italianità* into practice by creating the black-shirted *squadre d'azione* (shock troops); paramilitary

---

[102] Salvatore Lupo, *Il fascismo. La politica in un regime totalitario,* (Roma: Donzelli, 2000), p. 65. See also Anna Maria Vinci, 'Il fascismo e la società locale', in *Friuli e Venezia Giulia. Storia del '900*, pp. 221-58.

[103] Philip Cannistraro, *Historical Dictionary of Fascist Italy*, (London: Greenwood Press, 1982), p. 400.

[104] Quoted in Richard Bosworth, *Mussolini*, p. 153.

units for which Venezia Giulia became a veritable training ground. The official reason behind their creation was to provide support to the forthcoming seizure of Fiume by D'Annunzio and to prevent Slavs and Communists from carrying out a possible *coup* against Trieste,[105] a city which, in Mussolini's own words, was 'geographically, historically and morally Italian.'[106] In fact, *squadre* were meant to control and wipe out any real or possible resistance from the enemies deemed to be the Socialists and Slavs.

Left wing forces, the national foes par excellence, were perceived in Venezia Giulia as holding common ground with Slavs, in the guilt of eroding the national myth of *italianità* with un-Italian values and 'conspiring against the newly won integrity of the nation.'[107] In general, it was felt Socialists had become a sort of catalyst for all types of agitators who were dissatisfied with Italian order. However, there were other reasons behind such hostility. As Socialists had initially supported the idea of an independent Trieste, Italian nationalists feared the weight of their subversive political impact. Moreover, concern grew among the middle classes and industrialists that Slav socialists, who had merged with Italian socialists into one single Socialist Party, could have brought a more radical, Bolshevik-oriented and revolutionary trend into the unified party. Such fears, together with the inability of the Liberal state to control law and order during the upheavals of the red biennium, greatly advanced the triumph of *fasci,* and later of Fascism, as it was considered the only party capable of warding off the revolutionary threat. Closely linked to this apprehension was the fact that, in Trieste, Italian Nationalists were only a little less than half of the population, and a potential coalition of Socialists

---

[105] Claudio Silvestri, *Dalla redenzione al fascismo. Trieste 1918-1922*, (Udine: Del Bianco Editore, 1959), p. 50 quoted in A. Lyttelton, op. cit., p. 53.

[106] Benito Mussolini, *Opera Omnia*, (E. and D. Susmel eds.), (Firenze: Giovanni Volpe editore, 1978-1980), Vol. 7, pp. 345-8.

[107] Adrian Lyttelton, *The Seizure of Power. Fascism in Italy 1919-1929,* (London: Weidenfield and Nicolson, 1973), p. 53.

The Interwar Years

43

with Slovenian nationalists (each representing about a quarter) might jeopardise the success of their Italian opponents.[108]

The combustible character of ethnically mixed Venezia Giulia meant the other key enemy of fascism were Slavs. The threat they represented was twofold; firstly, they could expand from the east, which would have clashed with Italy's vital interests of national defence and the intention to create a monopoly of power in the Adriatic Sea and the Balkans. Secondly, the Slovene and Croatian minorities living in the Julian region were known, and considered, as 'Slav pollution' since their presence on Italian soil and socio-cultural assertiveness implicitly and explicitly challenged that form of Italian cultural compactness that Fascism wanted to achieve at any cost. Diversity could not be tolerated, and required the erasure of any traces of alternative identities, be they ethnical, linguistic or cultural. In this respect it may be worth remembering that even Italian anti-fascists were portrayed as non-Italians.

Slavophobia and anti-Bolshevism thus became the enduring essence and description of what became known as *fascismo di confine* (border fascism): a blueprint for the brutal actions, which would occur in Italy from the autumn of 1920 onwards.

In September 1920, upon his return from a journey in Venezia Giulia where he reviewed Julian Fascism, Mussolini telephoned an article to his paper *Il Popolo d'Italia,* in which he proudly stated that whilst 'In other Italian regions the *Fasci di combattimento* are hardly more than a promise, in Venezia Giulia they are the main and dominating element in the local political situation. Perhaps the Fascists of Venezia Giulia are the beginning of a great movement of national revival and constitute the generous and combative advance guard of the Italy of which we dream and for which we are preparing.'[109] Indeed, well before the March on Rome Trieste had the elite paramilitary organisation, which surveilled the city districts.[110] To

---

[108] Bogdan C. Novak, *Trieste 1941-1954. The Ethnic, Political, and Ideological Struggle,* (Chicago and London: The University of Chicago Press, 1970), p. 38.

[109] Stefano Buvoli, 'Il fascismo nella Venezia Giulia e la persecuzione antislava,' in *Storia contemporanea in Friuli,* XXVI, 27, 1996, p. 71.

[110] Adrian Lyttleton, op. cit., p. 53.

accomplish this aim, it used the military garrison, which occupied the city under the terms of the Armistice. For its swift punitive raids, it relied on lorries and support provided by the army, wealthy landowners and industrialists, such as the famous Dreher Brewery and the Cosulich shipping family, who were able to protect and advance their upper-class interests, thus ending working-class agitation.

Despite the major rift existing between Julian and Friulian Fascism, as well as disunity inside the latter, the fight against Socialists and Slavs seemed to galvanise efforts and strengthen factions in the common anti-Socialist and Slavophobic programme of erasing the alien inhabitants. Between 1918 and 1940 the policy, based on the notion of superiority, would pave the way for Italy's ambitions in the Kingdom of Serbs, Croats and Slovenes (as Yugoslavia was called then). It was believed to be a logical consequence that Italy would one day enjoy the prestige denied to her by the 'mutilated victory,' and as befitted a great nation, she would one day dominate the Adriatic and the Mediterranean. However, Slavs and Yugoslavia were the major obstacles standing in Italy's way and they had to be removed, a gamble which proved destined to fail.

THE BAPTISM BY FIRE

The fact that interwar politics was dominated by an anti-Communist and anti-Slav crusade had very predictable effects before the fascist seizure of power, but the official language initially used towards the Slav minority employed mellifluous words and sensible statements. A prime example of this, in the aftermath of the First World War, was during a speech by Prime Minister Francesco Saverio Nitti, who stated: 'Slavs must have the feeling that Italy does not desire their denationalisation.'[111] Instructions were given 'to pursue a policy of freedom, justice, and sympathy for the people of another race.'[112] But instead, growing hostility and a poisonous campaign

---

[111] Dennison Rusinow, op. cit., p. 97.
[112] Ibid.

The Interwar Years

of violence against Slav minorities was started as soon as the Italian Army occupied Venezia Giulia. An early draft of the Italian memorandum, which Italy submitted at the peace conference in Paris, clearly showed the Italian sense of superiority toward, and priority over, the Slavs. The document stated that whilst Italians were indigenous in the territory, Slavs were migrants and therefore Italian claims to the area were based on 'communal traditions, indissoluble interests, the will and the conscience to safeguard the fatherland.' Further it was claimed that Italy needed to have 'the territory that would allow her to defend the West from the barbarians to the East.'[113]

As early as November 1918, Prime Minister Vittorio Emanuele Orlando complained to General Pietro Badoglio, deputy to Commander-in-Chief General Armando Diaz, that as 'Yugoslavs, clericals and socialists [...] are conspiring against us,' the military government based in Trieste was being too permissive.[114] The 'conspiracy' mentioned by Orlando referred to Yugoslavia's claims over Trieste, Istria and Dalmatia and expressed his fear that the presence of Slovenian and Croatian people would jeopardise Italian territorial demands in the area.

Badoglio therefore devised a program to counteract Slav resistance to the Italian annexation of the region. The detailed plan of action, which was not limited to areas under Italian military control, but included territories outside that zone, was approved by Prime Minister Orlando, the Minister for Foreign Affairs Sidney Sonnino, and General Armando Diaz, on 9 December 1918.[115] Special squads were established, tasked to watch over and control former mayors and civil servants of Slav origin, who had been

---

[113] 'Les Revendications de l'Italie sur les Alpes et dans l'adriatique,' Prima stesura del memorandum preparato dalla delegazione italiana alla Conferenza della Pace per esser presentato alla Conferenza stessa, Doc. 574 in *I Documenti Diplomatici Italiani* sets serie: 1918-1922, vol. 2 (1980), pp. 399, 403, quoted in Glenda Sluga, op. cit., p. 97.

[114] A. Canavero, 'Le terre liberate e redente nel dibattio culturale e politico,' in *Commissione parlamentare di inchiesta sulle terre liberate e redente (luglio 1920-giugno 1922),* vol. I, (Roma: Camera dei Deputati Archivio storico, 1991), quoted in Mark Thompson, op. cit., p. 380.

[115] Ivo Lederer, *Yugoslavia at the Paris Peace Conference: A Study in Frontiermaking,* (New Haven: Yale University Press, 1963), pp. 71-5.

46   *Luisa Morettin*

dismissed due to the change of territorial borders, and to deport recalcitrant clergymen because 'the population, religious as it is, is in their hands.'

A little known fascist attack against Slavs was sparked by the incident of the War Memorial on Mount Nero (Krn) in June 1922. The monument was erected in memory of *Alpini*, the mountain units of the Italian Army, killed there during the First World War. One week after the unveiling, the Italian authorities in Trieste reported the destruction of the memorial, accusing the local population from the local Slav villages at the foot of the mountain. As a result, there followed multiple arrests of Slavs and their subsequent discharge from public offices, and a furious press campaign directed against the minority in the area who had recently been annexed to Italy. In retaliation, armed fascists smashed a statue of the Slovene composer Hraboslav Volarič in Caporetto, and revelled in acts of looting and destruction of public places. Although this group of fascists set out to murder the town mayor and vicar, they narrowly escaped the round-up by fleeing into the woods. Yet, locals were still terrorised by more fascists, who arrived from the nearby towns of Udine and Cividale and revelled in shooting at closed doors and windows of houses.[116]

The summer of 1919 saw the decision to change the Julian administration from military into civilian:[117] General Carlo Petitti di Roreto was replaced by Civil Commissioner Augusto Ciuffelli. Upon Ciuffelli's arrival, on 3 August, a violent incident took place, and although minimal, it aides in understanding the political and social climate in Venezia Giulia, particularly the extent of the political struggle and the union of interests that brought Fascism and Mussolini to power. The altercation began with a group of young nationalists, (not yet Fascists), who attacked a procession of Socialist children and their guides, who were returning to their summer camp after an excursion. A police intervention followed and, during the clashes, one of the nationalists was accidentally killed by the police themselves, who then went on to arrest many Socialists, but none of the

---

[116] *Italian Genocide Policy against the Slovenes and the Croats. A Selection of Documents*, (Belgrade: Institute for International Politics and Economics, 1954), pp. 154-8.
[117] Dennison Rusinow, op. cit., p. 93.

The Interwar Years

nationalists. As a result of this partiality, the Socialists expressed their protest by declaring a strike, which was immediately followed by a nationalist counter-demonstration during which Socialists were wounded and their trade unions building attacked.[118]

Ciuffelli's role was later taken by Antonio Mosconi, who did not share Nitti's cautious policy of the treatment of national minorities. It was during Mosconi's governorship when the first Julian violent exploit against Slavs took a dramatic turn. As a reaction to a petty incident in the Dalmatian city of Spalato (Split), on 13 July 1920, Francesco Giunta ordered a demonstration, culminating in *squadristi* setting fire to the Trieste *Slovenski Narodni Dom* (Slovenian National House). The building, which was burnt to ashes, was not only the most prominent cultural, economic and political centre for Slav organizations in town, but metaphorically, it was the tangible sign of their presence on Italian soil. On that same day, the headquarters of the Slovene newspaper *Edinost* were raided, the offices of Slav lawyers, banks, shops, restaurants were demolished and the equipment of the Slovene and Serbian private schools were destroyed. The premises of the Yugoslav delegation in the city were also targeted by the violent campaign, whilst only one day after the Trieste attacks, the *Narodni Dom* in Pola suffered the same fate as the one in Trieste. To mark what was defined as a 'patriotic' event, in September 1920, Mussolini joined a celebration to commemorate the fire,[119] whilst the violent fascist expansion spread out from Trieste to the Istrian peninsula, engulfing both Socialist and Slav targets in small towns, villages and hamlets. This use of violence was supported by the nationalist press as, on 20 October 1920, the newspaper *Idea Nazionale* applauded a fascist attack on *Il Lavoratore*, the Socialist newspaper of Trieste, by stating, 'The example of the veterans of Trieste must be immediately copied in the whole country,' encouraging veterans to 'voluntarily, *on their own initiative,* deal with the new enemy which stabs the nation in the back.'[120]

---

[118] Ibid., pp. 95-6.
[119] Ibid., p. 105.
[120] *Idea Nazionale*, 20 October 1920, quoted in Alexander J. De Grand, op. cit., p. 120.

Mosconi's reaction to the *Narodni Dom* incident in Trieste was lukewarm. Whilst he publicly condemned the arson, he failed to take any action against the culprits. Ambiguity toward the 'Slav problem' was evident in his declarations and, less than a month later, he resorted to Francesco Giunta's squads in order to stop a general mass strike, which was spreading from the shipyards in Monfalcone, where workers had already been ferociously attacked by fascists.[121]

Well before the Fascist March on Rome in October 1922, Fascism usurped traditional powers in Venezia Giulia, thus becoming a powerful, parallel movement. Trieste was now an example of proto-fascist misrule with the *Narodni Dom* attack marking the birth of organised *squadrismo* (the fascist movement based on armed squads), whose aim was the sabotage of Giolitti's negotiations with Belgrade. The Adriatic question was far from solved.

THE SLAV PERSECUTION DISCOURSE

Every dictatorship has a specific national enemy. Before Italy's African conquests and growing drift to Nazi Germany, as the first signs of racial consciousness started to emerge, Mussolini could not adopt the same policy as Hitler, which defined Jews as *Todfeind*, the mortal enemy. Pursuing the principle of racial purity in a country as heterogeneous as Italy would have meant the end of the nation.[122] Therefore, the 'Slav question' conceptually evolved in the context of what had to become a new order of Italian cultural supremacy and a strong nation. The figment of the Western imagination, 'the dark Slav soul,' presented eastern populations as inferior, uncouth and barbarian, and to make the situation worse, the Treaty of Rapallo, signed on 12 November 1920, did not include any protection clauses or guarantee of their civic rights.[123]

---

[121] Elio Apih, op. cit., p. 127.
[122] Stefano Bartolini, op. cit., p. 42.
[123] Ibid., p. 61.

The Interwar Years 49

Some of the most influential support, and 'rational' basis, for anti-Slav attitudes and policies came from historical sciences as archaeology, classics and history that provided the central narrative of Italian pre-eminence throughout the centuries. In the same way the Roman Empire, with its Caesars and Augustuses, had dominated the world and the Italian Renaissance had contributed to the progress of humanity, it could now be argued that fascism's historic mission was to fulfil its imperial duty and usher in a new civilisation. This unofficial stigmatisation of Slavs found many highly placed champions in Italy, and not only Mussolini, who would 'easily sacrifice 500,000 barbaric Slavs for 50,000 Italians,' adding that 'when dealing with such a race as the Slav - inferior and barbarian - we must not pursue the carrot, but the stick policy.'[124]

In September 1927, from the pages of the leading party journal *Gerarchia*, politician Giuseppe Cobol, denied the existence of a Slav problem as 'Fascism cannot tolerate any deviation and distortions.' Socially Slavs were seen as subservient peasants who, 'in a not too far away future will be attracted by our civilisation [...] and will be proud to be part of the Italian nation.'[125] Similarly, the Member of Parliament Giorgio Bombig and Livio Ragusin-Righi, the *reggente* of the National Fascist Party in Trieste, supported the paranoid ideological struggle, which eventually resulted in a state-based Darwinism endorsed by the local and national press. As early as 1919 the daily *La Nazione*, the Triestine *Il Piccolo*, and even the left-wing paper *L'Unità,* portrayed Yugoslavia as 'backwater,' which needed civilising. This ruthless and arrogant campaign continued well into the 1940s: in an editorial in *Il Piccolo*, the Yugoslavs

---

[124] Mussolini delivered this speech during his visit to Pola on 20 September 1920. Armando Sestani, *Il confine orientale: una terra, molti esodi*, (Istituto storico della Resistenca e dell'Età Contemporanea in Provincia di Lucca, 2012), pp. 12–13.

[125] Giuseppe Cobol, 'Il fascismo e gli allogeni,' in *Gerarchia*, VII, 9, settembre 1927, pp. 803-6, quoted in Stefano Bartolini, op. cit., p. 50. A so-called 'Fascist of the first hour,' Giuseppe Cobol, later changed his name into the Italian form Cobolli-Gigli. Between 1935 and 1939 he was Minister of Public Works.

50   *Luisa Morettin*

were openly and contemptuously considered below 'the most obscure tribes of central Africa.'[126]

It is difficult to ascertain how much the propaganda machine of national and local authorities mobilised public opinion against Slavs, and if neutrality of bystanders actually covered up their support. It seems reasonable to assume that the indoctrinating of Italian national identity must have held a special place in the imaginations of the ideologically committed. Thus progressively, it instilled prejudice and an aggressive spirit in ordinary people, who would react more or less violently against the alien and anti-national minority. On the one hand there exist mild testimonies; a militant in the Trieste Communist Party stated: 'Although we live in the same geographical area with the Slav people, we are not close at all in terms of mentality. [...] First of all we have to take into account the contrast between city and country, [...] to that element we should add our national prejudice against them. [...] The level of education of these [Slav] members of the party is very low.'[127] On the other hand, however, the national belief could take on the form of violent activism. This is explicit in the diary annotations of an Italian school teacher in Dalmatia, who passionately supported fascism and cheered the killing of forty rebels and the destruction of their houses, accusing them of being 'brutalised through enslavement by Moscow.'[128]

The *Gestalt* of Italian national supremacy and cultural anxiety quickly underpinned ordinary life in Venezia Giulia and became tantamount to a 'cultural genocide.'[129] The regime's forcible denationalisation process developed in three phases: the first, the so-called *pertinenza*, which implied the ethnic mapping of eligibility for citizenship; the second, the crushing of the national paradigms, marginalisation and humiliation of the minority

---

[126] Editorial in the Trieste newspaper Il Piccolo, 28 May 1942, quoted in James Walston, 'History and Memory of the Italian Concentration Camps,' in *The Historical Journal*, Vol. 40, No. 1 (Mar., 1997), pp. 169-83.

[127] Stefano Bartolini, op. cit., p.70.

[128] Christopher Duggan, *Fascist Voices*, (London: The Bodley Head, 2012), pp. 213-5.

[129] Enzo Collotti, 'Sul razzismo antislavo,' in Alberto Burgio (a cura di), *Nel nome della razza: il razzismo nella storia d'Italia, 1870-1945*, (Bologna: Il Mulino, 1999), p. 57.

The Interwar Years 51

group; and the third, the imposition of the national patterns of the persecutor.

Well before the Gentile School Reform of 1 October 1923, the Italian Supreme Army Command forced Slav teachers out of their jobs and caused schools and kindergartens to be closed without the consent of the communes and provinces concerned. Some of them were later re-opened as Italian schools, whilst in the ones which had been allowed to stay open the study of Italian became compulsory. The progressive Italianisation of the education system was complemented by school children's holiday homes and colonies, which served the purpose of keeping boys and girls away from the influence of their families, thus continuing the denationalisation project. Failure to enrol pupils in the organisations resulted in parents being liable to arrest, to lose their jobs or their trade licence, and be deprived of their pensions. It is not surprising that the forcible imposition of the Latin culture caused students to move to Yugoslavia to attend secondary schools and universities.[130]

A Royal Decree, dated 15 October 1925, institutionalised what was already a widespread practice in the region – the ban on using the Slovene and Croatian languages in courts, public institutions, and private businesses. Particular importance was given to the language change for shop signs, inscriptions, signboards, monuments and epitaphs.

The suppression of Slav languages and personal names did not spare the Church. In line with Article 22 of the Lateran Pacts, which banned the use of any language besides Italian in Catholic services,[131] all churches were ordered to replace the old-established custom of reading the Mass in the Old Church Slavonic and to use Italian or Latin for sermons, hymns, prayers, and in general, for teaching religion. The provision was then enforced by zealous clerics, who openly supported the Fascist authorities in their denationalisation work. In such a forcible, fanatical way, Venezia Giulia became an Italian province.

---

[130] Lavo Čermelj, *Life-and-Death Struggle of a National Minority: the Jugoslavs in Italy*, (Ljubljana: Tiskarna Ljudske pravice, 1945), pp. 37-40.

[131] Michael R. Ebner, *Ordinary Violence in Mussolini's Italy*, (New York: Cambridge University Press, 2011), p. 190.

52   *Luisa Morettin*

OPPRESSION

According to one Slav source, the only difference between the liberal and the totalitarian government in their treatment of the Slav minority was the fact that the latter 'displayed greater sincerity and brutality than the former democratic governments.'[132] Especially after the unsuccessful assassination attempts of Mussolini in 1926, earlier authoritarianism was accentuated and further repressive legislation passed. Amongst the harshest measures introduced to the national territory by the unconstitutional 'Law for the Defense of the State' was the establishment of OVRA (the secret police), *confino* (internal exile), and the creation of the Special Tribunal, which was a court for political trials.

Even if the data of the sentences passed by the Special Tribunal are incomplete, the comparison of the following figures shows how the persecution and repressive rates were much higher among the Slav minority. It is estimated that of the 2,907 defendants sentenced by that court until the end of 1935, over 150 were Slavs and of the nine people condemned to death by the Fascist Special Tribunal, only four were Italians.[133] If these data are compared with the size of the population (the Yugoslav community in Italy at the time represented only 1.5 per cent of the entire population), the number of Slavs sentenced turns out to be more than five per cent. Despite the secrecy of the trials themselves, or maybe as a direct result of it, the trials were extremely intimidating, especially when the severity of the rulings is taken into account. This is seen in the following numbers: 16,917 is the aggregate number of imprisonment years passed upon the above-mentioned, 2,907 convicted; of those more than 1,600 years were inflicted upon the 150 Slovenes and Croats judged by the Special Tribunal.[134]

Due to its strong importance amongst the masses as a repository of Slav cultural identity and self-awareness and as a 'gatekeeper' of the

---

[132] *Italian Genocide Policy against the Slovenes and the Croats. A Selection of Documents*, p. 65.
[133] Martin Clark, *Modern Italy 1871-1982*, (London: Longman, 1984), pp. 252-3.
[134] Lavo Čermelj, op. cit., pp. 190-1.

The Interwar Years

53

Slavic language and religion in Venezia Giulia, it was unavoidable that Slav clergy would be persecuted by the regime. To this effect, Henry R. Cooper stressed that the Church Slavonic Bible, 'forged a bond among the Slavs that is as enduring as the related languages they speak and certainly more cohesive than their rivalrous histories and national cultures [...] might suggest.'[135] Also, the Slav Church had a distinctive historical identity within Roman Catholicism in respect to its ecclesiastical administration. Even though Slav priests adhered to Roman ritual, in the sense that church services were conducted in Latin, there were some differences that made them unpopular amongst fascists. These were that the Slav seminarians dressed differently and priests read the entire liturgy in the Old Church Slavonic, a custom recognised also by the 1906 papal decree '*Decretum de usu linguae slavonicae in sacra liturgia*'.[136] Countless priests refused to use Italian, a language their congregation did not understand, and were labelled as 'enemies of Italy and faithless servants of God.' This resulted in priests under constant police supervision, as well as being subject to the most traditional fascist methods of threats, outrages, beatings, force-feeding of castor oil, and the invasion of churches while mass was being celebrated - as in the infamous case of Christmas Day 1920, in Baška, on the island of Veglia (Krk). Eventually it escalated to expulsions and replacement by 'pious' Italian clergymen.[137] It is known, for instance, that Bishop Trifone Pederzolli of Pola and Parenzo 'fell over backwards to please the authorities.'[138]

The Holy See's stance in respect to racial minorities was unclear. Even if the 28 January 1924 circular issued by the Sacred Congregation of the Vatican Consistory ratified that in regions inhabited by a non-Italian population the clergy would speak the language of the parishioners, when fascist violence turned toward the Slav clergy in Venezia Giulia, Pope Pius

---

[135] Henry R. Cooper, *Slavic Scriptures: The Formation of the Church Slavonic Version of the Holy Bible*, (London: Associated University Presses, 2002), p.15.

[136] Lavo Čermelj, op. cit., pp. 95-6.

[137] Michael Ebner, op. cit., p. 190.

[138] John F. Pollard, *The Vatican and Italian Fascism, 1929-32: A Study in Conflict*, (New York: Cambridge University Press. 1985), p. 93.

54   *Luisa Morettin*

XI, unlike his predecessor Benedict XV, did not condemn the unfolding events. Unsurprisingly, since as early as 1926 relations between Mussolini, 'the man sent by the Providence,' and the Vatican had become so cordial that they resulted in the Lateran Pacts of 1929. The Vatican 'sold the Slav minority to Fascism!' stated the anti-fascist historian Gaetano Salvemini. In the same way Pontius Pilate had washed his hands, Pius IX 'did all that was possible by praying.'[139] As a result, the Slav clergymen's appeals for intercession of the highest echelons of the Holy See fell on deaf ears, with a few exceptions. One such case was of Luigi Fogar Bishop of Trieste-Capodistria who, for his unbiased sense of justice and Christian support to the Slav minority, was eventually forced out of his diocese in 1936.[140]

Also the Slav press was hit hard by the denationalisation campaign. Notwithstanding existing press freedoms, the year 1918 marked the beginning of preventive censorship of Slav periodicals and papers, such as the Croatian weekly *Pučki Prijatelj*, the *Narodna tiskarna* and the famous Slovenian *Edinost*, which were repeatedly raided, bombed or burnt down.[141] Newspapers played an essential role in the support of fascism, hence not only the Slav press in Venezia Giulia was outlawed and closed down, but in the period 1925-1928, also the Italian press suffered censorship, suppression and dismissal of their journalists. This was seen in the case of the well-known liberal editor of Milan's *Corriere della Sera*, Luigi Albertini, who was removed from his position in November 1925.

In April 1929, Mussolini took it upon himself to order the prefect of Trieste to ensure 'no Slav newspaper' appeared on the city streets.[142] Books formed an intellectual continuum with the press, especially at a time when all Slav libraries and cultural societies were closed, and as such they suffered a similar destruction campaign. Commandants of *carabinieri* (the national gendarmerie), Fascist *podestà* (mayors) and schoolmasters imposed their control over the production, circulation and ownership of

---

[139] Gaetano Salvemini, op. cit., pp. 25, 28.
[140] Dennison Rusinow, op. cit., pp. 202-3.
[141] Lavo Čermelj, op. cit., p. 71.
[142] R. J. Bosworth, *Mussolini*, cit., p. 249.

books, whether they were novels, history books, prayer books, or pocket calendars written in Slovene.

In its desire to protect the Italian population from the sources of what was called 'criminal infection which are ignited and fed from beyond the frontier,'[143] the increasing power of fascism failed to acknowledge that by increasing fear, it lost ground. The only real achievement of the official demonology was the nurturing of deep resentment and hatred of the Italians amongst the Slavs in the region.

---

[143] 'Report of 7 May 1931 on the Parliamentary bill for the prorogation of the Special Tribunal,' quoted in Gaetano Salvemini, op. cit., p. 20.

Chapter 3

YUGOSLAVIA: WAR AND OCCUPATION

There is nothing intelligent to say about a massacre.
Everybody is supposed to be dead,
to never say anything or want anything ever again.
Everything is supposed to be very quiet after a massacre
and it always is,
except for the birds.

Kurt Vonnegut
Slaughterhouse 5

FASCIST FOREIGN POLICY

When fascism came to power in 1922, the Adriatic question evolved into the first test bed for Mussolini's foreign policy. The government's practical attitude to foreign relations was still informed by Italy's wish 'to be treated by the great nations of the world like a sister and not like a waitress.'[144] For

---

[144] Richard J. Bosworth, *Mussolini*, p.184.

the Duce, and his then minister of Foreign Affairs, Dino Grandi, strategy was forged by geopolitics and national prestige – as Italy's ultimate aim was the creation of an Italian empire in the Mediterranean. That in turn would require securing the Adriatic, an area of historic interest for Italy. Success would revive the Roman Empire's dream and that of the Venetian supremacy during the Middle Ages and Renaissance, thus rising Italy's profile. To achieve that goal Mussolini had devised a geostrategic 'grand design:' a territorial expansion that could only be realised through force and war and would dissipate the bitterness of the 'mutilated victory.' Italian interwar irredentism thus opportunistically evolved from the ethnic character of populations to the geographical and historic dimension of territorial claims, and only later introduced the notion of *spazio vitale* (vital living space) in order to justify wider hegemony. This explained the double standards of the Italian Fascist foreign policy during the 1920s until 1933. Despite the peaceful diplomatic strategy during the so called 'verbal pacifism' period and the success of the 1924 Rome Treaty of neutrality and friendship between Italy and Yugoslavia, in practice Mussolini pursued an aggressive policy aimed at the breakup of the neighbouring country. As a result, the relationship between Italy and Yugoslavia remained strained for most part of the 1920s and 1930s.

After taking direct control of the War Ministry in April 1925, Mussolini created the chief of the armed forces general staff, appointing Marshal Pietro Badoglio to the new office. In October 1926, he shared his strategic plan with Badoglio urging him to 'inflict on Yugoslavia one of those lessons which are sufficient to correct the mental and political deformities of any people.'[145] But things were not as easy as they seemed, as Badoglio warned the Duce. There was no guarantee that Germany or France would not intervene on the side of Yugoslavia; the required quick mobilisation of Italian divisions would not be possible until 1928, with the end of railway improvements; organising suitable tactics would require

---

[145] DDI, Serie 7, IV, 446, pp. 346-7, Mussolini a Badoglio, 2 October 1926.

time and preparation.[146] This was in contrast to Mussolini's plan to 'deal a robust blow' very quickly.

The situation did not improve after the 1927 Franco-Yugoslav Treaty of guarantee and security. The new diplomatic development would mean Italy would not face a 'one-front' war anymore, but a 'two-front' one. In January 1928 Badoglio's successor, General Giuseppe Ferrari, warned Mussolini that the Yugoslav Army was improving its resources thanks to French support and was in a position to allocate twelve divisions on the border with Venezia Giulia. For Rome, this implied that the twenty-one divisions at her disposal would not be sufficient in a joint war against France and Yugoslavia, as Italy needed at least thirty-one divisions to defend herself and a total of sixty (full Italian armoured capacity) to defeat her Adriatic enemy. In addition, not all divisions were completely efficient, therefore 'very burdensome sums' of money were needed to prepare for a victorious war.[147] Once again, Mussolini's war timetable was not realistic, and yet he would not give up. In February 1929, he urged the Fascist Grand Council to accelerate Italy's war preparations, as before long, Serbia would be involved in war.[148] Again in the winter 1932-33, Mussolini tried to convince the king and military advisers to invade Yugoslavia, but once more to no avail.[149]

Undeterred, the Italian Government continued to contemplate an invasion of its neighbouring state. In the meantime Italy resorted to another, more extensive way to subdue the Kingdom of Yugoslavia by means of a constant erosion of its internal unity. The Orthodox Serbs hated the Catholic Croats and both loathed the Muslim Bosnians. So, Mussolini viewed Yugoslavia as an inorganic construct, an 'artificial creation' of Versailles, which might collapse under the two front pressure represented by internal ethnic and religious questions on the one side, and Italian

---

[146] AUSSME, Rep. L-10 racc. 1/1. Badoglio a Mussolini, 4 October 1926.

[147] John Gooch, *Mussolini and His Generals. The Armed Forces and Fascist Foreign Policy, 1922-1940*, (Cambridge: Cambridge University Press, 2007), p. 84.

[148] DDI, Serie 7, VII, 185, pp. 212-3, 26 February 1929.

[149] MacGregor Knox, *Hitler's Italian Allies. Royal Armed Forces, Fascist Regime, and the War of 1940-1943*, (Cambridge: Cambridge University Press, 2000), p. 10.

60 *Luisa Morettin*

sponsored terrorism on the other.[150] By taking advantage of the unresolved conflict between the rival movements of Yugoslavia's constituent peoples, the Rome Government clandestinely supported and subsidised Montenegrin separatists: the subversive Internal Macedonian Revolutionary Organisation (IMRO), an ultranationalist organisation, and the Ustaše, the Croatian Revolutionary Movement, which under the lead of the nationalist exile Ante Pavelić, favoured an independent Croatia. The IMRO turned to terrorism in response to the dictatorship of Alexander Karađorđević, the Serb king, who was striving to create a united state out of his politically and ethnically divided people. Italy helped the Ustaše to set up terrorist training camps, chiefly at Borgotaro and Gaeta (Italy) and Janka Puszta (Hungary), and further supplied everything from military uniforms and provisions, to weapons, money and printing press for propaganda material, which were to be distributed in Yugoslavia and abroad. The highest echelons of the Italian state were aware of this subversive activity; from Emilio Manganiello, private secretary to the Chief Police Officer in Rome, to Pompeo Aloisi, Head of Cabinet at the Foreign Office.[151] Further, Italian training grounds were often visited by prominent Ustaše supporters such as Mile Budak, who was in charge of camps on the Liparis, and Branimir Jeli, a focal point for Croatian exile activities.[152]

The dangerous nature of the Ustaše became fully evident in October 1934 when, together with the IMRO, they participated in the assassination of King Alexander Karađorđević. Significantly, the murder took place during a state visit to France, which was meant to cement the close alliance between the two countries at a time when Italy's acts of imperialism were becoming more threatening. The murder of the Yugoslav king opened a period of disintegration for the Yugoslav state, the independence of which

---

[150] Denis Mac Smith, *Mussolini's Roman Empire*, (London and New York: Longman, 1976), p. 22.

[151] ACS, Documenti II G.M. Dainelli 1938 De Zoppis 1956, b. 161, Segnalazioni dei crimini italiani a danno della Jugoslavia e suoi popoli, 1946, pp. 5-6.

[152] Robert B. McCormick, *Croatia Under Ante Pavelić: America, the Ustaše and Croatian Genocide*, (London: I.B. Tauris, 2014), p. 16.

Yugoslavia: War and Occupation

61

slowly declined. By supporting Pavelić's dreams of separatism, Mussolini wanted to realise two objectives: first to maximise Italian influence in the whole Balkan region, thus fulfilling the last aspirations of irredentism; and second, to justify fascism by a successful invasion of the Adriatic neighbour that would enhance Italy's 'space' and provide an accessible source of raw materials. For this purpose, Venezia Giulia would serve as a bridgehead for the Italian expansion eastwards.

The fascist regime's geopolitical ambitions were exemplified by the increase in the military budget, which enabled Mussolini to engage in the African campaign that was centre-stage throughout the 1930s. After the Duce's invasion of Ethiopia in October 1935, he linked the existing colonies of Eritrea and Somalia, thus enlarging his African Empire. The Ethiopian annexation was presented to be one of the great successes of the regime, which would eventually command the Red Sea, and challenge Britain at the Suez. Yet, it cost Italy dearly as the territorial expansion weakened the military and ruined the country financially. Worse still, the Ethiopian war provoked the condemnation of all members of the League of Nations and the introduction of economic sanctions toward Italy. This in turn shifted most of Italian trade towards Germany and drove the Duce towards his fatal alliance with Adolf Hitler.

In the middle of the 1930s, after the fall of liberalism had given way to left wing revolutions, fascist ideology continued to spread abroad in a sort of 'travelling political universe,'[153] as did Mussolini's foreign policy miscalculations as Italy constantly engaged in an aggressive policy. Within three months of the Ethiopian enterprise, Italy was again at war in Spain, where Mussolini sent volunteers to intervene on the insurgent side of General Francisco Franco. The Duce's intervention in Franco's attempt at seizing power cost Italy almost eight and a half billion lire; 3,819 soldiers killed in battle; 12,000 wounded, and the waste of 759 planes, 3,436 machine guns, and 6,791 trucks.[154]

---

[153] Federico Finchelstein, *Transatlantic Fascism: Ideology, Violence, and the Sacred in Argentina and Italy*, 1919-1945, (Durham: Duke University Press, 2010), p. 6.

[154] Renzo De Felice, *Mussolini il Duce. Lo stato totalitario 1936-1940*, (Torino: Einaudi, 1981), p. 465.

Later, in April 1939, Mussolini invaded Albania. He had to act swiftly if he was to outmanoeuvre Hitler, who after invading Czechoslovakia in March 1939 had the potential to expand into Croatia. The occupation of Albania, which guarded the southern approaches to the Adriatic, offered Italy two strategic advantages. First, it secured the entire eastern coast of Italy from attack by giving her the right to control the Straights of Otranto. Second, it created a foothold in the Balkans from which Italy could stir Albanian irredentism in Kosovo, thus conveniently threatening Yugoslavia in its sensitive southern areas.[155] Yet, the occupation proved to be another costly enterprise: although the war was short and the weak Balkan state was quickly defeated and annexed, Albania turned out to be a burden, rather than a profitable acquisition for Italy.[156]

The continuous state of hostilities between 1936 and 1940 implied that the country was completely depleted of resources it could not replace, and that Rome had neither the necessary new technology nor industrial output at a crucial time when other countries were preparing for an approaching European conflict.[157] It is not by chance that between 1940 and 1943, Italy could produce only 11,000 warplanes, compared to Germany, which built 25,000, Britain with 26,000 and the United States at 86,000.[158] Also in 1940, Italy possessed only two searchlights, 230 anti-aircraft batteries for the defence of the whole national territory, 42,000 vehicles for the army, and no modern artillery. At the outbreak of war in June 1940, the Italian Army could rely on 700 tanks, a number similar, or even higher than what other major powers had available. Yet, closer examination revealed that in fact they were 'tankettes,' with armour which was too thin to be used as protection from machine gun fire.[159] In addition, combat units received

---

[155] Dragan Bakić, 'The Italo–Yugoslav Conflict over Albania: A View from Belgrade. 1919–1939,' in *Diplomacy and Statecraft*, Vol. 25, 4, 2014, pp. 592-612.

[156] Denis Mack Smith, *Mussolini's Roman Empire*, p. 149.

[157] Christopher Duggan, *The Force of Destiny. A History of Italy since 1796*, (London: Allen Lane, 2007), p. 507.

[158] Philippe Foro, 'L'Italie dans la seconde guerre mondiale,' in Jean-François Muracciole and Guillaume Piketty (eds.), *Encyclopédie de la Seconde Guerre Mondiale*, (Paris: Éditions Robert Laffont, 2015), p. 634.

[159] Philip Jowett, *Italian Army, 1940-1945*, Vol. 1, (Oxford: Osprey Publishing, 2000), p. 4.

Yugoslavia: War and Occupation

inadequate training, which limited the effectiveness of operations and prevented Italy from performing to her full potential in battle.[160] Realistically, Italy would be capable to meet the needs of the army, the navy and the aviation in full, only by 1944.[161]

The financial strain of the Ethiopian war ushered an improvement in Italo-Yugoslav relations with the five-year nonaggression Treaty of Belgrade, signed on 25 March 1937 by Foreign Minister Galeazzo Ciano and Prime Minister Milan Stojadinović. The agreement was supposed to mark the beginning of a cordial political and economic relationship between the two countries, as well as acting as a deterrent for German expansion towards Trieste and south-west Europe.[162] Rome had promised that she would respect Yugoslavia's territorial integrity and oversee the Ustaše organisations based in Italy. This marked a temporary decline for terrorist organisations, whose members were persuaded to return home or were transferred from Southern Italy to Tuscany. Further, special attention was devoted to the treatment of minorities in Venezia Giulia, who could be granted concessions, such as the revival of particular cultural and economic organisations, the publication of a Slovene-language newspaper, and use of Slovene in churches. But neither the Yugoslav political friendship nor substantial cultural freedoms were properly established and minority rights were barely implemented by the resistant Slavophobic Fascist officials in the region.[163] In fact, the 1937 treaty did not prevent Rome from conspiring against Yugoslavia and Rome used the treaty to bide their time until they were able to invade Yugoslavia. A document written in 1939 by Italo Sauro, an advisor of the Fascist Government and the son of famous irredentist Nazario Sauro, who was executed by Austria-Hungary in 1916, attested to the continuance of anti-Slav feelings in Italy and the possibility of invasion into Yugoslavia. In his report for Mussolini,

---

[160] See MacGregor Knox, *Common Destiny. Dictatorship, Foreign Policy, and War in Fascist Italy and Nazi Germany*, (Cambridge: Cambridge University Press, 2000), pp. 148-85.

[161] Francesco Rossi, *Mussolini e lo Stato Maggiore: avvenimenti del 1940*, (Roma: Regionale, 1951), p. 21.

[162] Jacob B. Hoptner and Henry L. Roberts, *Yugoslavia in Crisis 1934-1941*, (New York: Columbia University Press, 1962), pp. 73, 301-3.

[163] Dennison Rusinow, op. cit., pp. 236-7.

Sauro advised that 'the purge [of Slavs] in Venezia Giulia must be a prerequisite of any future conquest.'[164] In July 1940, he also wrote to Osvaldo Sebastiani, the personal secretary to the Duce from 1934 until 1941, saying: 'When events will come to their happy conclusion [the invasion of Yugoslavia], ... I beg you to tell the Duce to allow me the privilege to be at the forefront of the fight against the enemy of my blood: the Slavs.'[165]

In the meantime, the radical Italianisation programme of Venezia Giulia could not and did not mould the hearts and minds of the Slavs, who met violence with violence. The detailed reports, sent to Rome by the Prefect of Istria, describe an atmosphere of war, which was similar to the partisan guerrilla that raged in Venezia Giulia after 1943. He described anti-Italian riots, armed attacks toward Italian military and police, the arson attacks of Italian schools, and the burning of forests, which the Slavs had now been banned from by the Italian regime. The revolutionary activities were supported by two irredentist societies based in Ljubljana, the Orjuna and the TIGR, active altogether from 1921 to 1941. Next to them existed a net of communist cells, which clandestinely operated throughout the fascist period.[166]

In Venezia Giulia, the fascist assault on the enemy's cultural history and the divisive political thinking of 'us vs them' made both Italians and Slavs fearful. A well-informed Istrian Fascist, (possibly a certain Maracchi), noted in his eyewitness account:

Identifying nationalism with Fascism the [Italian] Istrians fought in the ranks of Fascism, as the Slavs ranged themselves under the red banner. From that day onward was created the situation in which in Istria Communism was equivalent to Slav nationalism and Fascism was equivalent to Italian nationalism.[167]

---

[164] ACS, b. 161, p. 4.
[165] Ibid., p. 4.
[166] Dennison Rusinow, Op. cit., pp. 204-9.
[167] Ibid., p. 210.

Yugoslavia: War and Occupation

Whilst the regime endeavoured to indoctrinate Italians and Slavs alike, there were new developments on the international front. First, the internationalisation of Fascism gave Mussolini confidence and caused the evolution of Italian-German relations. This would soon lead to the May 1939 'Pact of Steel,' the alliance formalising the 1936 Rome-Berlin Axis agreement of political and military support. As a result, the existing Slavophobia and the minority issue in Venezia Giulia did not improve, as Nazi Germany categorised Slavs as non-Aryan *Untermenschen* (subhumans). Second, the new Yugoslav regent, Prince Pavle Karađorđević, attempted to resolve the conflict with the Croats through a *Sporazum*. The agreement, signed in August 1939, created an autonomous Croatian *banovina* that incorporated a quarter of Bosnia-Herzegovina and was largely self-governing, except in regard to defence and foreign affairs. But the *Sporazum* split the country in two and provoked bitter resentment, not only among the Serbs, but also among the Ustaše, which saw it as a betrayal of the ideal the movement's ideal of a complete independence for Croatia. And, indeed, such form of internal appeasement was not to last.

On 23 January 1940 the Italian Foreign Minister and Mussolini's son-in-law Galeazzo Ciano, together with his *chef de cabinet* Filippo Anfuso, received Ante Pavelić and Josip Bombelles (who was probably a Yugoslav double agent), to discuss the arrangements to give Croatia independence from Yugoslavia. The plan agreed upon involved an Ustaše revolution in Croatia against the Belgrade government and, after taking the main Croatian cities, the Ustaše would invite Italy to occupy and keep control of the new independent state of Croatia. In this way, and without bloodshed, Italy could take over Croatia, which would become an Italian vassal. However, due to the existing international situation Ciano was convinced that it was not yet the right time and it would be unwise to act prematurely.[168] Five months later, on 10 May 1940, Pavelić once again met with Ciano, who realised the Croatian situation was at a pivotal point and feared that if Italy further delayed supporting the Ustaše, they would turn

---

[168] DDI, Serie 9, III, no. 194, pp. 162-4. Galeazzo Ciano, *Diario 1937-1943*, (a cura di Renzo De Felice), (Milano: BUR, 2006), 23 January 1940, pp. 389-90.

to Germany.[169] In June 1940, Ciano received an appeal from the members of the Croatian National Committee for the Liberation and Reestablishment of the Independent State of Croatia, in which they asked for Italian military assistance to separate Croatia from Yugoslavia.[170] But the Duce's focus had temporarily shifted from Yugoslavia to a greater objective: he had decided that Italy would enter into what would soon become the Second World War.

By the mid-summer of 1940, France, Poland, Holland, Belgium, Denmark, Norway and Luxembourg had fallen quickly to the advancing Wehrmacht and British forces were expelled from the continent. During this predatory climate, Hitler's victories proved to be irresistible for Mussolini, who began to emulate his Nazi ally. After nine months of neutrality, on 10 June 1940, the Duce announced that the Rome government had declared war on Britain and France. Italy entered into the conflict as the 'first ally' of Germany, holding fatal delusions about herself and her enemy forces. The over-confident Mussolini bragged about having 'eight million bayonets' at his command, believed that the United States would not enter into the war, and called Britain 'a declining power,' which would last only a few months in battle. Emboldened by Hitler's victories, he thought Rome had to take advantage of the situation swiftly and join in what he assumed would be 'a high-speed war,' sacrificing some thousand men in order to be able to sit at the peace table as an outright victor. However, Italy did not have the industrial basis needed for a modern war. The poorly executed offensive into the French Alps and the early blow during the Greek winter of 1940-41 would soon expose the extent to which Italy's strength had been overestimated.

By sending his army across the Albanian border into Greece, Mussolini was hoping to conduct 'a parallel war.' He had tried to match Hitler's previous success in Czechoslovakia, but poor leadership, lack of equipment and training meant the Italians were driven back by Greek forces. Therefore, Germany had to intervene to restore Italy's position,

---

[169] Galeazzo Ciano, op. cit., 10 May 1940, p. 428.
[170] DDI, Serie 9, IV, pp. 631-2.

Yugoslavia: War and Occupation

leaving Italy humiliated at being defeated by such a small country as Greece. This was later compounded, in the spring of 1941, by the collapse of the empire in AOI (Italian Oriental Africa).

Despite such setbacks Mussolini still nursed the dream of controlling the Balkans and avenging Italy's 'mutilated victory.' Italy had already disclosed her ambition to Germany during a visit of Galeazzo Ciano to Hitler in Salzburg in August 1939. During the three-hour long meeting while the Führer outlined Berlin's offensive and defensive plans, complaining about Poland's alleged provocations, Ciano openly revealed Italy's need to invade Yugoslavia.[171] Hitler promptly advised Italy to strike the blow as soon as possible, thus reiterating what Ribbentrop told Ciano the day before with regards to Croatia and Dalmatia.[172]

In July 1940 the Italian ambassador in Berlin, Dino Alfieri, was told about French and Allied documents, which had been found by the Wehrmacht in a train at La Charitié-sur-Saône. These documents attested to the fact that since Belgrade was looking for Allied support against the fascist countries, it clearly displayed an 'equivocal and hostile' Yugoslav policy towards Italy. This made Hitler support Italy in her endeavours and showed that this Italian retaliation was necessary 'at the opportune moment.'[173]

On the eve of 6 July 1940 and Ciano's trip to Germany, the Duce briefed his son-in-law to express to the Führer Rome's support for Operation Sea Lion (the invasion of Great Britain) and to mention the need to 'liquidate Yugoslavia, a typical Versailles creation of anti-Italian bent.'[174] However, on this occasion Hitler changed his mind and backtracked, fearing that 'action would be dangerous except if a general Balkan war had already broken out.'[175] The German order 'to halt all along the line' was reiterated on 17 August when Ciano had a meeting with the

---

[171] Galeazzo Ciano, op. cit., 12 August 1939, p. 327.
[172] DDI, Serie 8, XIII, 1, Conversazione tra Ciano e Ribbentrop, 12 August 1939.
[173] DDI, Serie IX, V, 161, Alfieri a Ciano, 1 July 1940.
[174] Galeazzo Ciano, op. cit., 5 July 1940, p. 450.
[175] MacGregor Knox, *Mussolini Unleashed 1939-1941: Politics and Strategy in Fascist Italy's Last War*, (Cambridge: Cambridge University Press, 2008), p. 142.

68   *Luisa Morettin*

Foreign Minister of the Reich, Joachim von Ribbentrop,[176] who revealed how the thinking in Berlin was that an attack against Yugoslavia and Greece would have caused a dangerous Russian intervention in the Balkans.

On 19 September 1940, during Ribbentrop's visit to Rome, Mussolini renewed the plans for Contingency E, (war with Yugoslavia). Ribbentrop reassured the Duce that 'Yugoslavia and Greece were two spheres of Italian interest in which Italy could adopt the policy she chose with the full support of Germany,' but Berlin held the view that 'in the existing circumstances the principal effort should be directed against Britain.' [177] Once again Rome had to accept Germany's decision and Contingency E had to be put on hold. Mussolini's desire to assert his position as a worthy ally and launch a 'parallel war' was being dampened. An evident competition between the two allies had emerged and Rome became aware of her inferiority. In this respect Ciano's recorded conversations with his father-in-law highlighted the difficult relationship with Berlin, which would not improve over time. 'One wonders,' the Duce would say later, 'if we [Italians] are also a vassal nation [to Germany].'[178]

WAR IN YUGOSLAVIA

Whilst Italy invaded Greece (October 1940-April 1941) in what would prove to be a disastrous military campaign for the Duce's forces, the Yugoslav domestic situation was deteriorating. After Romania, Hungary, and Bulgaria joined the Tripartite Pact, Yugoslavia found itself surrounded by Fascist countries. Although Belgrade had previously declared its neutrality, on 25 March 1941 Prince Regent Pavle was forced by Berlin to become an ally of the Axis powers. The move was a success for Italy in

---

[176] Galeazzo Ciano, op. cit., 17 August 1940, p. 458.

[177] Mario Cervi, *The Hollow Legions. Mussolini's Blunder in Greece. 1940-1941*, (New York: Doubleday, 1971), pp. 312-6.

[178] Galeazzo Ciano, op. cit., 20 July 1941, p. 535.

Yugoslavia: War and Occupation

that she could eventually expand into Yugoslavia and Germany could fulfil its wish to exterminate the forces of Bolshevism by launching Operation Barbarossa – the massive assault on the Soviet Union. Yugoslavia gave Hitler the much needed secure southern flank to enable him begin the offensive and the oil resources of Romania and Hungary would now be at his disposal, too.

The opinion of pro-Western Serb-nationalist army and air force officers, led by General Dušan Simović, was that Yugoslavia's drift toward the Axis meant not just compromising the country's integrity, but also a further marginalisation of Serbian classes and favouritism to the Croats. Such resentment led to a coup d'état on 27 March 1941 which ousted Prince Pavle in favour of the much younger, pro-British Prince Peter, the legitimate heir to the throne. Overnight Yugoslavia became a risk to Germany and the unexpected move shocked Mussolini, who was longing for his Balkan expansion to become reality. The Duce was eager to act and take the Balkan territory, yet he feared that his German ally might take Dalmatia and Croatia.[179]

In Berlin an enraged Hitler blamed the British BBC Serbian-language broadcasts as well as the activities of the British Secret Service in Belgrade for 'pulling the strings.'[180] For propaganda purposes London insisted that it was a strictly Yugoslav rebellion, but in fact both the British Secret Intelligence Service and the Special Operations Executive (SOE), the British secret organisation in charge of espionage and aid to local resistance movements, had been involved in the coup d'état.[181] The Yugoslav rising infuriated Hitler, who promptly wrote to Mussolini on 27 March 1941 claiming: 'I have done everything possible and have made tremendous effort to make Yugoslavia join our common cause. These efforts have been in vain.' And then, urging the Duce to consider the

---

[179] H. James Burgwyn, *Empire on the Adriatic. Mussolini's Conquest of Yugoslavia 1941-1943*, (New York: Enigma Books, 2005), p. 25.

[180] David Stafford, 'SOE and the British Involvement in the Belgrade Coup d'État in March 1941,' *Slavic Review*, Vol. 36, No. 3 (Sep., 1977), pp. 399-419.

[181] Neil Balfour and Sally Mackay, *Paul of Yugoslavia. Britain's Maligned Friend*, (London: Hamilton, 1980), p. 257.

70   *Luisa Morettin*

matter now closed, the Führer added some orders. 'I consider it necessary that you should try to man and guard the most important passes between Yugoslavia and Albania [and] … reinforce your forces on the Italo-Yugoslav frontier with all the means at your disposal and with maximum speed.'[182] The following day, Mussolini reassured Hitler that he would send infantry units to take up positions on the three lines of a possible attack: in Venezia Giulia, in Zara and in Albania. He promised he would also send seven divisions to join the six already present along the eastern alpine border where 15,000 frontier guards had already been put on alert; at the same time the second air squadron was ready to operate in the area.[183]

Dark clouds were gathering on the horizon for Yugoslavia and the storm began when Hitler launched 'Operation 25,' or 'Operation Punishment,' the aptly chosen codename for the simultaneous invasion of Yugoslavia and Greece, which had to be carried out – in the Führer's own words – 'with merciless brutality.' More specifically the order stated that 'the city of Belgrade [had to be destroyed] from the air by continual day and night attacks.' For that purpose, 600 Luftwaffe aircrafts were redeployed to the Balkan area and were added to the existing 400 bombers.[184]

The offensive, which involved also the military units of the Axis powers, turned out to be a catastrophe for Yugoslavia. Operations commenced without warning at quarter past five on the morning of 6 April 1941 with a simultaneous attack on Greece and Yugoslavia. A German massive air assault on Belgrade that lasted three days took an estimated 17,000 lives and left behind a carpet of destruction. What once was the capital city, the centre of power and communications, lay in ruins. Chaos reigned.

The brutal assault forced the Yugoslav Government to leave Belgrade as the Wehrmacht's land invasion commenced. The first attack came from

---

[182] Mario Cervi, op. cit., pp. 342-3.
[183] Ibid., p. 344. Letter from the Duce to the Führer, 28 March 1941.
[184] Williamson Murray and Alan Millet, *A War to be Won: Fighting the Second World War*, (Cambridge: Harvard University Press, 2000), p. 103

Yugoslavia: War and Occupation

Bulgaria so that German forces could converge with Italian forces. In Southern Yugoslavia, the XL Panzer Corps launched its offensive on 6 April, the Wehrmacht entered Zagreb on 10 April, while on 11 April the XLI Panzer Corps attacked from the east.[185]

The Chief of the Italian Army Staff, General Rodolfo Graziani, who had been in charge for planning the Italian invasion of Yugoslavia, later declared that Rome's intention was 'to make a little war for the [local copper and bauxite] mines as they had done in Albania, and not a large-scale war alongside the Germans which they hoped to avoid,'[186] yet, in fact, Italy had launched a full scale offensive. This operation had been spearheaded by the Second Army of General Vittorio Ambrosio, who had moved from Venezia Giulia and Istria towards Ljubljana, and then southward along the Dalmatian coast. His 2nd Army was reinforced by three Army Corps, three divisions and several units, which had the task to push towards Spalato and Jajce, in central Bosnia, and join German troops coming from Graz. They would also link up with forces coming from the second front, located in Zara, where General Emilio Giglioli's division, was headed towards Sebenico, Spalato and Ragusa (Dubrovnik), as well as with four divisions of General Alessandro Pirzio Biroli's 9th Army, advancing upwards from the third front located along the Yugoslav-Albanian border.

The First Front

The border between Italy and Yugoslavia ran for approximately 136 miles, from the town of Tarvisio down toward the coast, and was divided into two defensive areas: the northern part of Varco di Coccau to Monte Grosso (excluded), and the southern part, running from Monte Grosso down to Fiume. The Italian 2nd Army, under the lead of General Vittorio Ambrosio,

---

[185] Percy E. Schramm, *Kriegstagebuch des Oberkommandos der Wehrmacht 1940-1945 - Eine Dokumentation*, Teilband. 1, (München: Weltbild, 1982), p. 368.

[186] *Processo Graziani: l'Autodifesa dell'ex Maresciallo nel Resoconto Stenografico*, Vol. 1, (Roma: Ruffolo, 1948) p. 137.

was deployed along this defensive line with the task to defend the frontier and to carry out various assaults. The command of the northern part of the boundary was allocated to General Mario Robotti and his XI Army Corps, whilst in the south General Riccardo Balocco commanded the V Army Corps.[187]

On 11 April 1941, the Italian 2nd Army began its advance from Trieste into Slovenia, occupying inner Carniola and the majority of lower Carniola. Crucially the Italian Army was informed by intelligence that a motorised German division was headed to Ljubljana, a city agreed to be within the Italian area of operations. The Italian Army managed to take Ljubljana and Italy now felt she was on an equal footing with Germany, as for Rome, it was not only a matter of military and political prestige, but also an endorsement of the Fascist regime's legitimacy.

After conquering the city of Karlovac on 12 April 1941, the 2nd Army swiftly headed south to defend the right flank of German forces, which were operating on an easier terrain, but were subject to potential Yugoslav counteroffensive actions from the Dinaric Alps. The 2nd Army also prevented the enemy from reaching the craggy mountains in Bosnia, where the natural features would enable an extensive resistance. They further swiftly occupied Dalmatia, so Yugoslav troops could not reach the coast and escape with the support of British naval forces. The 2nd Army was also used to intimidate Slav forces who were concentrated along the northern border with Albania.[188] In all of their operations speed was of upmost importance for the 2nd Army, yet they were delayed by difficult roads and inadequate military resources. Despite the difficulties, Italian Army units managed to proceed along the coast reaching the towns of Senj, Karlobag and Otočac and joined troops in Zara. Together, on 14 April, they took the city of Knin, in the Dalmatian hinterland, where Yugoslav troops had desperately struggled to hold on to.

---

[187] Salvatore Loi, *Le operazioni delle unità italiane in Yugoslavia (1941-1943)*, (Roma: Ufficio Storico dello Stato Maggiore dell'Esercito, 1978), pp. 50-2.
[188] Ibid., p. 61.

The Second Front

The garrison stationed in Zara, already an Italian enclave, was divided into a land and sea front, which consisted of artillery, XXX Corps of engineers, mechanised company, *Carabinieri* force, and navy units.

Within just a few hours of the Belgrade coup, the Italian Army Staff sent a ciphered telegram to all troops deployed in Zara, ordering them to occupy the city walls, gates and bastions, whilst also deploying a defensive line.

On 2 April 1941, the first voluntary civilians were evacuated from the city, and the following day, rural areas were cleared of inhabitants and cattle, so that by 4 April, all the fields were able to be set with mines. It was on the night of 5 April, at 23:40, when telegram number 4711 ordered Italian forces to launch an attack on the following morning.[189] Although there was a substantial difference in man power, it did not prevent the success of Italian operations. General Giglioli's 9,000 strong front lines were manned thinly in comparison to General Ivan Prpić's Jadranska Division, which was made up of the Benkovac, Knin, Mostar and Sinj Infantry Divisions, totalling 18,000 men.[190] Yet, on 8 April, during three incursions at 10:25, 11:35 and 16:35, Italian bombers targeted enemy shipping vessels, rather than any inland targets, as visibility inland was quite poor. In retaliation, the Yugoslav Air Force attacked, but failed to hit any Italian tank ships. The weather became worse the following day, when Italian forces suffered a few setbacks in Puntamica, on the island of San Clemente, and in Val di Bora, as thick clouds forced air units to strike at 300-500 ft, where they became easy targets for light automatic flak and infantry small-arms fire.[191] On the afternoon of 10 April, Italian squadrons made an offensive mission on the Benkovac area, as well as over the

---

[189] Ibid., pp. 67-8.

[190] Charles D. Pettibone, *The Organization and Order of Battles of Militaries in World War II. Germany's and Imperial Japan Allies, Co-Belligerent, and Puppet States*, Volume VII, (Bloomington: Trafford Publishing, 2012), p. 257.

[191] Christopher Shores, Brian Cull, and Nicola Malizia, *Air War for Yugoslavia, Greece and Crete, 1940-41*, (London: Grub Street, 1987), p. 213.

Croatian flying boat station of Slosella (Pirovac) where they bombarded ten enemy seaplanes, destroying four of them and seriously damaging the rest.

But the turning point of the war in Croatia came on 12 April, when Colonel Eugenio Morra's troops had to reach Zemonico Inferiore (Zemunik Donji), Nadin and Benkovac, all located in the Zara municipality, with the intent of surprising the enemy forces deployed east of Zemonico Superiore (Zemunik Gornji) and west of Biljane Inferiore and Nadin. The Italian units encountered a weak resistance, which easily allowed them to achieve their objectives. Given the easy victory, the garrison's commander located in Zara extended the occupation and, on 12 April at 12:00, Italian contingents drove inland and entered the towns of Dilko, Košino, Poljica, Murvica, Opacić, Smoković, San Cassiano (Sukošan), Polesnick, and Nona.

The Third Front

The third front was the most difficult due to the nature of the rugged and often inaccessible terrain and the lack of good roads. The scant number of Italian forces available and the width of the Albanian front meant the army could not employ a continuous squad of military personnel. Therefore, troops were deployed according to the importance of access lines: the most important were securely barred by troops, whilst less crucial lines were under surveillance. However, in case of enemy infiltration there existed fixed points where Italian troops could assemble in order to drive back the Third Yugoslav Army.

Pirzio Biroli's 9th Army consisted of two infantry corps: the XIV Corps under General Giovanni Vecchi and the XVII Corps under General Giuseppe Pafundi. The first could rely on 38th Infantry Division Puglie and 4th Alpine Division Cuneense, the second on 18th Infantry Division Messina, 32nd Infantry Division Marche and 131st Armoured Division Centauro. The two Corps were flanked by General Gabriele Nasci's Librazhd Sector, which included the 53rd (mountain) Infantry Division

Yugoslavia: War and Occupation

Arezzo, the 41st Infantry Division Firenze, and the 24th Infantry Division Pinerolo.

The XVII Corps' task was to defend the city of Scutari (Shkodër) in north-western Albania, which was one of the first targets of the Yugoslav air force. Scutari suffered only minor damage and the major Yugoslav offensive began in the Puka area. To prevent enemy infiltration, Italian troops blew up the Lumes River Bridge. On 7 April, the battle became more intense as regular troops and mobs crossed the Albanian border along the Vermosh salient. In the Puka district, the Yugoslavs overpowered the Italians; with two battalions each comprising 3,000 soldiers they occupied the Tropojë area, penetrating to Valbona (Valbonë), which lay on a wide plain surrounded by mountains, and as far as Fierzë. In the Kukës sector the Third Yugoslav Army enjoyed another success: Italian forces had to withdraw to avoid being surrounded by the enemy.

On 8 April, the Yugoslavian offensive of the Zetska Division continued steadily, as the Komski cavalry Odred crossed the dangerous Prokletije Mountains, breaking through Italian defences. Eventually it was stopped also as a result of the fall of Skopje at the hands of the Germans. In one day, the losses sustained by the Italian forces reached a total of 201 men, which included those killed, wounded and missing in action.[192] On 9 April, the Zetska Division advanced toward Scutari and dogged fighting became the defining feature of the following days. Between 11 and 13 April 1941, German and Italian troops advanced and forced the retreat of the Zetska Division to the Pronisat River, where it remained until the end of the campaign.[193]

Three days later, Montenegro was taken over by the Messina Division, part of the XIV Army Corps stationed in Albania. After penetrating Yugoslav defences, Italian troops rapidly moved to the coastal town of Bar, in southern Montenegro, and then advanced toward the Yugoslav fleet based at Kotor, occupying Cettigne (Cettinje) and Podgorica. On 17 April,

---

[192] Salvatore Loi, op. cit., p. 79.

[193] Fortunato Fatutta and Franco Covelli, '1941: Attack on Yugoslavia,' *The International Magazine of Armies and Weapons*, 4 (15–17), 1975, pp. 15-7.

76 — Luisa Morettin

Italian forces captured the Bocche di Cattaro (Bay of Kotor) and much of the Yugoslav fleet. Operations became easier when General Cesare Amé's *Servizio Informazioni Militari* (SIM), the military intelligence organisation for the Italian Royal Army, managed to crack the Yugoslav code which detailed the composition and position of Yugoslav forces.[194]

Despite their fight Yugoslav forces succumbed to the combined onslaught as its army, caught half prepared and with weak defences, could not withstand the Axis offensive. The Yugoslav air force had just a few modern aircrafts and there was a short supply of tanks, anti-aircraft artillery, and motor transport. Further, the army was made up of 250,000 soldiers and only thirty per cent of the 500,000 men called up had answered within the prescribed time.[195] Hence, when the Italo-German attack began, it caught an army which was still mobilising and only some 11 divisions were in their planned defence positions at the start of the invasion. Yet, for all of the inadequacy of the Yugoslav Army, no European forces could have hoped to stand up to the superiority of the Wehrmacht combined with the Italian armed forces.

The Axis victory was swift and Yugoslavia's collapse complete. On 11 April, four days after the initial attack, Croatia seceded under the Poglavnik Ante Pavelić's Ustaše, German troops marched into Zagreb and on 17 April 1941 they entered Belgrade. Eleven days after the invasion, Yugoslavia had been wiped off the European map, its conventional military forces ceased to exist, and 344,162 Yugoslav soldiers became prisoners of war.[196] The Axis invasion marked the beginning of an occupation, which would last four years and would be characterised by chilling, immeasurable, and ubiquitous violence where civilians were as much of a target as soldiers, and often more so.

---

[194] Fortunato Fatutta, *La campagna di Jugoslavia. Aprile 1941-settembre 1943*, (Campobasso: Opportunity Books, 1996), p. 35.

[195] Stevan K. Pavlowitch, *Hitler's New Disorder. The Second World War in Yugoslavia*, (London: Hurst & Company, 2008), p.17.

[196] Enzo Collotti, op. cit., p.199.

THE DISMEMBERMENT OF YUGOSLAVIA AND POLICING

The speed with which the Axis powers defeated and dispersed the Royal Yugoslav Army was surprising and immediately afterwards the country was divided between its captors. As Germany had a superior military to Italy and due to Mussolini's dependence on Hitler, Germany decided how Yugoslavia would be split. This meant Berlin would keep all of Serbia, with a separate German administration for the Vojvodina east of the Tisza River and most of the Slovene territory almost as far as Ljubljana. The partition enabled Germany to control all copper mines and bauxite deposits, vital to the German aircraft industry, as well as the important Maribor-Zagreb-Belgrade rail line. Hungary annexed the Slavonian Medjumurie and Prekomurje, the Vojvodina's Baranja and Bačka, whilst Bulgaria occupied part of Macedonia.

Even though the disparity produced a future inevitable clash between Rome and Berlin, the April campaign at least gave Italy what she had coveted for over twenty years – the expansion eastwards at the expense of Yugoslavia. Rome was left with the larger, but poorer part of Slovenia south of the Sava River which became the new Province of Ljubljana. It was immediately annexed to the Kingdom of Italy in order for it to become a buffer zone between the German and Italian territories.[197] The occupation, in Ciano's words, 'inspired by very liberal ideas would attract sympathies in the part of Slovenia subject to German rule where the most horrible excesses had been recorded.'[198] The province, officially created on 3 May 1941, was allocated to High Commissioner Emilio Grazioli, a Fascist officer who to maintain public order relied on the police, the financial police and border guards.

Italy also acquired some Croatian territory in the hinterland of Fiume, which was incorporated into the Italian Province of Fiume, and discontinuous portions of the coastal region of Dalmatia, from the island of

---

[197] Marco Cuzzi, *L'occupazione italiana della Slovenia* (1941-1943), (Roma: Stato Maggiore dell'Esercito, 1998), p. 27.
[198] Galeazzo Ciano, op. cit., 29 April 1941, p. 506.

Arbe (Rab) to the Bocche di Cattaro to the south. The annexed part of Dalmatia became the Governorship of Dalmatia under Giuseppe Bastianini and was divided into three provinces: Zara, Spalato and Cattaro. Italy's claim to the annexed areas was justified not just by the historical evidence, which stated the 'Italianness' of the once Roman and Venetian territories, but also by their strategic position in the control of the Adriatic Sea.

Macedonia and most of Kosovo were annexed by Italian-ruled Albania. Italy also occupied Montenegro, promising its inhabitants that it would reinstate independence under the tutelage of Queen Elena, daughter of the exiled King Nikola I Petrović and wife of the Italian king, Victor Emmanuel III. Italy's initial idea was to restore the Petrović-Njegoš dynasty and make Montenegro a satellite under the lead of the late King Nikola's grandson, Prince Mihajlo. But Prince Mihajlo's strong Yugoslav and Allied sympathies prevented him from accepting the throne. Therefore civil affairs were managed by Count Serafino Mazzolini, who was appointed High Commissioner.

From the ashes of the former Kingdom of Yugoslavia an Independent State of Croatia, (Nezavisna Država Hvratska, NDH), was established. Proclaimed in Zagreb by Colonel Slavko Kvaternik on 10 April 1941, one week before Yugoslavia's capitulation, the NDH was a puppet state run by Pavelić's Ustaša movement. It was nominally included in the Italian sphere of influence, whilst its main natural resources were under German control and it would not be until the second half of 1942 that Berlin would play a more important role in Croatian political and military matters.

Since May 1941 in the NDH a 4,500 strong Ustaše Militia was established and was under the command of Ante Pavelić. It was reinforced by some 25,000-35,000 irregular Ustaše men, whose task was to defend the regime and the Poglavnik. Further, the Domobrani, the Croatian Home Guard (*Hrvatsko domobranstvo*), was responsible for defending the state from internal and external enemies and was accountable to the Ministry of

Yugoslavia: War and Occupation

the Croatian Home Guard. The relationship of the Ustaša to the Domobrani has been described as similar to that of the SS and the German Army.[199]

Given the strategic importance of the new Yugoslav territorial acquisitions, policing the new territories became a major undertaking. The 2nd Army was given the responsibility of controlling the territory. Initially it was comprised of around 200,000 men and was under the command of General Vittorio Ambrosio, from April 1941 until his promotion to Chief of Staff in January 1942, when Italy had engaged almost thirty divisions and one quarter of the army's manpower.[200] Ambrosio was succeeded by General Mario Roatta, who was commander until January 1943, when General Mario Robotti took over until the Italian Armistice on 8 September 1943.

Even though high-profile generals had commanded the troops in the newly conquered territories, it was still clear that the units which had defeated the Yugoslav Army were actually unprepared to control the new area as fierce guerrilla warfare had broken out and spread like wildfire throughout the country in the summer and autumn of 1941. The surrender of the Yugoslav Army and Belgrade's capitulation had not marked the end of the war, as armed resistance forces emerged in remote and almost inaccessible mountain areas. The soldiers and officers who escaped capture relied on an abundance of weapons, which they used in the brutal and unrelenting guerrilla war against the occupation troops which patrolled Yugoslav territories.

Throughout the war three movements emerged: the Chetniks, the partisans and the Ustaše, who fought against each other whilst the Axis occupying powers were using the animosities and different ideologies of the Slavs to 'divide and conquer.' The Chetniks, led by Draža Mihailović, supported the Royal government-in-exile and the restoration of the pre-war political order. The Communist-sponsored underground National Liberation Movement, the partisans, under the leadership of Josip Broz

---

[199] Fred Singleton, *Twentieth Century Yugoslavia*, (London: Macmillan, 1976), p. 87.

[200] Lucio Ceva, *La condotta italiana della guerra. Cavallero e il Comando Supremo 1941-1942*, (Milano: Feltrinelli, 1975), p. 196.

80 Luisa Morettin

Tito, fought instead for social revolution: a new Communist order in a federative Yugoslavia. The common aim of both groups was to defeat the Ustaše and the Axis powers, but at the same time their different ideological outlook resulted in them being in conflict with each other. Over time the Chetnik movement welcomed Serb peasants who had fled the Ustaša persecutions in Croatia. This transformed the movement from being an extension of the Yugoslav Royal Army into a Serb national force that employed a cautious, if not a collaborationist strategy toward the Axis powers. This would later contribute to the Allies' abandonment of the Chetniks in favour of the Communist partisans who recruited fighters from all nations and nationalities of Yugoslavia. The power struggle among the Chetniks and the partisans added layers of complexity to the Venezia Giulia issue and to the bloodiness of the foreign occupation.

ITALIAN ATROCITIES IN YUGOSLAVIA

As noted in chapter two, Italy's aggressive foreign policy and the use of propaganda against the Slavs found fertile soil in a state and regime which was not only authoritarian and militarist, but also racist. Italian Fascists depicted Slavs as subservient, primitive, and dangerous Bolsheviks, who had to be re-educated. This attitude towards the conquered people of Yugoslavia was clearly seen within the Italian colonialist experience in Africa, especially in the Libyan province of Cyrenaica and Ethiopia, which was a tried and tested repertoire of brutal repression. Its justification had more to do with imperialism than with the 'civilising mission' of the higher Italian race operating in what were perceived as backward regions.

In a speech dated 10 June 1941 Mussolini outlined how he intended to proceed with the nationalisation policy of occupied Yugoslav areas including, if necessary, the deportation of part of the population so that the political border would coincide with the ethnic one.[201] It was in this period

---

[201] *Corriere della Sera*, 11 June 1941, quoted in Enzo Collotti, *L'occupazione nazista in Europa,* (Roma: Editori Riuniti, 1964), p. 522.

Yugoslavia: War and Occupation

81

that the substantial push of propaganda and polarisation of regional politics gained strength as they were placed into a formula which equated 'Partisans/Slavs with Communists' and 'Italians with Fascists.'[202] In the light of this, Italian soldiers stationed in Yugoslavia did not see themselves as aggressors, but as fighting a just and defensive war against Bolshevism. Not only did this myth encourage an increase in aggressive attitudes of the troops, thus condoning any degree of violence committed against the 'agents of Moscow,' but also developed a deep mistrust of the civil population who were believed to be allies of the insurgents.

In many areas armed resistance started immediately after the invasion campaign, however, it was in January 1942-43 that Communist insurgency grew and strengthened the body of its militants. This was during General Mario Roatta's tenure as commander of the Italian 2nd Army in Yugoslavia, responsible for all units deployed both in the former Yugoslav territories annexed in the spring of 1941 and for the new-born reign of Croatia. The partisans' knowledge, mobility, and exploitation of the rough terrain, as well as their capacity to blend in with the local population, meant they were able to live in safe areas whilst expanding and at the same time gain tactical advantages.

In order to respond to such insurgency warfare Roatta devised a detailed strategy of counter-insurgency that was carefully thought, encouraged and demanded. On 1 March 1942, he circulated a pamphlet entitled *Circolare 3C*, outlining the measures to be taken to re-establish order in the provinces. This is now known as the manifesto for repression in Yugoslavia. Roatta devised the infamous pamphlet with two objectives in mind: first, it was aimed at the civilians who supported the insurgents; and second, it meant to extinguish the notion of '*buon italiano*,' (good

---

[202] Amedeo Osti Guerrazzi, *The Italian Army in Slovenia: Strategies of Antipartisan Repression, 1941-1943*, (New York: Palgrave, 2013), pp. 25-6. See also Dennison Rusinow, op. cit., p. 278.

82 *Luisa Morettin*

Italian), and dissuade good-natured soldiers from being sympathetic and friendly with the local population.[203]

In the document, which marks the radicalisation point of the anti-insurgency campaign, the General assured that 'excesses of reaction, undertaken in good faith, [would] never be prosecuted' and specifically foresaw the possibility of destroying farms and their goods, raze houses to the ground, arrest and deport family members of suspected rebels, and finally, carry out immediate executions, shootings and hangings.[204] The formula used was not in the vein of justice as an *'eye for an eye'* but in the form of revenge, as a *'head for an eye.'*

On 7 April 1942 new clauses were added to the original pamphlet by General Roatta and included in the so-called 'Appendix B.' The orders imposed the immediate killing of armed insurgents, with the exception of minors and women, who instead would be sent to appear in front of ordinary tribunals. Further, the appendix outlined the evacuation and arrest orders for singular civilians, families, or if necessary, whole villages. According to the Slovene historian and partisan Tone Ferenc, the content of 'Appendix B' was deliberately excluded by the *Circolare 3C* because the language and contents of Roatta's orders were a blatant violation of the Hague Conventions of 1899 and 1907, that banned certain acts as 'war crimes' and ensured the protection of civilians in times of conflict.[205] In spite of the legal contravention, Roatta's ruthless repression plans received support amongst Rome's highest Fascist echelons. The Secretary of the National Fascist Party was at the time the Triestine Aldo Vidussoni[206] who, well before *Circolare 3C* had been introduced, was convinced that in those lands it was imperative to take a hard line against partisans and civilians.

---

[203] A copy of the 3C Circular is reproduced in Massimo Legnani, 'Il "ginger" del generale Roatta. Le direttive della 2a armata sulla repressione antipartigiana in Slovenia e Croazia', *Italia Contemporanea*, 209 (10), 1997, pp. 159-74.

[204] Brunello Mantelli, 'Gli italiani in Jugoslavia 1941-1943: occupazione militare, politiche persecutorie, crimini di guerra,' in *Storia e memoria*, n. 13, 2004, pp. 23-30.

[205] Tone Ferenc, *'Si ammazza troppo poco:' condannati a morte, ostaggi, passati per le armi nella provincia di Lubiana: 1941-1943: documenti*, (Ljubljana: Istituto per la storia moderna, 1999).

[206] Martin Kitchen, *A World in Flames: A Short History of the Second World War in Europe and Asia, 1939–1945*, (New York: Longman, 1990), p. 252

Yugoslavia: War and Occupation

Indeed in January 1942 Vidussoni candidly told Galezzo Ciano that he wanted to kill all of the Slav population. Ciano protested that there too many of them - a million or more, but Vidussoni insisted: 'We must behave like *askari* and exterminate them all.'[207]

At the end of July 1942, at a conference in Gorizia, General Roatta was encouraged by the Duce who ordered him to 'respond with *il ferro e il fuoco*' [with an iron fist] to the partisans' terrorist attacks.[208] As a result of the decisions taken at the conference, a policy of internment was implemented. Mario Robotti, General of the XI Army Corps, reported to his commanders:

> 'We have transported and interned all able bodied [of those arrested] to the island of Arbe. It does not matter if during the interviews you get the impression you are dealing with harmless people. Bear in mind that for many reasons they can turn into our enemies. Hence, total elimination. ...
> I would not be opposed to interning all Slovenes and replace them with Italians (the families of war-wounded or fallen soldiers).'[209]

In other words what Robotti said in July 1942 was stressing what Mussolini had ordered in June 1941: 'Make sure that political borders correspond with racial ones.'[210]

Another turn of the screw on Slav insurgents came towards the end of 1942 when the rules toward prisoners changed for the worse. The original Italian military instructions had imposed a distinction in the treatment of able-bodied and injured prisoners from the People's Liberation Army of Yugoslavia. The former were shot immediately, whereas the latter were

---

[207] Galeazzo Ciano, op. cit., 5 January 1942, p. 578. *Askari* from the Arabic meaning 'soldier' was a local soldier serving in the armies of the European colonial powers. In general *askari* became famous for their fighting skills and loyalty to their colonial masters, but in fact reality was more nuanced. In the specific case of Ethiopian troops in Italian pay many *askari* deserted and joined the cause of their country's independence. See Alberto Sbacchi, *Ethiopia under Mussolini: Fascism and the Colonial Experience*, (London: Zed Books, 1985).

[208] Ugo Cavallero, *Comando Supremo. Diario 1940-43 del Capo di S.M.G.*, (Bologna: Cappelli, 1948), pp. 297 and following.

[209] ACS, b. 161, p. 60.

[210] Ibid.

84   *Luisa Morettin*

judged by a war tribunal. Although few Italian commanders had complied with the instructions, it was after September 1942 that orders were changed. War bulletins no longer reported the capture of prisoners: they were simply killed. An example of Italian extreme measures and unfettered violence is given by the incident at the hospital of Jelenov Žleb, in Southern Slovenia, where Italian soldiers shot all wounded partisans who were interned there. Likewise in the war journal of General Umberto Fabbri, commander of the V Group of the *Guardia alla Frontiera* (Border Guard), it was written that 'on 15 February 1943 the partisan hospital in Cinj-Potek [sic] was set on fire.'[211]

Such measures, together with Mussolini's instructions dated June-July 1942, to deport 30,000 Slavs from the Ljubljana province and send them to internment camps,[212] reveal how the Italian repression went beyond the need to tame the local guerrilla warfare and instead was comparable to ethnic-cleansing. According to a memo prepared for the Duce in the summer of 1942, at least 52,800 Slavs had already been taken to fascist camps scattered throughout Italy and the occupied territories.[213] However, the Italian government refused to provide the International Committee of the Red Cross with data on the amount, names and citizenship of civilian internees, their detention place and the reason for their arrest.[214]

The most infamous fascist camps operational until September 1943 were located at Monigo di Treviso, Chiesanuova di Padova, Gonars, Arbe, Aidussina (Ajdovščina), Renicci di Anghiari, Colfiorito, Tavernelle, Cairo Montenotte, Visco, Fraschette di Alatri, Zlarino, Melada (Molat), Ugliano (Uljan), Vodice, Zabjelo, Prevlaka, Forte Mamula (Lastavica), Bar (Antivari), Scoglio Calogero (Ošljak), Porte Re (Kraljevica), and Buccari

---

[211] ACS, Ibid., pp. 56-7.

[212] ACS, PS Massime, b. 109, Alto Commissariato Provincia di Lubiana a Ministero dell'Interno, 6 June 1942.

[213] Tone Ferenc, *Rab-Arbe-Arbissima: confinamenti, rastrellamenti, internamenti nella provincia di Lubiana, 1941-1943*, (Ljubljana: Institut za novejso zgodovino: Drustvo piscev zgodovine Nob, 2000), p. 237, doc. n. 266.

[214] ACS, PS Massime, b. 110, Alto Commissariato Provincia di Lubiana a Ministero dell'Interno, 18 January 1943.

(Bakar).[215] Living standards in these camps were appalling: unhygienic conditions caused dysentery; water supplies were meagre and medical facilities non-existent; inmates, including women and children, suffered from cold and hunger in open-air tents as some barracks were not yet completed. As anticipated, such conditions led to the death of thousands. Often it was not only the physical conditions, but also the psychological humiliation that would affect the sense of self and made difficult for prisoners to retain their human dignity and self-worth.

Overcrowding in the camps was another issue. In the Arbe complex, made up of three camps located in the south-eastern part of the Italian-annexed island by the same name, it is estimated that more than 100,000 people were held. One of the detainees, a Slovene student called Metod Milač, recalled that the camp was so overcrowded that three people had to roll 'in unison' on their shared beds because they were simply too narrow to sleep so many people.[216]

The Fascist policy of unbridled territorial expansion, the scorched-earth campaign of de-Balkanisation followed by forced Italianisation proved to be understandably hideous to the local populations. What the Italian repressive measures ultimately reveal is that Mussolini's troops failed to control the conquered territories and, most importantly, to find a balance between between the policies of attraction and chastisement. As the war continued, it eventually backfired.

Occupied Montenegro

In the aftermath of the Italian occupation of Montenegro the complex political landscape of the area presented the authorities with difficulties.

---

[215] Alessandra Kersevan, *Lager italiani. Pulizia etnica e campi di concentramento fascisti per civili jugoslavi 1941-1943*, (Roma: Nutrimenti, 2008), pp. 80, 100. See also Martin Dean and Geoffrey Megargee (ed.), *The United States Holocaust Memorial Museum Encyclopedia of Camps and Ghettos, 1933-1945*, Volume II, (Bloomington: Indiana University Press, 2012).

[216] Metod Milač, *Resistance, Imprisonment, and Forced Labor: A Slovene Student in World War II*, (Bern: Peter Lang, 2002), p. 75.

86 *Luisa Morettin*

Divisions within the autonomist movement, Italy's annexation of the bay of Kotor, and allocation of Montenegrin areas to Albania, fanned the flames of discontent leading it into rebellion. Milovan Djilas, the influent Yugoslav Communist politician and a native Montenegrin, was sent home to organise the insurgence.[217] On 13 July 1941, the day after the proclamation of the Montenegrin independence, a ferocious uprising took place against the Italians near Cettigne and quickly spread to the rest of Montenegro.[218] The revolt, started by Communist Party adherents and former Yugoslav Army officers who had returned home, revealed to the surprised Italian authorities that the restoration of Montenegro enjoyed scant support amongst the populace. Indeed, it was seen as a regime of military occupation, rather than one of independence. In Governor Serafino Mazzolini's account for the Rome Government, it was reported how the uprising was carried out by not more than 5,000 men with light arms. In contrast, Yugoslav sources state that the revolt was a wider phenomenon, involving approximately 32,000 citizens, of which 1,800 were members of the Yugoslav Communist Party, whilst 3,000 belonged to the Communist Youth Organisation.[219] Both sources were unanimous, however, in stating that the insurgents were well equipped with weapons that former army officers had brought with them and due to the backing of the peasant population, almost all of Montenegro was conquered by rebels within three weeks. This success can be explained by the fact that in Montenegro the Italians had retained only one Army Corps, that could hardly cover the whole territory, and lax procedures meant Italian troops were unable to face insurgents.

Mussolini responded to the emergency by recalling Mazzolini to Italy and appointing General Alessandro Pirzio Biroli as Military Governor, who had complete civil and military power.

The speed of the uprising prompted a series of violent reprisals by General Pirzio Biroli, who assigned 70,000 Italian troops to suppress the

---

[217] Milovan Djilas, *Wartime*, (New York: Harcourt, 1977), p. 22.

[218] Kenneth Morrison, *Montenegro. A Modern History*, (London: I.B. Tauris, 2009), pp. 51-4.

[219] Batrić Jovanović, *Crna Gora, u narodnooslobodilačkom ratu i socijalističkoj revoluciji*, Vol 1, (Belgrade: Vojno delo, 1960), p. 257.

revolt, declaring martial law, and ordering the surrender of weapons and the confiscation of insurgents' properties.

Unfamiliar with guerrilla warfare, Italian troops struck back blindly against civilians[220] and, as had happened in Italy's African colonies and in the occupied areas of Yugoslavia, the worst of the fascist's terror was unleashed as extreme violence. According to the 'Bulletin of Italian crimes against Yugoslavia and its Populations,' in Montenegro Italian occupation forces immediately carried out the first wave of indiscriminate killings. The document reports how Italians, like Germans, resorted to large scale deportations, arson, and plundering to force occupied areas into obedience. In particular troops belonging to the Alba Division, directly under the command of the Military Governor, committed many atrocities. On 17 July 1941, during a 19 miles coastal march from Bar to Buvda, an Italian motorised battalion killed inhabitants in the villages where they passed through and looted their homes. The following day, Italian troops set fire to the village of Brajice, captured all male inhabitants and killed four of them whilst the rest were deported to Albania. More villages were burnt in the coming days in areas from Cettigne to Čevo and the town's men interned in camps.[221]

The inhabitants of the towns and hamlets which the Division Cacciatori delle Alpi met during their march from Podgorica to Danilovgrad encountered an even worse fate: whoever had not fled was brutally killed. The Division Pusteria set fire to almost all villages they went to and deported approximately 900 people from the coastal areas in Montenegro. Similar merciless counterinsurgency strategies were employed by the Divisions Taro, Messina, Venezia, and Puglie in their attempt to defeat local insurgencies.[222]

Documentary evidence shows how, in a number of places, violence included torture. A woman, Milena Bakumir, recalled her experience in the prison of Berane, a town in north-eastern Montenegro. She and other

---

[220] ASMAE, GABAP, b. 5, 22 July 1941.

[221] *Bollettino sui crimini italiani*, quoted in Enzo Collotti, op. cit., pp. 538-9.

[222] Enzo Collotti, op. cit., pp. 538-9.

88 *Luisa Morettin*

prisoners were repeatedly kicked and beaten with clubs and rifle butts for four or five hours on end. If the victims fainted, they were placed under a shower to regain consciousness, enabling the beating to continue.[223]

Another witness testimony by Dalibor Mestanek reported how he was ferociously beaten time and again from his ankles to his knees.[224] Yet another witness recalled how he was collected from the hospital whilst still ill and taken to the police station in Spalato in order to be tortured. He could remember how every night he heard the harrowing pleading of the tortured prisoners that came from the security room.[225]

By mid-August 1941 the brutality of the counterinsurgency operations enabled the Italians to re-establish control over the territory. Attempts were later made to establish or estimate the number of victims: according to Francesco Fatutta, the July uprising cost 4,000 Italian casualties, a third of Italy's occupying force, in dead, wounded, and dispersed. At least 4,000 insurgents were killed, but he reported the number of civilians who had lost their life, as unknown.[226] Gino Bambara's estimate was lower, stating that the Italians suffered a total of 1,079 dead and wounded,[227] whilst Stephen Clissold reported Montenegrin losses at 5,000, with 7,000 wounded and 10,000 deported to concentration camps.[228]

With the revolt quashed, the Military Governor tried to set up a collaborationist regime, which would win over the populace of Montenegro, aiding him to defeat the communist threat. Showing a degree of moderation towards the Montenegrins, General Pirzio Biroli promised to punish Italian soldiers guilty of mishandling prisoners, proclaimed an amnesty to the insurgents and released 3,000 internees.[229] However, his ambition to be seen as an enlightened and conciliatory ruler did not work,

---

[223] ACS, b. 161, p. 22.

[224] Ibid., p. 23.

[225] Ibid.

[226] Francesco Fatutta, *La campagna di Iugoslavia. Aprile 1941 – settembre 1943*, (Foggia: Italia editrice, 2008), pp. 61-3.

[227] Gino Bambara, *Jugoslavia settebandiere. Guerra senza retrovie nella Jugoslavia occupata 1941-1943*, (Brescia: Vannini, 1988), p.102.

[228] Stephen Clissold, *Whirlwind. An Account of Marshal Tito's Rise to Power*, (London: Cresset Press, 1949), p. 80.

[229] H. James Burgwyn, op. cit., pp. 94-5.

as toward the end of 1941 the rebels resumed their guerrilla acts. The insurgents' attack on the Italian garrison in Pljevlja, in the northern part of Montenegro, caused Pirzio Biroli to abandon his former ruling ways and revert to cruelty to restore order, involving a repression that proved to be beyond brutal. On 12 January 1942 he issued a command in which he specified the ferocious reprisal measures to be used by Italian troops. For every Italian officer wounded or killed, in retaliation 50 Montenegrin civilians would be executed and for every Italian private citizen wounded or killed 10 civilians would be shot.[230] 'The fable of the *buon italiano* [good Italian] must cease!' – Pirzio Biroli told his soldiers – 'The Italian soldier is above all a warrior. He who does not wish to understand the generosity of a friendly hand will now feel the force of our fist. ... He who hates Fascism hates Italy.'[231] Such an ominous identification with Fascism would soon prove to be a disaster for the Italians in Venezia Giulia.

In Montenegro the fight against the invader exposed the lack of unity of the resistance front. It soon became apparent that the Communist-led partisans and the Serbian-oriented Chetniks had started to fight each other in an attempt to gain control of post-war Yugoslavia. The Communist troops of Milovan Dijlas and Mosa Pijade tried to lead insurgency operations whilst carrying out pitiless actions against the foreign occupier and against those who did not embrace the communist creed. Likewise, the Chetniks' leader Draža Mihailović, who wished to fight the partisans and Axis forces, considered the former a much more dangerous enemy than the latter in the long run. These ideological hatreds would make it difficult for the Special Operation Executive (SOE) to understand which faction was actually fighting the Germans and Italians. The Italo-Chetnik co-operation in Montenegro started in February 1942 and operated in such a way whereby the Italians controlled the towns and the Chetniks the countryside,[232] whilst the partisans were ousted. But during a series of

---

[230] Jozo Tomasevich, *War and Revolution in Yugoslavia, 1941-1945: Occupation and Collaboration*, (Stanford: Stanford University Press, 2001), pp. 141-2.

[231] Giacomo Scotti and Luciano Viazzi, *L'inutile vittoria. La tragica esperienza delle truppe italiane in Montenegro*, (Milano: Mursia, 1989), pp. 153-4.

[232] Jozo Tomasevich, op. cit., p. 143.

battles in the Neretva Valley in mid-March 1943, during the last part of Operation Weiss aimed at the annihilation of partisan forces, the Chetniks experienced a complete military and political defeat. The partisans had gained significant ground when in the spring of 1943 the SOE established direct relations with them, which would lead to their recognition as an Allied force. In the meantime the Military Governor Pirzio Biroli was replaced by Curio Barbasetti di Prun on 1 July 1943, but by then the end of Italian rule in Montenegro was already in sight.

Occupied Slovenia

After the invasion of April 1941, due to a certain cultural autonomy enjoyed by the new provinces and the fact that Italians wanted to make their rule more acceptable to the Slovenes, they initially did not allow themselves to engage in the violent excesses, which Germans had shown in northern Slovenia. Therefore, the Information Office of the Italian Second Army, triumphantly claimed the local population 'appreciate[d] [...] the liberality which inspired the rules that governed the annexation of the province of Ljubljana to Italy.'[233] But in fact, the Slav population was far from welcoming the arrival of a foreign occupier, who had fiercely suppressed the 'oppositional' Slav minority within Venezia Giulia. The feelings of ordinary Slovenians during the invasion of Yugoslavia are best exemplified by a passage from the memoir of Peter Starič, an electronics engineer.

> On the next day [of the invasion], the posters and newspapers brought the messages of the occupational authorities: *Noi ordiniamo!* [We order!] as well as in Slovenian language. Pictures of the hated Mussolini and of the king Vittorio Emanuele accompanied the news.[234]

---

[233] AUSSME, M 3, b. 53, circular of the "I" Office of the Second Army, 12 May, 1941, quoted in Amedeo Osti Guerrazzi, op. cit., p. 24.
[234] Peter Starič, *My Life under Totalitarianism 1941-1991*, (Augusta: Sotina Publishing, 2015), Loc. 393 of ebook.

The main problem facing the Italian occupation forces in Slovenia was the organised resistance in the city of Ljubljana and countryside. In February 1942 the Italians erected a barbed wire fence and eleven check points, which enclosed the city, in a vain attempt to cut it off from the surrounding areas and prevent communication between the partisans in Ljubljana and those in the countryside.[235] The Communist Party of Slovenia (CPS) became active early on by setting up the *Protiimperialistična Fronta* or PIF (Anti-Imperialist Front). Their aim was to engage in armed struggle in order to liberate Slovenia with the help of other political groups who joined the PIF. These groups included some Christian Socialists, a dissident group of Slovene Sokols known as 'National Democrats,' a group of left-leaning and liberal intellectuals around the journals *Sodobnost* and *Ljubljanski zvon*, and more than ten smaller groups.[236]

The first episodes of rigid Slovenian resistance against Italian officials and collaborators, took place in May 1941.[237] After Germany's attack on the Soviet Union in June 1941, the PIF was renamed *Osvobodilna Fronta Slovenskega Naroda* (OF, Liberation Front of the Slovene Nation) and, on 27 June, the Supreme Command of Partisan Contingents was formed under the lead of Marshal Tito. By September 1941 the Communist forces within the OF had virtually taken over the other groups. Indeed, in the face of representing a small minority the Communist forces managed to control the Slovenian resistance. This was the result of their organisational skills, superior tactics and long-standing underground apparatus, which had been previously persecuted by the Royal Yugoslav Government and this made other political groups who joined the OF soon lose their identity. The OF operations were so intense and well organised that by the end of the same year the partisans had already recruited 1,500 men and women.[238]

---

[235] Jozo Tomasevich, op. cit., p. 103.

[236] Leopoldina Plut-Pregelj, Gregor Kranjc, Zarko Lazarevic, and Carole Rogel, *Historical Dictionary of Slovenia*, (Lanham: Rowman & Littlefield, 2018), p. 314.

[237] Giuseppe Piemontese, *Ventinove mesi di occupazione italiana nella provincia di Lubiana. Considerazioni e documenti*, (Ljubljana: s.n.ö, 1946), p. 3.

[238] Rudolf Wördörfer, *Confine orientale. Italia e Yugoslavia dal 1915 al 1955*, (Bologna: Il Mulino, 2009), p. 180.

The spread of the armed resistance in the province of Ljubljana helped the OF to enter into collaboration with Italian Communism and by the end of 1942, in Trieste alone, there were approximately thirty resistance committees.[239]

The Slovene partisan operations soon became minutely organised and perfectly carried out. The nature of the rough terrain, covered in forests and mountains, allowed swift ambushes and attacks against Italian garrisons or isolated soldiers – a form of resistance which was supplemented with disconnecting communications, blowing up bridges and derailing trains. In this way, no one could predict the time and location of the next partisan attack. The success of these activities seems to have been made possible due to the location of Italian troops, who were spread too thinly over the territory, and the Italian police methods that were not as uncompromising as Nazi methods. Stung by a sense of inferiority towards the Germans who criticised Italian troops, General Mario Robotti, commander of the 11th Army Corps, and General Mario Roatta, commander of the 2nd Army, urged their soldiers to engage in a merciless fight without quarter thus showing their allies that they were equal partners in cruelty and perseverance. General Robotti asked for propaganda to be increased relentlessly and for it to include episodes of barbarous Slav attacks on Italian civilians and soldiers fallen prisoners. Such a strategy would both facilitate the tension erupting into full-fledged hatred against partisans and support the narrative of 'Balkan ferocity' that featured in Italian propaganda.[240]

Having to show results to their military superiors and prodded into more ferocious violence by the Italo-German antagonism, Italian troops carried out heavy handed actions. A vicious example of this was the arson of the village of Ravne, where 'the burning, [...] which destroyed 31 houses, was caused by incendiary bombs and explosive fired from an airplane. The populace, which fled terrified, was mowed down by gunfire from above. An old woman and a twelve-year-old girl were killed and

---

[239] Dennison Rusinow, op. cit., p. 278.
[240] Amedeo Osti Guerrazzi, op. cit., p. 36.

Yugoslavia: War and Occupation

many men were wounded and burnt.'[241] Italy now spread their ruthless treatment to the Balkans, treatment normally reserved for their 'brown' colonies.

Circular 3c's emphasis on pitiless violence, confiscation and violent excesses nailed down the concept that the enemy was everyone and everywhere. This was further documented in General Roatta's gruesome mass deportations plans. However, as the High Commissioner for Ljubljana, Emilio Grazioli, explained to Roatta in a meeting at the Headquarters of the High Commission on 14 June 1942, the planned forcible expulsions presented a logistical challenge and could not take place for one reason only: no internment camps had been prepared.

This hindrance was soon overcome. A camp was created in Cighino (Čiginj), in north-western Slovenia, by using existing military huts where approximately 600 people were interned for a few weeks. [242] However, it was the camp in Gonars, a village south of Udine in Friuli, which became the first proper Slav civilian camp, especially used for Slovenian political prisoners. Although the camp was originally built in autumn 1941 with the intention to intern Russian prisoners of war, who were believed to be numerous after the Axis aggression toward Russia, yet it was where many Slavs were interned instead. The concentration camp consisted of three sectors surrounded by barbed wire and security towers, from which the guards machine gunned anyone who got too close to the fence. Despite its maximum capacity to hold 2,800 prisoners, 4,200 people were detained there in June 1942. Once the huts were full, the surplus were held in tents where the living and hygienic conditions were extremely harsh.[243] Milan Cimprić described his time as a nine years old interned at Gonars. He experienced hunger so 'unimaginable' that he and other children collected peelings from a pit near the camp kitchen and ate them. [244]

---

[241] Tone Ferenc and Pavel Kodrič, op. cit., p. 159.

[242] Alessandra Kersevan, op. cit., p. 53.

[243] Ibid.

[244] Metka Gombač, Karl Stuhlpfarrer, Dario Mattiussi, *Als mein Vater starb: Zeichnungen und Zeugnisse von Kindern aus Konzentrationslagern der italienischen Ostgrenze (1942-1943),* (Klagenfurt: Wieser Verlag, 2009), p. 89.

94 *Luisa Morettin*

In order to solve the problem of overcrowding, Italian authorities later established camps not only in north-eastern Italy, but also in occupied territories. According to historian Giacomo Scotti, 'around 200 internment camps were set up, large and small' in Italy, Yugoslavia and Albania.[245] It is difficult to describe in meaningful terms the barbarous treatment and deportations of Slavs at the hands of Italian authorities and soldiers. Figures do not help since they are somehow elusive, inflated or lessened on the basis of political views and ethnicity of reporters. If the letter-testimony by Amleto Giovanni Cicognani is to be believed, the nuncio in Washington wrote to an Italian Cardinal in August 1943 stating that approximately 100,000 Slavs were interned in Italy and left without food and clothes. The mortality rate amongst them was of 300 every day, as they were either killed or succumbed to malnutrition, hypothermia, and other effects of their ordeal.[246]

The Italian anti-insurgency operations inflicted losses, which made no distinction between insurgents and civilians and caused demoralisation in partisan units.[247] Overall, fascist failure to tame the serious guerrilla war caused the Italian government to resort to methodical punitive expeditions which got worse with time. In turn the regime's brutal response to armed opposition fuelled greater radicalism amongst insurgents. Records show episodes of calculated violence and terror inflicted upon the civil population multiplying amidst the chaos caused by telegraph and telephone communications being cut, roads, bridges, electricity and water mains being sabotaged, or blown up by the local resistance. As a result, during 1942 the partisans seized municipalities and in the summer the forced Italianisation of the new province was discontinued.

Increasing economic difficulties, the loss of the 8th Army in Russia, and the Allied landings in North Africa indicated Italy's possible exit from the war. This could be seen in the province of Slovenia, where civil

---

[245] Giacomo Scotti quoted in James Walston, 'History and Memory of the Italian Concentration Camps,' in *The Historical Journal*, Vol. 40, No. 1 (Mar., 1997), pp. 169-83.

[246] Tone Ferenc, *Rab – Arbe – Arbissima*, p. 401.

[247] Jozo Tomasevich, op. cit., p. 111.

authorities, unable to hold power and perform their duties, were taken over by military organisations in January 1943.[248]

During the last few months of Italian occupation, the partisans still continued their attacks against Italian targets, but on a smaller scale.[249] Insurgents were saving their manpower and resources for one particular moment: the takeover of power in Yugoslavia under the Communist banner.

Occupied Croatia (NDH)

The situation in the Independent State of Croatia (NDH) was more complex, as the Ustaša's 'new order' mirrored the radically nationalistic Italian-German model, from an ideological and institutional viewpoint. The unwritten Ustaša plan identified the Axis occupation with extensive national autonomy and aimed at the creation of a homogeneous state out of a heterogeneous population. Pavelić's policy, therefore, involved the extermination of Serbs, Jews, Roma, and any opposers to the regime for whom regular and irregular courts were introduced, mass shootings organised, and concentration camps established.

The first concentration and work camp was set up at Danica, 55 miles north-east of Zagreb. Although there were overall around twenty-six camps throughout the NDH, it was the Jasenovac concentration camp complex which became the most infamous. The camp, which was established in Slavonia at the confluence of the Sava and Una rivers, was described by Croatian demographer, Vladimir Žerjavić, as a horrifying place: 'Nowhere was the torture comparable to Jasenovac.'[250] The camp became known as

---

[248] Davide Rodogno, *Fascism's European Empire. Italian Occupation during the Second World War*, (Cambridge: Cambridge University Press, 2003), pp. 258-9.

[249] Jozo Tomasevich, op. cit., p. 116.

[250] Vladimir Žerjavić, *Population Losses in Yugoslavia 1941-1945*, (Zagreb: Dom & Svijet, 1997), p. 79.

the 'Yugoslav Auschwitz,'[251] where an estimated 80,000-100,000 people were murdered.[252]

Pavelić and his closest followers developed and conducted a policy using the formula of thirds: kill one third, deport one third, convert one third to Catholicism. Such a plan triggered a deadly reign of terror made up of direct executions and mass crimes, such as the massive bloodbath in the village of Gudovac, where in retaliation for the killing of a Croatian soldier, 176 Serbian men were collectively shot by a firing squad of up to 70 Ustaše guards.[253] Such reprisals became the norm. Historian Ian Kershaw, described one episode of sadistic horror, where 250 Serbs of the Glina district, after being locked in a church, were murdered one after another by Ustaše who hit them on the head with spiked clubs,[254] as the use of hammers to bludgeon victims to death was a common procedure utilised by the Ustaše. The Croatian terror's uniqueness lay in its brutality: photographic and eye-witness evidence demonstrates forms of violence and rape that are, in historian Misha Glenny's words, 'so obscene that it would be pornographic to detail them.'[255]

Records show that the spate of massacres against Serb and Jewish civilians, their women, elderly and children included rape, shootings, torture, burning and savage brutality. By 1942 even German officers and the German Plenipotentiary General in Zagreb, Edmund Glaise von Horstenau, lamented the Ustaša orgies of killing. His concern was not dictated by humanitarian qualms, but by strategic reasons as he considered the negative impact the atrocities had on the security on the Balkan area, which was strategically important, serving as the line of communication between the Eastern Front and the Mediterranean area.[256]

---

[251] Vladimir Dedijer, *The Yugoslav Auschwitz and the Vatican: The Croatian Massacre of the Serbs During World War II*, (London: Prometheus Books, 1992).

[252] Ivo Goldstein, *Croatia. A History*, (London: Hurst & Co., 1999), p. 138.

[253] Ibid., p. 137.

[254] Ian Kershaw, *To Hell and Back. Europe 1914-1949*, (London: Penguin, 2016), pp. 363-4.

[255] Misha Glenny, *Balkans 1804-2012: Nationalism, War and the Great Powers*, (London: Granta, 2012), p. 501.

[256] Ann Lane, *Yugoslavia: When Ideals Collide,* (Basingstoke: Palgrave Macmillan, 2004), pp. 78-9.

Yugoslavia: War and Occupation

General Lothar Rendulić, who in 1943 was in charge of destroying the local guerrillas, reported how, after his appointment to the role, over 1,000 German soldiers requested to be moved to any other theatre of operations rather than face the savage conditions in the area.[257] The Italian Civil Affairs Office noted that the frenzy of the atrocities committed by the Ustaše were so cruel that 'their equivalent is only to be found in the darkest times of the Middle Ages.'[258] Indeed, it is possible to read evidence reporting how 'famished women in prison ... were offered their spit-roasted children to eat' and how Orthodox Christian children were killed, their 'livers and hearts cut out' and 'hung on the doorknobs of the abandoned houses.'[259]

In order to avoid problems with Croatia, not an occupied enemy but an allied state, Italian authorities initially decided to adopt a neutral stance and did not intervene. Despite that, the Ustaša government organised a violent anti-Italian propaganda campaign and demonstrations, which were fuelled by a deep resentment toward Rome's occupation of portions of Dalmatia.

Relations between the erstwhile partners soon became tense as the extreme violence in the NDH set off a wave of refugees fleeing from the Ustaša massacres to seek some refuge in Serbia, where many were recruited by Communist partisans for guerrilla actions.

Hatred of the invader and local quislings enabled the Yugoslav Communist Party (KPJ), and its energetic leader Tito, to gain further support and to develop his bands into an extremely mobile and aggressive fighting force. Moreover, the Soviet Union's entry into the war on 22 June 1941 encouraged partisan forces to continue their relentless struggle. This was further reiterated when, despite the initial catastrophic losses, the Red Army and the Soviet Air Force, did not break down, something which Nazi military commanders had not anticipated.

---

[257] Lothar Rendulić, *Gekämpft, gesiegt, geschlagen*, (Heidelberg: Welsermühl Verlag, 1952), p. 210.

[258] Davide Rodogno, op. cit., p. 185.

[259] ASMAE, GABAP, b. 34, 'Ministero dell'Interno – DGPS Divisione polizia politica, 12 July 1941, quoted in Davide Rodogno, Op. cit., p. 187.

At the end of August 1941 Italian authorities and the Command of the 2nd Army, alarmed by an increase in the massacres of the civilian population by the Ustaša, urged by Serbs and Jews' pleas for protection, and fearing that chaos could spill over and spread to Dalmatia, occupied Croatia in agreement with Germany. As decreed by the *bando* (announcement) of 7 September 1941, the Ustaša militia lost civil powers that were assumed by General Vittorio Ambrosio, the commander of the 2nd Army, who issued orders for his officers to neither interfere in religious affairs nor engage in pro-Serbian actions. The totalitarian NDH regime did not take well to such a move, which was seen as a disempowerment of the ruling Ustaša, and a spate of accusations, counter-accusations and lack of co-operation between Rome and Zagreb ensued. However, the spread of the national liberation struggle in Croatia meant the Italian 2nd Army became engaged mainly in counter-insurgency operations. By the end of 1941, partisans in Croatia relied upon 7,000 armed men and around 20,000 helpers.[260]

It was between May and June of 1942 that General Mario Roatta attempted to return to collaborative engagements with Croatian troops. Although the Croats accepted Roatta's agreement, which involved the withdrawal of Italian garrisons from some localities, brutal violence and abuse erupted again against Ustaša enemies.

As Italian influence in the NDH diminished, German influence increased. In late 1942 and at the beginning of 1943, Berlin took advantage of Germany's military and economic control in the NDH as well as of Croatian sympathies (not least due to the area's Hapsburg history) to extend influence in the area. In the meantime, Tito's partisan movement seemed unstoppable. To counter the guerrilla's relentless advance, several German divisions were moved from Serbia to Croatia and all combat units of the NDH armed forces were placed under German command.[261] After February 1943, it became clear that although the Ustaša had gained control

---

[260] Ivo Goldstein, op. cit., p. 143.

[261] Mario Jareb, 'The NDH's Relations with Italy and Germany,' p. 66 and n. 54, p. 73, in Sabrina P. Ramet (ed.), *The Independent State of Croatia 1941-45*, (London: Routledge, 2007).

Yugoslavia: War and Occupation

99

in Croatia thanks to Mussolini's sponsorship, the disposition of the Croatian people was compactly against Italians. The time had arrived for Italy to admit defeat and withdraw her garrisons.[262]

Occupied Dalmatia

In Dalmatia, Governor Giuseppe Bastianini, appointed in May 1941, established a policy of Italianisation and Facistisation affecting every aspect of the social, economic, political, and religious life of the annexed area. Convinced, as he was, that the Italian 'political and military expansion would only have a provisional character without *civiltà italiana* (Italian civilisation),[263] Bastianini introduced the following measures: Italian as the official language in schools bringing teachers from Italy; changed place names from Croatian to Italian; imposed after-work recreational programmes; insisted that the press had to publish in Italian; tried to reorganise the hierarchy of bishops; introduced the Italian lira as sole legal tender; and made sure that all banks, insurance companies, and business establishments were taken over by Italian interests.[264] Such a programme of denationalisation met with the resistance of Dalmatian Croats, but their armed struggle, which broke out toward the end of July, was immediately subdued by Italian forces as the insurgent groups tried to link up with other Communist rebels who came from an uprising in Bosnia and the Croatian region of Lika.[265]

On 11 October 1941, Bastianini established the death penalty for anyone belonging to subversive organisations and carrying out any form of civil disobedience.[266] To maintain order, the Governor of Dalmatia could

---

[262] For further details on the complex relationship between Italy and the Independent State of Croatia see Davide Rodogno, op. cit., pp. 185-203.

[263] Oddone Talpo, *Dalmazia. Una cronaca per la storia*, (Roma: Ufficio Storico Stato Maggiore dell'Esercito, 1994), p. 997.

[264] Jozo Tomasevich, op. cit., pp. 131-3.

[265] Frank P. Verna, 'Notes on Italian Rule under Bastianini, 1941-1943,' *International History Review*, Vol. 12, No. 3 Aug. 1990), pp. 528-47.

[266] Ibid., p. 535.

100 *Luisa Morettin*

rely on several forces, which included not just the Blackshirt militia, but also the financial guards, the gendarmerie, border police as well as units from the 'Milano' squads and two Fascist 'M' battalions.[267] Despite that, throughout 1941 and 1942 there was no sign that the subversive attacks and armed resistance would stop. Initially, Bastianini did not implement the provisions of Mario Roatta's circular 3C of 1 March 1942, but the ambush and assassination of Vezio Orazi, the prefect of Zara, by partisans on 26 May of the same year, convinced him that stricter measures were necessary to deal with insurgent turbulence.[268]

Italian history books conspicuously omit the widespread atrocities committed in Dalmatia by the Italian occupation forces, which used the collaboration of civil servants and primary school teachers to create lists of hostages who would be hunted down during thorough searches.[269] Italian armed forces used ferocious reprisals against civilians for partisan attacks, even if their involvement was not proven. Their counter-insurgency operations included burning houses and entire villages, shooting hostages, withdrawing ration cards, and deporting the inhabitants of villages to concentration camps. Reprisal actions were often exemplary. The most infamous massacre carried out by Italians took place in July 1942 in Podhum, a village not far from Fiume, where as a reprisal for the killing of Giovanni Renzi, an Italian primary school teacher, his wife and two other Italian citizens, over 100 Slav civilians were shot.[270] Following the massacre, the rest of the population, including women and children, was interned and the village razed to the ground. Imprisonments and reprisals against Slav insurgents were quick and often exaggerated. During three weeks of July 1942, 975 people from Sebenico and surrounding villages were arrested and 240 people were shot.[271] Military instructions coming from above were diligently obeyed and have been preserved in unguarded, private letters, such as one written by an Italian soldier, Salvatore Seldi, to

---

[267] H. James Burgwyn, op. cit., p. 121.
[268] Frank. P. Verna, op. cit., p. 538.
[269] ACS, b.161, p. 12.
[270] Jozo Tomasevich, op. cit., p. 134.
[271] *Bollettino sui crimini italiani*, quoted in Enzo Collotti, op. cit., p. 542-3.

Yugoslavia: War and Occupation

101

his family on 1 July 1942. In this letter, he described the Italian raids: 'We've destroyed everything from top to bottom without sparing innocents … We're killing entire families, every night, beating them to death or shooting them.'[272]

On 16 November 1942, in retaliation for a partisan attack on an Italian convoy where 14 Italian soldiers were killed and 7 wounded, the Italian forces stationed in northern Dalmatia bombed the village of Primošten killing 150 people and further arrested 200 citizens during a massive four-hour combined, land, air, and naval attack. The disproportionate retaliation provoked the outrage of the Bishop of Šibenik, Jerolim Mileta, who protested with Bastianini and even requested for the Vatican's intervention.[273] These and many more witness testimonies are convincing enough to reassess the view that Mussolini's regime was only mildly repressive.

In February 1943, the anti-Yugoslav Francesco Giunta succeeded Giuseppe Bastianini as the Governor of Dalmatia, imposing a rule that was even more brutal than Bastianini's as Italian forces increased their terror-based repression in Dalmatia.[274] Immediate killings of insurgents were motivated if one or more of the following situations occurred: aiding and abetting partisans; if a police order to stop was not followed; and, if prisoners tried to flee during transfer.[275] However, such specific regulations did not mean that police forces could not have a free hand in administering justice and, if necessary, even forge official reports. On an April day in 1943, at the police headquarters in Spalato, a seventeen year old student, Ivan Pejkvic, was arrested and killed on the same day together with two other young men at the hand of a police officer. Allegedly, the prisoners had tried to run away. In fact, a later report revealed how the killing of the three young men was ordered by the Marshal of Security Services, a

---

[272] ACS, b.161, p. 35.
[273] Jozo Tomasevich, op. cit., p. 135.
[274] Ibid., p. 13.
[275] ACS, b.161, pp. 16-7.

102 *Luisa Morettin*

certain Franceschetti, who then recommended his subordinates to present 'the fact with intelligent tact.'[276]

Summary, extrajudicial justice was extremely common. An episode on 29 April 1943 is revealing: four people were killed in the village of Sonković, and three in Bratiškovci, for allegedly helping partisan groups, but it was in fact a prostitute who had pressed charges against them. Although the truthfulness of her testimony was not ascertained, the men were murdered by Lieutenant Giuseppe Gaetano, who compelled the father of two of the victims to watch the execution and then arrested him.[277]

Soon the politics of reprisals took on the proportions of a full extermination of Yugoslavs in compliance with what Mussolini and the Army Chief of Staff had previously decided at the Gorizia Conference in July 1942. As a result, General Mario Robotti circulated the following order amongst Italian troops stationed in the occupied territories of Yugoslavia.

> It is not important if the questioning proves that the prisoners are inoffensive. Remember that, due to various reasons, these people can become our enemies. Therefore [the strategy is] total deportation.
> … We should not restrict ourselves only to imprisonment. I will not oppose that all Slovenians are interned and replaced by Italians families of Italians who were wounded or who died. In other words, make sure that the political borders will correspond to ethnic borders. [278]

In reprisal for the partisan destruction of electricity supply pillars along the railway line of Sebenico-Spalato on 16 May 1943, General Gaspero Barbera, the *prefetto* of the Zara area, issued the order to shoot 65 hostages and asked for his instructions to be precisely followed.[279]

Then, on 7 July 1943, the Secretary of the Fascist Party in Zaravecchia (Biograd na moru), reported how members of the Division Granatieri di

---

[276] Ibid., pp. 18-9.
[277] Ibid., p. 19.
[278] *Bollettino sui crimini italiani*, quoted in Enzo Collotti, op. cit., p. 541.
[279] Ibid., p. 540.

Yugoslavia: War and Occupation

103

Sardegna had arrested five people, amongst them a young woman from Pašman. Before the arrested were all killed near the village church, heartrending scenes occurred when the victim's families pleaded for the lives of their loved ones. Due to this, the general public became terrified knowing that the five victims had no reason to be executed.[280]

Both in camps and prisons starvation of captives was the norm. Prisoners would receive 4.5 oz of bread a day and on some occasions they were fed salty fish and then given soapy water to drink.[281]

Survivors recall the horror of torture at the police station of Spalato, where it was routine to force the victims' mouths open so that they could be fed the policemen's excrements.[282] In some prisons a common torture tool was a wire mesh, which would be tightened around the abdomen of the victims so that their bowels would be compressed against other inner organs causing terrible pain and eventually death.[283] Sadism was not only the radical negation of the other, but also a way to prolong the victim's pain and the tormenter's perverse pleasure infinitely.

After suffering every kind of physical and psychological abuse, some prisoners chose to take their life. Some hanged themselves. In the prison of Sebenico, on 15 June 1942, Frane Djuba from Slarino (Zlarin Island), cut his coat and made a fabric rope with which he hanged himself. Others chose other ways. On 9 May 1943, Sergio Grubic stabbed himself in the stomach with a blunt instrument. He was taken to hospital in Zara, but he died three days later. In Spalato, on 8 March of the same year, Zorka Rosandic tried to kill himself by biting his wrists open.[284] The surge in suicides demonstrated the scale and brutality of torture, which was carried out by Italian forces.

This was to come to an end when the tide of war turned. On 19 August 1943, the Italians abolished the Governorate of Dalmatia, which was substituted by direct rule of the three *prefetti* who were governing the

---

[280] ACS, b.161, p. 20.
[281] Ibid., p. 20.
[282] Ibid., p. 24.
[283] Ibid., p. 23.
[284] Ibid., p. 24.

104 *Luisa Morettin*

provinces of Zara, Spalato and Cattaro. Italy's surrender on 8 September marked the end of Italian occupation not only in Dalmatia, but throughout Yugoslavia. Rome's imperial dream was over and Italy was a nation left almost in tatters. Yet, the legacy of violent occupation and destruction, which Italians left in Yugoslavia was not easily forgotten.

ITALY'S ARMISTICE

Whilst Italy struggled to bring order to her new Balkan territories that were confronted with a ferocious resistance, the East African empire was almost lost by the spring of 1941. The battle of Gondar in Ethiopia, in November 1941, forced the surrender of the Italian forces. As the situation grew grimmer and the five month long battle of Stalingrad marked the turning of the tide of the war in favour of the Allies, some leading Fascists tried to get Italy out of the conflict. They had come to the conclusion that the country could be saved from complete disaster only by removing Mussolini. To accomplish this, they needed to reach out to the British Government. In the spring of 1942, Luigi Rusca, an emissary of former Chief of Staff General Pietro Badoglio, started secret negotiations for Italy's surrender to the Anglo-Americans. Yet, his attempts floundered when the British War Office concluded Badoglio's forces had no real military power.[285]

After this, a number of peace-seeking efforts continued and one of them possibly originated from Galeazzo Ciano.[286] Also Giuseppe Bastianini, former Governor of Dalmatia and, from February 1943, Ciano's successor at the Foreign Ministry, tried to approach British officials through Francesco Fransoni, the Italian ambassador in Lisbon. The British were willing to meet with him as long as he was the authorised spokesman

---

[285] FO 954/13B/It/43-1, Eden Papers, 14 January 1943.
[286] Llewellyn Woodward, *British Foreign Policy in the Second World War*, Vol II, (London: HMSO, 1971), p. 461.

of the alternative leader to Mussolini, but since Fransoni only acted on behalf of Bastianini the invitation for a meeting was dropped.[287]

Yet, Italian efforts continued undeterred, and a proposal from an 'unnamed person' in the entourage of the Italian Crown Prince Umberto of Savoy, (later to be identified as the Duke of Aosta, formerly Duke of Spoleto, and brother of the late Duke of Aosta), declared his intention to lead an armed uprising against Mussolini and the Fascist regime.[288] In the royal family only Umberto of Savoy's wife, Princess Marie José of Belgium, had retained some contact with the Italian anti-fascist opposition and in September 1942, out of her own initiative, used the Vatican to contact the Anglo-Americans.[289] But when the King Victor Emmanuel III discovered that his daughter-in-law had been dealing in politics, her plan was immediately blocked. The king declared that 'In the House of Savoy women should not intervene in public affairs.'[290]

The British Foreign Secretary Antony Eden decided not to continue on any of the attempts to secure Italy's removal from the war out of fear that contacts with the existing Italian regime could jeopardise the genuineness of the British declaration, and intention, to destroy fascism.[291] The Italian proposals did not convince the Foreign Office and neither did they convince the American Department of State: until Germany proved itself as powerful as to not be defeated, no party in Italy would be able to conclude a separate peace with the Allied forces.

Amongst the Italians outside Italy possibly only the anti-fascist politician Count Carlo Sforza had the most influence, but in the view of senior allied officials he had been out of the country for too long and would not enjoy much support. And rightly so: even if Sforza had famously led the anti-fascist opposition in the Italian Senate, he had then been forced into exile in 1926 and had lived abroad ever since.

---

[287] Ennio Di Nolfo and Maurizio Serra, *La gabbia infranta. Gli Alleati e 'Italia dal 1943 al 1945*, (Roma: Laterza, 2010), p. 13.

[288] PMM/42/303, R8802/3700/22, 12 December 1942.

[289] Adele Cambria, *Maria José*, (Milano: Longanesi, 1966), pp. 88-9.

[290] Paolo Puntoni, *Parla Vittorio Emanuele III*, (Bologna: Il Mulino, 1993), p. 153.

[291] PMM 42/292, R8802/3700/22, 2 December 1942.

At the end of 1942, Germany suspected a potential defection of its weak ally from the Axis and developed operational plans for operations Alarich and Konstantin, later codenamed Operation Achse, devoted to the invasion of Italy and the Balkan areas occupied by the Italian Army. In Italy support to the Fascist regime was quickly eroded by bombings, food rationing and years of misery and sacrifice. The military situation was deteriorating quickly. General Giovanni Messe surrendered the last Axis forces in Tunisia on 13 May 1943, and on 10 July, Anglo-American forces landed in Sicily encountering little resistance. On 19 July Rome was heavily bombed in broad daylight by over 500 Allied planes. Four days after the landings in Sicily, whilst General Vittorio Ambrosio advised the Duce to give up a hopeless fight and surrender, a group of senior Fascists pressurised Mussolini to summon the 1923 established Grand Council of Fascism, a private advisory council of the Prime Minister. Mussolini agreed. Before the Grand Council met Hitler asked Mussolini for a meeting in Feltre, near Belluno, where the Duce failed to clearly state Italy's right to withdraw from the conflict. It was one of the last mistakes of a dictator who had progressively lost touch with reality and was nearing a mental breakdown.

During a long meeting on the night of 24-25 July 1943, the Grand Council, by a majority vote of nineteen to seven, suggested a motion of no confidence in Mussolini, who had to give up command of the armed forces. This would be continued by the King, who had the Duce arrested the following day. Thus, the powerful dictator was overthrown by the party which he had created.

Publicly Italy continued in the war as a member of the Axis, yet privately, she was still negotiating with the Anglo-Americans the terms of Italy's surrender, which was finally signed on 3 September 1943 in an Allied military camp at Cassibile, Sicily. However, the capitulation failed to extricate the country from the war. Despite the expectation of millions of Italians that the conflict would end, the only order which troops received on 8 September by new Prime Minister, Pietro Badoglio, was to retaliate in case they were attacked.

Yugoslavia: War and Occupation

The Germans immediately snapped into action and on 9 September, their troops swiftly poured from the north thus beginning Italy's occupation and the disarmament of the Italian Army. Ahead of the advancing German troops, the royal family, Badoglio and senior generals quickly left Rome for the safety of Brindisi, in Southern Italy, which was already in Anglo-American hands, and there they set up a Kingdom of the South. By irresponsibly leaving the armed forces without clear instructions, they caused the disbanding en masse of the army in Italy and in the occupied territories, all which led to disastrous consequences.

In the unliberated north of Italy, on 9 September the *Comitato di Liberazione Nazionale* (CLN), or National Liberation Committee, was formed. It was a political umbrella organisation, representing the Italian resistance movement that, under the chairmanship of Ivanoe Bonomi, comprised of five political parties: the Liberals, the Christian Democrats, the Socialists, the Communists, and the Actionists (*Partito d'Azione*). Their guerrilla units joined forces with scattered army bands and took to the hills.

However, after the liberation of Rome in June 1944 it was the CLN of Milan, known as the Committee for National Liberation for Upper Italy (CLNAI) and recognised by the Allies as the supreme underground authority, which was to become more closely involved with the events of Venezia Giulia. Within the CLNAI, the best organised, largest and strongest units were communist, known as the Garibaldi Division, which together with the Action Party, controlled almost 70 per cent of the guerrilla forces, thus giving the CLNAI a distinctive, left-wing predominance.

In Yugoslavia, whilst the non-Communist parties in the Slav Resistance sought co-ordination and co-operation in order to fight the common German occupier, the strong position of the Communist forces and the prospect of winning the territorial battle prompted Palmiro Togliatti, the new leader of the Italian Communist Party (PCI), to agree to a Yugoslav takeover of the whole of Venezia Giulia, thus eliciting the

108 *Luisa Morettin*

resentment of the CLNAI that accused him of 'selling out Italian interests.'[292] Indeed, Togliatti, together with his friend Antonio Gramsci, was not only a founding member of the PCI in 1921, but had been Vice-Secretary of the Comintern. Thus, due to his close relationship with Stalin, he was suspected to go against Italy's cause.[293]

The Allies were not able to gain much advantage from their surprise invasion of mainland Italy. Whilst the bulk of their forces were required for the landings in France, they made very slow progress up the Italian peninsula as the Germans strongly resisted. Still, they were able to land at Salerno, just south of Naples, and at the port city of Taranto on 9 September 1943, in Sardinia on the 14, eventually entering Naples on 1 October.

In the meantime, Mussolini was rescued from his prison on the Gran Sasso Mountain by German paratroopers and installed at the head of a German-dominated puppet state called *Repubblica Sociale Italiana* (Italian Social Republic), also known as RSI or Republic of Salò, located around Lake Garda. Fascist officials, who had not already abandoned fascism, joined the RSI, thus collaborating with Germany as the conflict continued in the north and centre of the country. When the Italian Government declared war against Germany on 13 October 1943, General Albert Kesselring was already receiving reinforcements and consolidating Germany's hold on central and northern Italy. German forces moved rapidly taking over Italian zones of occupation in the Balkans and Southern France and disarming the Italian forces in Italy.

In such a difficult situation, Italian soldiers faced a serious dilemma. Whilst some held onto the idea that the fatherland was represented by fascism, and fought for Mussolini's Republic of Salò, others believed the way forward was to see that the real fatherland worth serving and fighting for was 'that of the poor devils who ha[d] paid for the sins of others with

---

[292] Bogdan C. Novak, op. cit., p. 102.
[293] Elena Aga-Rossi and Victor Zaslavski, *Stalin and Togliatti. Italy and the Origins of the Cold War*, (Stanford: Stanford University Press, 2011), chaps. 3, 6.

Yugoslavia: War and Occupation 109

their lives.'[294] The latter group took to the hills and became active partisans joining an estimated 80,000 fighters.[295] Others deserted and went into hiding, waiting for the end of the conflict. To further complicate this divisive picture, in some areas class antagonisms triggered armed uprisings against not only the Germans and Fascists, but also against local landowners. Depending on their motives and objectives, combatants fought different types of war: a civil war against Italian Fascists, a war of national liberation against the German occupiers, and a class war against the ruling class that was aimed at a greater social justice. Such ideals would often turn into strong political beliefs and it was not uncommon that different partisan groups came into vicious conflict with each other, as it happened in February 1945, between a group of Communist partisans belonging to the *Gruppi di azione patriottica* (GAP) and the Brigata Osoppo, a formation of Catholic inspiration. Several members of the Brigata Osoppo, accused of hindering the collaboration with Communist partisan troops, were brutally murdered by the GAP in the border area of eastern Friuli, in what became known as the Porzûs massacre.[296]

In the light of the complex nature of the Italian civil war, Italian politician Concetto Marchesi defined the period of 1943-1945 as 'the most ferocious and sincere of all wars.'[297] Indeed, civil war did not aim at a just peace, but rather at the complete and brutal annihilation of the enemy.

---

[294] Nuto Revelli, 'La ritirata di Russia,' in Mario Isenghi (ed.), *I luoghi della memoria. Strutture ed eventi dell'Italia Unita*, (Bari: Laterza, 1997), p. 374.

[295] The figure was given by the Salò government by the early summer of 1944. Christopher Duggan, *The Force of Destiny*, p. 536.

[296] Pier Paolo Pasolini, 'Mio fratello,' *Vie Nuove*, Numero 28, 15 July 1961.

[297] Claudio Pavone, *A Civil War. A History of the Italian Resistance*, (London: Verso, 2013), p. 270.

Chapter 4

A JOURNEY INTO DARKNESS

To punish the enemies of the fatherland,
we must find out who they are:
but we do not want to punish them;
we want to destroy them.

Maximilien de Robespierre
Report on the Principles of Political Morality

THE ARMISTICE IN VENEZIA GIULIA AND YUGOSLAVIA

When the Italian armistice was made public, chaos spread not only throughout mainland Italy, but also in the occupied territories of the Balkans, southern France and Greece.

In Yugoslavia, where 305,000 Italian soldiers were stationed, (representing slightly less than half of the troops in the Balkans where a total of 650,000 men had been posted), troops were left to fend for themselves.[298] The inertia of Italian military's high commanders and their lack of willingness to issue their subordinates with clear orders, that instead were so ambiguous as to be unintelligible, meant that a large army was abandoned in a grim and bitter struggle. In Yugoslavia, Italian troops had to choose between desertion or captivity either by the Germans, furious at the betrayal of the Axis alliance, or by the Yugoslav partisans, resentful of the Axis invasion of their country that had led to thousands of deaths and the bloodstained destruction of entire villages.

News of the armistice reached General Mario Robotti, commander of the Italian 2nd Army, by radio on the evening of 8 September 1943. In turn he ordered troops of the Italian Second Army nearest to Ljubljana to gather. However, it later emerged that some garrisons were never informed by their immediate superiors. Amidst great uncertainty officers were often unable to take on a resolute attitude and show their own initiative, something unusual for them due to the cult of passive obedience to superiors they had been strictly trained under.[299] Being Venezia Giulia and Ljubljana closest to Austria, they were the first areas to be occupied by German troops in September 1943. Indeed two weeks before the Italian surrender, the Germans had moved two regiments to the Slovene Littoral and around Trieste, while stationing another regiment in the area of Ljubljana.[300] Their first violent actions against Italians on the morning of 9 September forced General Robotti to contact the Chief of Staff in Rome to get further instructions in relation to *Memoria 44*, a vague and general order issued by General Mario Roatta on 2 September ahead of Italy's capitulation and directed only to the high military commands. But in vain: by then the king and all high commands had precipitately departed from Rome leaving behind no commander for the troops that were still engaged in the war and were not ordered how the Germans were to be opposed. At the local level there was no clear idea of the way forward as well as no

---

[298] Gerhard Schreiber, *I militari italiani internati nei campi di concentramento del Terzo Reich. 1943-1945*, (Roma: Ufficio Storico SME, 1992), pp. 180-2.

[299] Giorgio Rochat, *Le guerre italiane. 1935-1943. Dall'impero d'Etiopia alla disfatta*, (Torino: Einaudi, 2005), p. 180.

[300] Jozo Tomasevich, op. cit., p. 121.

A Journey into Darkness

113

clear divide between military and political objectives. Amidst the chaos following the announcement of the Italian armistice, the state of war continued while the borders of irregular and regulated occupation became blurred.

Faced with the inevitably quick German counterattack, depressed and demoralised, most of the Italian army units disintegrated. In the early hours of 9 September a German unit entered Ljubljana, arrested the commanders of the XI Army Corps and the divisions Cacciatori delle Alpi, Lombardia and Isonzo, thus preventing them from carrying out Robotti's orders.[301] Trieste was occupied by Wehrmacht troops and became the headquarters of a newly created *Operationszone Adriatisches Küstenland* (Operational Zone of the Adriatic Littoral), the details of which will be examined later. In the port town of Fiume although 50,000 men were stationed, their commander General Gastone Gambara surrendered to a Wehrmacht colonel accompanied by two soldiers on motorbicycles. In Pola, Italian soldiers together with about 40,000 sailors of the naval base under the command of Admiral Gustavo Strazzeri refused to hand over their weapons to the Italian anti-Fascist Committee and instead capitulated to a small German unit.[302]

It is Dalmatia that better exemplifies the dramatic, large-scale collective tragedy of Italy's mishandled armistice. In September 1943 the situation along the Italian occupied Croatian coast was particularly chaotic due to the simultaneous presence of Italian and German troops, Croatian collaborationists, Chetniks, and Tito's partisans. The outcome was political and military upheaval, which was due not only to the lack of clear commands, but also to the location and the individual circumstances of each unit and division. In Cattaro and Ragusa, Italian forces refused to continue fighting on the German side; in Spalato and Sebenico, Italian troops held simultaneous negotiations with both Germans and partisans; whilst in Zara, they reached an agreement with their former ally, Germany,

---

[301] Gino Bambara, *Non solo armistizio. Autunno 1943. Tragico sfacelo dell'Armata italiana in Jugoslavia e ai confini orientali*, (Gussago: Società Editrice Vannini, 2003), p. 49.
[302] Dennison Rusinow, op. cit., p. 291.

114 *Luisa Morettin*

in order to avert a partisan occupation of the town. [303] As a result, on 10 September 1943, two days after the Italian surrender was announced, the 114th German Jäger Division entered Zara and this Dalmatian coastal town, one of the oldest in Croatia, was placed under the control of Major Hans Teissl. In the afternoon of the same day Croatian aircrafts repeatedly flew over Zara and dropped leaflets signed by Ante Pavelić. They read:

> Dalmatians! The leader of the Reich has acknowledged the annexation of wonderful Dalmatia to Croatia ... Together with the heroic Croatian liberation troops also German forces are bringing you freedom ... The Italian behaviour did not surprise us.[304]

Such 'paper bombs' conveyed a subtle yet powerful message by targeting Italian troops at a crucial time in warfare, and demoralising the already psychologically weakened populace, by focusing on the future ethnic identity of their city. The text had been a product of a top secret meeting held on 2 August 1943 between Siegfried Kasche, the Ambassador of the German Reich to the Independent State of Croatia, and General Edmund Glaise von Horstenau, Plenipotentiary General in the NDH,[305] who had discussed the destination of Italian occupied territories. In the case of Dalmatia, the two senior Germans decided it would be annexed by Croatia and the Ustaša Government should organise irregular forces that would take over the coastal area, as well as the Italian enclave of Zara. The German decision was shared with Mladen Lorković, the then Foreign Minister of the NDH. On 8 September, Hitler agreed to the plan, the details of which were radio broadcast by Ante Pavelić in person the very same day.

The arrangement was met with bewilderment by the compactly Italian city of Zara, whose representatives stressed the city's Italian nature to Major Hans Teissl of the Jäger Division. An agreement was therefore reached, according to which General Umberto Spigo and his 5,000 Italian

---

[303] Oddone Talpo, op. cit., p. 1042.
[304] Ibid., p. 1331.
[305] Ibid., p. 1495.

soldiers would retain their weapons in order to maintain and guarantee public order in Zara, Spalato and Sebenico.[306] The concession was granted in order to prevent the much feared arrival of partisan units. As the Artillery Captain Ernesto Cuneo had highlighted, the Italian forces wanted to remain in Zara not as German collaborationists, but rather to protect citizens from external attacks.[307] However, during the next three months, only a few Italian units remained in the area, as the Germans had decided to relocate Italian troops and disband the Italian Army.

Ivo Venturini, sublieutenant of the Third Battalion 'Spalato' from the Zara division, recalled how the war-weary Italian soldiers were caught between two fires: on one side the Germans, on the other the partisans. Their deepest desire was to return home and wait for the end of the hostilities. One evening, Venturini remembered, the battalion decided to join the partisan Garibaldi division that disarmed them, stripped them of their clothes and left them to fend for themselves. After a three weeks long march, with no clothes and no food, they reached Fiume, where the Germans arrested them and sent them to the prisoners of war camp located in Markt Pongau (Sankt Johann im Pongau), near Salzburg, Austria.[308] Some, like Venturini, eventually returned home yet many others did not.

Gorizia was the only major town of Venezia Giulia not to have surrendered to the Germans. Instead, the commander of the local Infantry Division Torino, General Bruno Malaguti, formed a tacit alliance with the partisans of the Slovene OF and attempted to resist the German advance in the Isonzo Valley with the help of the newly formed Trieste Proletarian Brigade.[309] Still, German forces managed to move into the town, and Mussolini's Special Tribunal for the Defence of the State investigated General Malaguti for betraying his country.[310]

---

[306] USSME, b. 2125/E Relazione sugli avvenimenti riguardanti il XVIII Corpo d'armata nel Settembre 1943.

[307] Oddone Talpo, op. cit., p. 1335.

[308] Ibid., p. 1449.

[309] Vittorio Leschi, *La Resistenza italiana nella Venezia Giulia, 1943-1945: fonti archivistiche,* (Gorizia: LEG, 2007), p. 106.

[310] AA.VV., *Storia contemporanea in Friuli,* (Udine: Istituto Friulano per la storia del movimento di liberazione, 2003), p. 23.

116   *Luisa Morettin*

The Germans were not the only ones to capitalise on the weakness and disorientation of the Italian Army. Indeed, due to a lack of resources the Wehrmacht only managed to seize the strategic coastal cities of Trieste, Pola and Fiume, leaving out large pockets of territory in the hinterland, which became a no man's land. The first to take advantage of such a vacuum in authority in the Istrian countryside were Tito's partisans, who swiftly replaced the Fascist rule in the more rural areas of Venezia Giulia. They secured and took control of large countryside sections, which devoid of strategic importance for fascist forces, were left to their own devices. The partisans acted rapidly. Stating they were the only movement recognised by the Allies, (something which only happened later at the Tehran Conference of November 1943), they managed to get Italian forces formations to surrender, turning over their weapons and enlist as soldiers, thus expanding their ranks of partisan combatants.[311]

Tito's troops further strengthened their positions by defeating their old enemies, the Chetniks. Due to the general confusion following the Italian Armistice, the local conservative forces, known as *Guardia Civica* or *Vaške straže* (the Village Guards) who opposed the partisans, were organised by the Mayor of Ljubljana, Leon Rupnik, into a new military force called the *Domobranci* (Home Guards), also including what was left of the Chetnik troops. Tito's forces encircled and defeated the Slovenian Chetniks in a brutal fight at Grčarice, after which Mihailovič's followers surrendered.[312]

Local partisans and even unarmed Croatian peasants acted quickly and confronted the Italian units, which led to the surrender of their commanding officers. This happened widely throughout Istria, as seen with the troops stationed in the centre of Albona (Labin), Pisino (Pazin), and Pinguente (Buzet), where thousands of Italian soldiers abandoned their weapons and surrendered to scant numbers of locals.[313] In this way the

---

[311] Jozo Tomasevich, op. cit., p. 299.
[312] Bogdan C. Novak, op. cit., p. 81.
[313] Marina Cattaruzza, *Italy and Its Eastern Border, 1866-2016*, (London: Routledge, 2016), p. 181.

partisan movement stepped in and organised their Communist rule from 9 September until the beginning of October 1943.

The scholarly consensus surrounding the Italian northeastern border at this pivotal moment is that there were two waves of Yugoslav violence in Venezia Giulia; one, which occurred in 1943, and the other in 1945. Yet, it is more apt to say that the development of terror and violence continued through three interrelated, but very distinct periods. The first wave of this kind occurred from 9 September, when Yugoslav partisans took hold of the Istrian countryside, until 1 October 1943 when the Germans reconquered the whole region. The second happened between October and November 1944 when, after the German withdrawal, Tito's troops entered the city of Zara and carried out indiscriminate and swift executions. A third, and the fiercest wave of atrocities, took place from 1 May and continued until 13 June 1945, (or at times until 1946-1947, depending on the areas involved), during which the cities of Trieste, Gorizia and Fiume, together with some towns in the Istrian hinterland became the main targets for the campaign of widespread ethnic and political cleansing.

THE FIRST WAVE OF VIOLENCE. 1943

During the transitional period, prior to the arrival of German troops, which is mentioned above as 'the first wave of atrocities,' the partisans imposed a Communist rule during which they killed not only Italians involved with the Fascist regime, Village Guards, Home Guards and Chetniks in Ljubljana Province, but also harmless civilians. Allegedly their violent actions were spontaneous, as their sense of retribution and settlement of old accounts did not distinguish between guilt and innocence. In some areas, the killings did not suddenly end when the Germans conquered the whole of Istria on 1 October, instead they slowly dwindled and continued to occur until November 1943.

For the violence perpetrated during this period there are very few Anglo-American witness reports available as it was only two years later, in the spring of 1945, that Allied forces finally reached Venezia Giulia to liberate it and they could then collect extensive witness testimony from Italian survivors who described the Yugoslav atrocities, which took place between the 9 September 1943 and 1 October 1943. Despite the scarcity of Allied sources, the documentation available offers a glimpse into a conflict that had taken on the hallmarks of barbarism.

One survivor, Fedele Casolari, Sergeant Major of *Carabinieri Reali* (Italian State Police) stationed on the island of Cherso, recalled:

> All the men belonging to the class 1908 have been obliged to join their [Tito partisans'] files and had to leave for Yugoslavia. ... Fifteen persons, the most prominent Italians, have been deported and four of them (Antoni, Baici, Zadro and another one whose name I do not remember) were killed with the excuse that they were Fascists. ...
>
> On 2 November 1943, with a pre-announcement of two hours, they [Tito's troops] obliged all Italians to go on board of a sailer with the promise that they will be sent to Bari. On the sailer were about one hundred twenty persons, almost all of them militaries and [Italian] government employees with their families. On the sailer came also an armed guard of twenty Slav partisans. In the meantime all the houses of the deported ones were robbed (we knew later that they have been deported).
>
> The vessel made a short stay at Ossero (Lussino) where more Italian deportees came on board. The guard proceeded to an accurate search in the luggage of the deportees and on the persons. We have been literally robbed of everything we had, even shoes.
>
> Instead of Bari, we arrived at Cerquinizza (Dalmatia) where, after another particular search and another robbing, we were sent in a column with rapid march in direction northward. After a few kilometres the leader of the escort whistled several times and to this signal all the partisans fled, leaving us alone. We continued our march for fear of being shot at, carrying our children, and after one kilometre we met German armoured cars and tanks.[314]

---

[314] WO 204/430.

A Journey into Darkness

The casual encounter with German vehicles saved the lives of this column of Italian prisoners to which Casolari belonged. However, at the nearby Croatian island of Lussino things went tragically differently for another group of prisoners. Casolari continued:

> The sailer which took the Italians [from Lussino] sailed before we did and returned into the harbour after a few days completely stained in blood. The captain of the sailer gave signs of mental haziness. It is said that all Italians who were on board were first robbed, then massacred and finally thrown into the sea. Indeed of no one was heard any more.[315]

Another survivor, *Senatore* Antonio Tacconi, who was Mayor of Spalato from April 1941 until September 1943, recalled that after the armistice, 'bloody and violent persecutions started against Italians, many people were arrested and then shot.' On that occasion, most of the Italians left their houses and took shelter in communal homes. The partisans took particular aim at teachers who had taken shelter in an Italian school, that the soldiers continually visited and where they ill-treated the refugees. 'Some of the partisan soldiers' – Tacconi added – 'used violence against the Italian women.'[316] It is not clear if rape was considered legitimate by Tito's forces, either on the grounds of revenge for previous Italian brutality or simply as a casual right of conquest, or still, as in the case of collective sexual violence, as a bonding process.

It certainly echoes the indiscriminate violence and systematic rape carried out by large numbers of soldiers of the Red Army during their advance toward Central Europe. Even if reports from Venezia Giulia do not record the same methodical violence against women as Stalin's troops, it is highly unlikely that sexual abuse was punished, and it is not known of any partisan leader that intervened to stop it. On the contrary, some cases of collective rape became infamous, such as that of Norma Cossetto, the young daughter of a landowner and Fascist Mayor of Visinada (Vižinada),

---

[315] WO 204/430.
[316] WO 204/11202.

who was repeatedly tortured and raped by her captors for several days in a school turned prison, before she was thrown into a *foiba* near Pirano (Piran), in north-western Istria between 4 and 5 October 1943. When they retrieved Norma's body from the 443 feet deep pit, her breasts had been removed and a long piece of wood was found inside her genitals.[317] Since then, Norma's death is remembered as emblematic of the fate of the Italian victims of partisan violence in Venezia Giulia.

Three sisters, Albina, Caterina, and Fosca Radecca, aged from 17 to 21, met with a similar fate: the three of them were raped before being thrown into the pit of Terli (Trlji), but only Albina was shot, meaning that the other two sisters were thrown in alive.[318]

Arnaldo Harzarich, a Fire Marshal born in Pola in 1903, is inextricably linked to the tragedy of the *foibe* killings, since he headed a team of firefighters, who between 16 and 25 September 1943, pulled out 84 bodies that had been thrown into the foiba in Vines, near Albona, in south-western Istria. Twelve of them were of German soldiers.[319] The corpses of many other victims could not be retrieved due to the depth of the pit, the danger of its walls collapsing, and out of fear of the partisans' ambushes. Indeed, Harzarich was often the target of shooting attacks intended to hinder his search for victims.[320]

He later wrote a detailed report on the findings retrieved from the local *foiba:* all bodies had been handcuffed with a wire behind their backs, and in many cases, they had been clamped so tightly that the metal had cut into their flesh and broken their wrists. In addition, many prisoners had been tied one to the other in pairs or in small groups, but only one of them resulted in being shot. Such a detail reveals that, as in the case of the Radecca sisters, the first prisoner, who had been killed, would drag into the pit the rest of the victims who were still alive.

---

[317] Gianni Oliva, *Foibe. Le stragi negate degli italiani della Venezia Giulia e dell'Istria*, (Milano: Mondadori, 2003), p. 78.

[318] Ibid., p. 79.

[319] Raoul Pupo and Roberto Spazzali, *Foibe*, (Milan: Mondadori, 2003), p. 57.

[320] Giuseppina Mellace, *Una grande tragedia dimenticata. La vera storia delle foibe*, (Roma: Newton Compton, 2018), pp. 90-1.

A Journey into Darkness

Near the *foiba* in Vines a perfectly round hole of thirty centimetres was also found. Initially it was believed to be the place where a machine gun was positioned to kill the victims, but a partisan woman from Barbana revealed it was the location of the platform for a mobile radio station, from which the killings were broadcast live. Allegedly, the radio telegrapher was a woman in her mid-twenties who reported the atrocities in Russian.[321]

Quarries were also used as dumping sites by Yugoslav partisans as seen at the bauxite mining site in Montona (Motovun) and Villa Catuni south of Pisino; in Lindaro (Lindar), west of Gallignana (Gračišće), and in the nearby Villa Bassotti (Bacsoti); the coal mine in Val Pèdena in the vicinity of Pisino; and others in the San Martino woods at Vettua. It was estimated that over one hundred Italian victims were dumped into these quarries in 1943.[322]

In coastal towns and villages, the bodies of those executed were not thrown into pits or mines, but rather into the sea where there was a minimal risk of the body being returned to shore by strong currents. Yet, occasionally, the sea would return a corpse. On 21 October 1943 Carmine De Giovanni, head of the police station at Medolino (Medulin), and police officer Angelo Martinello, were found tightly tied to one another at Porto Badò (Porto Bado), a narrow waterway extending into the land, along the eastern coast of the Istrian Peninsula.[323]

It is known that a similar fate met 19 people who were being held prisoners in the isolated barracks of the *Guardia di Finanza* in Santa Marina di Albona (Sveta Marina) and then were flung into the sea where they drowned between 4 and 5 October 1943.[324] Indeed, the regularity of executions sped up at the beginning of October 1943 when the People's Authorities, chased by German troops, had to withdraw into the mountains

---

[321] Raoul Pupo and Roberto Spazzali, op. cit., pp. 57-8.
[322] Gaetano La Perna, *Pola-Istria-Fiume 1943-1945. La lenta agonia di un lembo d'Italia*, (Milano: Mursia, 1993), p. 184.
[323] Ibid., p. 182.
[324] Ibid., p. 183.

122   *Luisa Morettin*

and thus decided to leave behind no witnesses to the atrocities they had committed.[325]

Italian soldiers, who disbanded after the Armistice, were recruited into the Yugoslav forces. Adriano Horst, an Italian Lieutenant in the XXV Infantry Regiment Bergamo, confirmed that as soon as his soldiers joined the VIII Dalmatian Korpus, (a corps of the Yugoslav partisans formed in October 1943), on average, two Italians disappeared every day, and 'each disappearance meant death,' Horst recalled.[326] However, he did not specify if the killings were a form of punishment or if they were simply random and unmotivated.

It seems that the recruitment drive into the Yugoslav forces was aimed at both strengthening the ranks of the Yugoslav resistance to the German occupation and at persuading Italians to become Yugoslavs. Prima facie evidence shows that these Italians would have been included into the Yugoslav nation, but their refusal meant the death penalty. Diego De Castro, a member of the Venezia Giulia Committee in Rome and later a representative in the Allied Military Government (AMG), recalled how in the southern Italian region of Apulia, where shelters had been put up for ill and wounded Yugoslav combatants, who in 1944 reached 20,000 units, hospitalised partisans recruited many Italian soldiers to join their ranks. However, these Italians were compelled to declare that they were born in Trieste or Pola, hence that they were Yugoslav citizens, change their Italian surname into a Yugoslav one, and embrace the Communist faith. Those who refused were executed in the Adriatic island of Lissa (Vis), where from 1944 the Communist headquarters was located. The British forces called them 'the underground battalion,' referring to its clandestine origin and to the tragic end that awaited those unfortunate soldiers.[327]

Italian sources indicate that after the Armistice the number of Italian troops fighting alongside Tito's partisans in Yugoslavia was approximately 80,000. They were then sent to fight far from the Julian Front, scattered

---

[325] Raoul Pupo and Roberto Spazzali, op. cit., pp. 12-3.

[326] Paola Romano, *La questione giuliana 1943-1947. La guerra e la diplomazia. Le foibe e l'esodo*, (Trieste: Lint, 1997), pp. 41-7.

[327] Diego De Castro, *Il problema di Trieste*, (Bologna: Licinio Cappelli Editore, 1953), pp. 106-7.

throughout the territory, allocated to battalions where the majority of combatants were Yugoslavs. In doing so, Tito avoided the risk that a corps made up entirely of Italians could then later lay claim to territories they had liberated from German occupation.

THE GERMANS IN THE ADRIATIC LITTORAL

Despite the setbacks due to the collapse of Fascism and Italy's defection, Hitler still had reason to believe Germany could win the war and was adamant to clamp down on any dissent. When his troops recovered Venezia Giulia, it was the start of a brutal occupation lasting 18 months, which also saw the creation, on 15 October 1943, of the *Adriatisches Küstenland* (Adriatic Littoral) out of Istria and the provinces of Ljubljana and Udine. The takeover was of strategic importance since the region linked Germany, Italy and the Balkans, and granted sea access and a revival of the Nazi economic penetration towards east.

In the Adriatic Littoral, the Germans refused to recognise Mussolini's new appointees to the role of prefects. As an alternative, they placed the new civil and military administration under the governorship of two senior Austrian Nazis, Friedrich Rainer and Odilo Goblocnik, appointed respectively as High Commissioner in the rank of a SS–Obergruppenführer, and Higher SS and Police Leader of the Operational Zone of the Adriatic Littoral. The Italian Bruno Coceani was nominated *prefetto* of Trieste and supervisor of all other regional prefects, whilst Cesare Pagnini became the city's *podestà*. In January 1944, the Germans allowed Coceani and Pagnini to install the Trieste *Guardia Civica* (Civic Guard), a body that held the task of defending the city and, according to Coceani's plans, could also be used at the end of the war to defend Trieste against any advancing Yugoslavs.[328]

---

[328] Galliano Fogar, *Trieste in guerra 1940-1945. Società e Resistenza*, (Trieste, ISMLFVG, 1999), pp. 92-8. Bogdan Novak, op. cit., p. 76.

The German administration of the *Adriatisches Küstenland* performed independently from the RSI, signalling a move toward a pan-Germanic future in the event of a German victory, or at least a revival of the Habsburg era if Germany lost. Indeed, the RSI government was only allowed to carry out the payment of state employees' salaries and to have their own military troops, which always under German control, were employed to fight the partisans. As for the rest, the Austrian born or Austrian related officers, appointed to key roles in the Adriatic Littoral, controlled everything. Not only were Rainer and Goblocnik from Carinthia. Also Baron Ferdinand Wolsegger, Rainer's Deputy, Dr Hinterreger, the German advisor to the Prefect of Trieste, and Herr Schranzhofer, advisor to the Mayor of Trieste, were of Austrian origin or had studied in Austria. Likewise, Coceani and Pagnini were respectively born in Monfalcone and Trieste, then belonging to Austria-Hungary. In Gorizia, the prefect Count Marino Pace, and in Udine the prefect Riccardo de Beden had once been Austro-Hungarian officers.[329] To complement these appointments, the Adriatic Littoral Government placed great emphasis on the implementation of new legislation, which removed the control of the area from the Italian Social Republic and also suggested a separate nationality.

According to the new Nazi order, laws were not to be issued by the Salò Government, but by the Supreme Commissioner, who also ratified laws put forward by the RSI and further had the prerogative to pardon whomever they wished during court trials. Visits by Italians from the RSI required special permission and were limited to seven days. Further, customs barriers were introduced on the River Tagliamento and on the former Austro-Italian border, and officials were not allowed to take the customary oath of allegiance to the RSI. Lastly, there was a restriction on conscripting Adriatic Littoral soldiers for the Army of the Italian Social Republic.[330]

---

[329] Dennison Rusinow, op. cit., p. 307.
[330] Ibid., p. 301.

A Journey into Darkness

Under German occupation, the area was governed by a divide and conquer policy, which exploited the long-standing animosities between Italians and Slavs. As a result, Germany promised the Istrian Peninsula to both the Italians and Croats at differing times.[331] Germans also enhanced Slav culture: they re-established the linguistic and cultural rights of Slovenes, with Slovenian re-introduced for administrative purposes and in schools and the Slovenian press reinstated. This restoration of their culture was welcomed by a significant number of Slovenes, who would eventually collaborate, believing German rule to be the 'lesser evil' if compared to the alternative of the region being ruled by Slovenian pro-Communist partisans.[332] These Littoral anti-Communist Slovenes formed the *Primorska narodna straža* (Littoral National Guard), an armed body that despite having similar ideological goals as the Home Guards in the Ljubljana Province, was not permitted by Germany to operate together – a decision which proved detrimental to the development of a strong anti-Communist organisation.[333]

Similarly, local Italian collaborators, old Fascists who did not join the Republican Fascist Party, saw the German danger as transient as opposed to the Slav long-term danger. They also felt – as Bruno Coceani would later claim – that if they had abandoned their offices, 'the foreign arrogance would have been stronger and more uncontrolled and their successor would have contributed to ... new violence.'[334] Such a train of thought poses complex moral questions regarding the nature of collaboration and responsibility, for which it is difficult to infer judgement if the axiom of 'man is morally responsible for his actions, only if he has free choice' is taken into account. The Adriatic Littoral soldiers did not have many options available to them, as the scope between collaboration and resistance was often ill defined and long-standing assumptions

---

[331] Bogdan C. Novak, op. cit., p. 88.

[332] Gregor Joseph Kranjc, *To Walk with the Devil: Slovene Collaboration and Axis Occupation, 1941-1945*, (Toronto: University of Toronto Press, 2013), pp. 196-8.

[333] Bodgan Novak, op. cit., p. 86.

[334] Bruno Coceani, *Trieste durante l'occupazione tedesca 1943-1945*, (Milano: La Stampa Commerciale, 1959), p. 98.

regarding right and wrong were becoming jumbled. After Italy's armistice whichever choice the soldiers made the other party still considered them disloyal. It did not matter if they chose to join the partisans, or fight alongside the Germans, and even if they allowed themselves to be taken prisoners by the Wehrmacht and sent to labour camps; what one faction justified as legitimate, the other political and ideological side gave the label of traitor. This was seen clearly in the formation of the Civic Guard, which showed how the situation became even more ambiguous. When the Guard was established at the beginning of 1944, it was intended to be an apolitical municipal army. However, it soon became apparent that the Germans had an alternative plan for the unit, which they instead trained and used for their needs of territorial defence,[335] thus the Civic Guard recruits became involuntarily collaborationists.

Assuming that Coceani was correct that his collaboration and presence curtailed the Germanisation of Trieste and it further opposed the 'Red' danger of Yugoslav demands toward Italian borderlands, it still raised the question of whether it justified the acceptance of German cruelty and disproportionate retaliation. Indeed, Italians had no say in mitigating reprisal attacks or preventing deportations and this then became most evident in the case of Italian Jews.

The year of 1938 had marked the launch of the Italian Fascist's regime anti-Jewish campaign, aligning its racial policy to that of Germany. The freedom of Italian Jews was certainly limited as many lost their jobs and were exiled internally or forced to flee. However, in Fascist Italy the solution of the 'Jewish Question' was different to Germany's as anti-Semitism was not a constituent element of Italian Fascist ideology. Indeed, Italians were not indoctrinated to hate Jews, and the country's entry into the war in 1940 did not correspond in an upsurge to persecute them.[336] They were not sent en-masse to be killed in concentration camps, as the guiding thought of the Italian anti-Semitic policies was to retrain them, to 'Italianise' and 'Fascisticise' them, before reintegrating them into the

---

[335] Dennison Rusinow, op. cit., p. 336.
[336] Laurence Rees, *The Holocaust. A New History*, (London: Penguin, 2017), pp. 279-81.

A Journey into Darkness

127

fascist system.[337] A further example of Italy's relatively benign policy is shown by the Italian Army granting protection to those Jews who fled Ustaše Croatia to the Italian zone.[338] In mainland Italy, Mussolini did little to halt the Italian efforts to frustrate German plans of the 'Final Solution.'[339]

Therefore, the German occupation of Italy in 1943 held devastating consequences for those Jews living in Italy and the former occupied territories, since the active presence of German units in Italy, and in the Adriatic Littoral, meant that new leaders had the opportunity to identify, capture, deport, and murder Jews on a larger scale. Furthermore, Globocnik, the former Gauleiter of Vienna and Lublin SS and Police Chief, was an ardent anti-Semite, who had been in charge of Operation Reinhard when he built and oversaw many concentration camps, including Bełzec, Sobibor and Treblinka. Consequently, a plan for the hunt and extermination of Jews was implemented in the Adriatic Littoral by Globocnik's team, which included Christian Wirth, Franz Stangl, Kurt Franz and Josef Oberhauser.[340] They conducted a reign of terror in the region. On the outskirts of Trieste, they took over the *risiera*, a five-storey rice-husking factory, in San Sabba. It was called Stammlager (or Stalag) 339 and was transformed into a police detention and transit camp for Jews, who were to be deported to Auschwitz-Birkenau in occupied Poland, and for political prisoners and partisans, who were sent to Dachau, Buchenwald and Mauthausen. Later, expert master mason Erwin Lambert, who had already designed a number of ovens for concentration camps in Poland, converted the San Sabba *risiera* into a crematorium for the execution of political prisoners. It was tested on 4 April 1944, with the cremation of 72

---

[337] Renzo De Felice, *Storia degli ebrei italiani sotto il fascismo*, (Torino: Einaudi, 1972), p. 252.

[338] Susan Zuccotti, *The Italians and the Holocaust. Persecution, Rescue and Survival*, (Lincoln: University of Nebraska Press, 1996), p. 77.

[339] R. J. B. Bosworth, *Mussolini*, pp. 392-3.

[340] David Cesarani, *Final Solution. The Fate of the Jews 1933-49*, (London: Macmillan, 2016), p. 669.

128   *Luisa Morettin*

bodies, shot the day before at the Opicina shooting range in retaliation for the killing of seven German soldiers following a partisan attack.[341]

At the large complex, which made up the *risiera,* the Germans and their Fascist collaborators would beat, torture, and kill their prisoners in a number of ways including, shootings, lethal blows to the head, and gassings. The gassing of prisoners was carried out in the *risiera*'s garage where specially converted black vans had exhausts connected to the inside.[342] It is estimated that 69 convoys bound for various death camps departed from Trieste and to these should be added another 30 convoys, which were bound for labour camps.[343] According to Austrian historian Johannes Sachslehner, 5,000 prisoners lost their lives in the *risiera*, whilst more than 20,000 passed through it on their way to the camps scattered throughout the Reich.[344] The *risiera di San Sabba* would remain operative until the end of April 1945 and became the symbol of the Jewish tragedy on Italian soil.

In the Adriatic Littoral, the German manhunt targeted not only Jews, but also partisans and anti-fascists. Repression and reprisals against insurgents became frequent, as seen in Trieste, when following a partisan attack against the recreation centre, the 'House of the German Soldier,' that caused six deaths on 23 April 1944, the Germans then executed 51 prisoners held in the Coroneo jail, and hanged their bodies from the balustrades of the building's staircase, which was a warning for all those passing by who viewed the gruesome spectacle.[345] During the same month, and because of seven German soldiers who were killed by a bomb in a cinema in Opicina, 72 two locals were killed in reprisal.

The violence did not spare the countryside and during the course of 1944 many villages were razed to the ground in retaliation for partisans

---

[341] International Committee of the Nazi Lager of Risiera di San Sabba, *Risiera di San Sabba. History and Museum,* (Trieste: s.n., 2009), p. 2.

[342] For further details, see Francesco Fait (a cura di), *Scritte, lettere e voci. Tracce di vittime e superstiti della Risiera di San Sabba,* (Trieste: IRSML, 2014).

[343] International Committee of the Nazi Lager of Risiera di San Sabba, op. cit., p. 5.

[344] Johannes Sachslehner, *Zwei Millionen ham'ma erledigt: Odilo Globocnik - Hitlers Manager des Todes,* (Wien: Styria Verlag, 2014), p. 335.

[345] Dennison Rusinow, op. cit., pp. 332-3.

A Journey into Darkness 129

operations against German soldiers, vehicles and communication lines. On 30 April 1944, in the Slovenian village of Lipa, 257 inhabitants were murdered and their houses set on fire in retaliation. In the municipality of Trieste, alone 1,138 insurgents were killed as a result of the armed struggle between February and April 1945.[346] However, Germany's fortunes on the battlefield worsened, signifying that the Third Reich's days of cruelty were numbered.

THE SECOND WAVE OF VIOLENCE. THE FATE OF ZARA. 1944

In Venezia Giulia, the partisan movement did not end when the Germans began their occupation in October 1943, as despite heavy losses it still sought to re-organise its efforts in order to survive and due to its renewed tactics and determination, it gained momentum. Further, at the Tehran Conference, (28 Nov – 1 Dec 1943), Tito was recognised as the sole commander of all military units in Yugoslavia, whilst other resistance groups were to come under his command. This meant the Yugoslav partisans were given full Allied support at the expense of Draža Mihailović and the Chetniks, whose fate was now sealed. The British acted as an intermediary between the two factions and pushed for the Royal Yugoslav government-in-exile to succumb to the diplomatic demands, and agree to a coalition government with Tito. For the partisan leader, this was a short step from becoming the ruler of Yugoslavia, where his armed forces were ready to take control of Venezia Giulia.

Between 2 November 1943 and 2 November 1944, along the coastal area of Dalmatia the Italian enclave of Zara was the target of fifty-four Allied air raids, which included heavy and lighter bombings as well as machine-gun attacks on land, in the port and close to the suburbs of Barcagno, Ceraria (Voštarnica), Val de' Ghisi (Jazine) and Borgo Erizzo

---

[346] Marina Cattaruzza, op. cit., p. 191.

130 Luisa Morettin

(Arbanasi). The attacks ravaged the town where eighty per cent of the buildings was destroyed, and saw a high toll of civilian casualties. The reason behind such a high number of raids on Zara is still disputed. Local historians Oddone Talpo and Sergio Brcic describe how the Italian community suspected Titio's partisans called upon the Anglo-Americans for air support in their operations, since they were recognised as an Allied force. In the specific case of Zara, it is believed the partisans deliberately spread false news amongst the Allies, stating that many German units were holed up in the coastal town.[347] In this way, they were able to erase from the map a city inhabited by a large majority of Italians, which made its later annexation to Yugoslavia an easy task for Tito.[348] However, Yugoslav military historian Jozo Tomasevich claimed that when Allied planes operating against central Europe failed to dump their bombs on the designated targets, they instead dropped them on Zara 'since they were not supposed to return from their missions still loaded with materiel.'[349] However, it is difficult to understand why Allied planes would cause the death of civilians and the destruction of a whole city simply to return offloaded to their airbase.

According to the Committee of Assistance to the Italians in Dalmatia, the night after the bombardment of 16 December 1943 Zara became inhabitable and unsanitary. As a result, many inhabitants were forced to seek refuge in the neighbouring areas where they were killed by Tito's partisans.[350] With their houses destroyed and the fear of the communist advance, more and more civilians evacuated the city, heading north toward Venice and Trieste – the only cities with efficient transport, with a twice weekly service aboard the ship *Sansego*. It was impossible to reach Bari and southern Italy, not only due to lack of transport, but because German planes machine-gunned any boats, which were sailing from Zara in any direction other than Trieste. Those unable to flee flocked into neighbouring

---

[347] Oddone Talpo and Sergio Brcic, *Vennero dal cielo. Zara distrutta 1943-1944*, (Campobasso: Palladino editore, 2006), pp. 41-2.
[348] Ibid., pp. 25-46.
[349] Jozo Tomasevich, op. cit., p. 749.
[350] FO 371/48951/R17043/15199/92, 21 July 1945.

A Journey into Darkness

131

villages located on the mainland, and on the nearby islands. There, the displaced citizens lived in huts built with materials retrieved amongst the city rubble.[351]

The Italian Committee of Zara claimed that during the period of German occupation, the cooperation between partisans, the citizens of Zara, the representatives of the city authorities and police forces, became positively intense. Food, money, ammunitions, weapons, and clothes were given, in considerable amounts, to partisans. Released partisan and Italian prisoners were provided with money, false identity cards and work cards. Such joint Italo-Slav actions were not risk free, as arrests and executions by German forces were frequent. The collaboration was initiated in order to hasten the end of the German occupation so Zara would be handed back to Italy. But it became apparent much later that the partisans had different plans, despite their reassurance to the Italian community that, 'Once Zara would be freed from the Germans, any party of whichever nationality would be allowed to hoist their own flag, while the protection of public order would be left to the *Carabinieri* and the civil administration to Italians.'[352] Apparently Tito's partisans used their cooperation with Italians to quite different ends.

Toward the end of summer 1944, victory over the Axis powers in Europe was certain. When the Allied offensive reached the Gothic Line on mainland Italy in August–September 1944, German troops withdrew from the Balkans where crippling defeats and the ferocious Soviet advance meant crucial Axis allies, such as Romania, deserted. Despite Germany's will to hold onto every inch of territory, their presence in Zara was untenable and they had to leave, which they did on the night of 30 October 1944.

The following day partisans occupied Zara without encountering any resistance. The heavy Allied bombings had destroyed most of the city's buildings, which were looted by Tito's partisans, who now invested in a campaign of terror. Partisan commanders took possession of the town, in

---

[351] Ibid.

[352] FO 371/48951/R17043/15199/92, *Also at Zara Justice is Expected.*

132 *Luisa Morettin*

contradiction to previous promises made to the Italians, and proceeded to arrest those citizens who 'were considered guilty of nothing else but of being Italians.'[353]

The day after the German withdrawal, the Italian police were ordered by the partisans to go to nearby Boccagnazzo, where they were disarmed, declared prisoners, beaten and used as work force in the airfield at Zemonico. However, a few days later when an Allied Commission arrived at the airport, all prisoners were hidden from sight.

As the number of people eliminated increased, the definition of what it meant to be on the partisans' black list evolved. This now included not just Italians involved or suspected of involvement with the Fascist regime, but also representatives of the Italian State became fair game. For instance, the *Carabinieri* Lieutenant Terranova and Professor Fiengo from the local prefecture were targeted. During this time, approximately 400 citizens of Zara disappeared, leaving no trace at all; amongst them was the famous liqueur manufacturer, Pietro Luxardo, whilst his brother Nicolò and sister-in-law Bianca were executed by the partisans.[354] The Tolja brothers[355] were also arrested and shot, despite being American citizens and holding anti-fascist credentials, which was clear from when fascists had arrested them in the past for the support they gave to Slav partisans. It is likely that their activities as bankers, insurers and shipping agents negatively shaped their destiny under the new partisan rule.

Similar fates awaited members of the Catholic Church. Infamous examples include the parish priests of Cerno and Lagosta, who disappeared never to return, and the Pastor of Borgo Rizzo, who was sentenced to forced labour. Further, the Archbishop of Zara was forced by the OZNA (the security agency of Communist Yugoslavia) to confinement in Spalato; from there he was moved to the island of Lissa and then confined at

---

[353] Ibid.

[354] Nicolò Luxardo De Franchi, *Dietro gli scogli di Zara*, (Gorizia: Libreria Editrice Goriziana, 2017).

[355] FO 371/48951/R 17043/15199/92, *Also at Zara Justice is Expected.*

A Journey into Darkness

Lagosta where he was starved. It was only in February 1945 that he was finally allowed to return to Zara.[356]

The campaign of elimination showed no signs of abating in the following months. On the nights between the 7 and 8 November 1944, around 20 policemen and 25 civilians were carried on a lugger to the nearby Isle of Ugliano (Ugljan), led along a path, which ended at a precipice overlooking the sea, and killed.[357]

Wanton violence was another aspect of the terror occurring in Zara from which not even the poor could escape. A widow, and mother of nine children, begged for food from British soldiers. Upon receiving it, the partisans threw the woman and the food into the sea. Yet two Allied soldiers rescued her. Similar treatment was reserved to whomever asked the Anglo-Americans for help, which included children who tried to offer them some assistance with small jobs in exchange of food.[358] In the meantime, the Italian offices which still existed were suppressed, their documents burned, and their money and valuables seized.

Exorbitant sums of money were embezzled by the new occupiers: approximately five million Lire from the *Banca d'Italia* (Bank of Italy), two and a half million Lire from the local *Prefettura*, and one and a half million from the Municipality. Likewise, private companies suffered losses, which saw building materials stolen from their storage yards in Zara. The shipyards, companies and the few houses still standing were seized and the owners forced out. They were allowed to take with them only a small suitcase.[359]

Later, a report detailed how street and place signs had been removed, the armorial bearings on the front of the houses and of half-destroyed palaces were chiselled out, the Saint Mark's Lions, which decorated the monuments and gates of the town in memory of the dominion for centuries

---

[356] Oddone Talpo, op. cit., p. 1437.

[357] FO 371/48951/R17043/15199/92, *Also at Zara Justice is Expected.*

[358] Oddone Talpo, op. cit., p. 1438.

[359] FO 371/48951/R17043/15199/92, *Also at Zara Justice is Expected.* Oddone Talpo, op. cit., p. 1440.

of the Venetian Republic, were pulled down.[360] Also the registers of the municipality of Zara were destroyed. It is plausible to assume that, as pointed out by Italian witnesses, the aim of such destruction was 'to prevent, after the dispersion and partly transportation of its inhabitants, that it [...] would have been possible to evidence irrefutably with documents on the ethnical composition of its inhabitants the Italian character of Zara.'[361]

It is estimated that 2,500-3,000 Italians from Zara migrated to Ancona, Bari and Brindisi and approximately 3,000-4,000 towards northern Italy, with almost 6,000-8,000 people remaining.[362] Some people did not have the means to leave Zara and were thus considered by the new authorities as Slavs, leaving them no hope to be able to migrate to Italy. For those who left Zara behind, and for those who were forced to remain, hope for their future quickly vanished.

THE BEGINNING OF THE END

By the beginning of February 1945 the German Reich had lost Poland and the most important eastern areas of East Prussia, East Brandenburg and Silesia. The advancing Red Army, under the lead of Generals Ivan Chernyakhovsky and Konstantin Rokossovsky, forced German troops into pockets and, whilst liberating Europe from Fascism, they also committed crimes on a mass scale including the systematic gang rape of women of all ages, plundering, stealing, and unnecessary arson.[363] In April, throughout Northern Italy the withdrawal of German troops, the installation of Committees of National Liberation (CLN) and the setting up of the Allied Military Government (AMG) followed partisan insurrections.

---

[360] FO 371/48951/R 17043/15199/92, *Also at Zara Justice is Expected,* 21 July 1945. The Assistance Committee for Refugees from Zara to the Allied Military Government Regional Commissioner in Venezia Giulia.

[361] Ibid.

[362] Oddone Talpo, op. cit., p. 1444.

[363] Antony Beevor, *Berlin. The Downfall 1945*, (London: Penguin, 2002), p. 30.

A Journey into Darkness 135

When it was clear the war was drawing to a close, the final race for Venezia Giulia began. Not only was the region experiencing the same chaos and lawlessness sweeping the rest of Europe, but Trieste and the surrounding areas also presented one of the most complicated political pictures as it was the last Mediterranean battleground in the Second World War, where events were unfolding rapidly. At dawn of 30 April troops from CLN and CEAIS, (a Slovene proposed formation of a mixed Italo-Slovene Anti-Fascist Executive Committee, created on 13 April 1945) began to revolt. German troops withdrew to some defensible positions, such as in the Castle of San Giusto, the Palace of Justice, the free port and the railway station. In the afternoon of 1 May 1945, the Yugoslav IV Army entered and occupied a large part of Trieste, ahead of the New Zealanders, under General Bernard Freyberg, that arrived on 2 May.

The aim was to put the Allies in front of the *fait accompli* of a Yugoslav occupation of the Italian areas, which Tito had claimed. To achieve the objective of being the first to liberate the town and establishing their own military administration, partisans had left behind pockets of German troops within Yugoslav territory. With the view to avoid a clash with the Yugoslavs, the CLN commanders ordered their units not to fight Tito's troops that had seized the City Hall and the Prefecture setting up a Yugoslav rule that would last forty days.

Shortly after the arrival of Communist partisan forces in Trieste, posters began appearing in city streets proclaiming an autonomous Trieste inside a Federal and Democratic Yugoslavia. Tito's plan to create a new Communist Yugoslavia was in contrast to the 'Percentages Agreement,' decided by Churchill and Stalin at the Moscow Conference in October 1944, whereby Yugoslavia would be equally divided into a Western and Soviet sphere of influence.

The 'race for Trieste,' as it became known, and the ensuing struggle led to escalating and unbridled violence in pursuit of Tito's expansionist and revolutionary goals. The harsh measures introduced - the Belgrade authorities and the Yugoslav press explained - such as special permits needed to travel from one Venezia Giulia village to another and curfews during the night introduced so that the enemies could not escape, were justified by the fact that the war against the enemy was not over yet. This was especially true in Venezia Giulia, which was considered by Communist partisans as the last gathering place for many Fascists. Historians have agreed that the Trieste crisis was the first post-war confrontation between East and West.

THE THIRD WAVE OF VIOLENCE. 1945

It was on 14 June 1945 that the Allied forces located in Italy received the following report from the Italian Committee of National Liberation in Trieste:

> During the Yugoslav occupation of this city [Trieste], mass arrests were carried out by military and paramilitary forces and by the Guards of People's Defence. At any time, but especially at night long queues of arrested people walked on the streets of the city. Among them there were Fascists and collaborators of the Germans, but the vast majority was guilty of simply being Italian. However while many among the first two categories were released, many innocents were taken somewhere else; their families were never informed as to the whereabouts or the fate of their beloved.
>
> We have collected very precise and gruesome evidence about atrocities carried out in Basovizza on 2, 3, 4 and 5 May, so that we cannot nurture any positive hope as to the destiny that awaited our fellow citizens and country people.
>
> In the name of civility we plead that light is shed on these many crimes. The details that we are referring to relate only to the atrocities committed in Basovizza which are similar to those reported in Istria in September 1943 and probably they are not isolated episodes of cruelty.
>
> On 2, 3, 4 and 5 May several hundreds of inhabitants were taken to Basovizza to the disused mine-shaft and thrown into the pit which is 240 meters deep. Later approximately 120 bodies of German soldiers, killed during the fight of the following days, were thrown on top of the Italians. The decomposed carcasses of horses were thrown in last of all.

A Journey into Darkness

137

In order to identify the bodies of the victims and to bury them, we asked for the advice of experts that had previously helped us to retrieve bodies from the pits in Istria. However the equipment of our experts is not good enough due to the exceptional depth of the Basovizza mine-shaft, the number of victims and their advanced state of decay. We are therefore asking the Allied Command to provide us with the help and equipment that our experts need to carry out their merciful task. We also ask that the Allied forces to guard the mine-shaft in order to stop prowlers from preventing the identification of victims.[364]

The incident caused an immediate reaction amongst Anglo-American officials. An investigation was ordered two days after receipt of the letter, when the Allied Command Headquarters urgently wrote to the 13 Corps of the British Army, asking for a detailed report to include as much information as possible.[365] The Italian complaint was taken so seriously that two weeks later the Deputy Chief of Staff, Major General Lyman Lemnitzer, sent a memorandum to the assistant Chief of Staff instructing press correspondents to be given every facility to find out the truth as, 'Such action [may be] useful in the future to have the stick of publicity to beat the Yugoslavs with.'[366]

However, Philip Broad, from the Resident Minister's Office in Caserta, informed the Foreign Office the investigations had been unproductive. The mineshaft was 800 feet deep, and although lights had been lowered to the bottom, it was impossible to see through the fog. Efforts by engineers to raise bodies with grapnels only yielded fragmentary human bones and weapons, and technical difficulties hampered efforts to enable them to bring anything else to the surface. The work involved was defined as 'hazardous and unhealthy' and positive identification of the bodies was 'almost impossible.'[367] As a result, the HQ 13 Corps recommended that the exploration of the shaft be halted and the pit

---

[364] Document dated 14 June 1945 contained in WO 204/12753, Summary, 4 August 1945.
[365] WO 204/12753, 16 June 1945.
[366] Ibid., 16 July 1945.
[367] Ibid., 1 July 1945.

138   *Luisa Morettin*

hygienically sealed.[368] After all, Broad argued, no evidence from eyewitnesses had been forthcoming and unless such evidence was obtainable, it seemed fruitless to continue an enquiry into what really happened.[369] However, the State Department was inclined to take a serious view of the Basovizza incident and felt that unless full investigation was carried out, the Anglo-Americans would later be accused by the Italians of suppressing evidence regarding Yugoslav terrorist activities. Washington therefore suggested setting up a SACMED (Supreme Allied Commander for the Mediterranean) commission of inquiry, to which all members of the Advisory Council would be invited to send observers.[370] The same view was shared by Henry Hopkinson, a diplomat based in Rome, who wrote to the Foreign Office: 'My own feeling is that whatever the difficulties, every conceivable effort should be made to solve the mystery of this crime. Otherwise it seems to me that we should incur a terrible responsibility before history.'[371] With the full support of Churchill, who sent his approval from Germany[372] where he had arrived five days earlier in order to take part at the Potsdam conference, it was decided to continue the enquiry and to postpone sealing any *foiba* in the region. In the meantime, the US Army at the headquarters of the Mediterranean Theatre of Operations had received reports that pits, which held similar scenes to that at Basovizza, also existed at Corgnale (Lokev), San Servolo (Socerb), Racia and Matteria (Materija). In the latter two, there were reputed to be the bodies of members of Allied Missions to the partisans and of Allied aircrews shot down by the Germans.[373]

The 13 Corps' advice to close the pit was based on technical difficulties of bringing bodies to the surface and investigative difficulties, as witnesses to the events were not forthcoming. The Engineer Corps, in order to retrieve the bodies, needed to erect a form of derrick with a power-

---

[368] Ibid.
[369] FO 934/5, 14 July 1945.
[370] Ibid., 17 July 1945.
[371] Ibid., 18 July 1945.
[372] Ibid., 20 July 1945.
[373] WO 204/12753, paper 15 D, 29 July 1945.

operated cable and specially designed grab, which it was estimated might have brought up 10-30 bodies a day. The work, however, was deemed as hazardous and excessively unhealthy due to the stench of decomposing bodies.[374] As to the difficulty of obtaining witness reports, this was due to several factors: lack of official documents and police archives, feared reprisals for those in charge of the investigation, and a widespread feeling amongst the Italian community, where people refrained from reporting the disappearance of their family members out of fear of communist retaliation.

In spite of the issues, the Anglo-American forces managed to obtain some evidence regarding the Basovizza murders. Testimonies, gathered in a document dated 13 July 1945, report conflicting data to the number of victims, but all agree on the procedures carried out for the killings. According to witness reports, between 2 and 6 May 1945, 800 people were killed at the Basovizza mine-shaft. A doctor of the Urological Department of Trieste Hospital stated he heard a Yugoslav Commissar declare that by 5 May, 550 people had been killed at the mine.

Accounts detailed that the Yugoslavs carried out their executions by forcing their victims to try to leap over the mouth of the shaft, and when failing they would fall to their deaths. These are partly corroborated by the evidence of half a dozen Slovene-speaking children, who, near the pit, told two Allied officers that on 1 May more than 100 people were made to jump in this manner. The spontaneous comments of the children, such as, 'You should have heard how the Fascists screamed!' added an air of truth to their story. An Italian informant gave the names of five people who were killed in the way the children had described, amongst them was Andreina Pettarossi, the postmistress in the village of San Antonio in Bosco, her husband and their child aged just two.[375]

The British Embassy in Belgrade stated that they were unaware of the crimes committed and asked for further details, especially dates, before

---

[374] Ibid., 1 July 1945.
[375] Ibid., 13 July 1945.

140   *Luisa Morettin*

formally investigating on that matter with the Yugoslav General Staff.[376] Therefore, between 15 August and 20 September 1945 the Anglo-American forces began their investigation, which not only proved the validity of various official and unofficial reports pertaining to large scale atrocities, but also produced evidence of other war crimes (wholesale arrests, deportations, other abuses and excesses), committed between 2 May and 12 June 1945 by the IV Yugoslav Army and Yugoslav partisans in Venezia Giulia.[377] The Allied command decided to extend their investigation and collected further proof to the occurrence of a steady stream of violence against Italians and anti-Communist Slavs between 1 October and 8 November 1945.[378] Hundreds of cases were gathered from the reports of various military agencies, including the Military Government, Italian Committee of Liberation, Italian Red Cross, individual civilian sources, personal interrogations, and from censorship intercepts. The content of this dossier was meant to remain closed until 2021, but because of the end of the Cold War and the change in international affairs, they were released much earlier.

A CHILLING ACCOUNT

The following evidence is reported in full below as it deserves close examination. Indeed, such detailed testimonies by two priests, don Malalan and don Sceck, are the only Yugoslav sources admitting to crimes against Italians, which the Anglo-Americans were able to collect as there was continual denial by Yugoslav officials.

On 7 August 1945, an Allied informant codenamed 'The Source' visited don Malalan, the priest of San Antonio in Bosco, a little village in the province of Trieste not far from Basovizza. It was here where the clergyman had witnessed many of the Basovizza executions. Don Malalan

---

[376] Ibid., 28 July 1945.
[377] WO 204/430, undated.
[378] WO 204/431.

A Journey into Darkness

141

'proved to be a fanatic pro-Slav and bitterly anti-Italian,' the Allied source reports, who at first denied all knowledge of the killings. However, 'The Source' made him aware that the Fascist reactionaries were conducting an exaggerated campaign against the Yugoslavs stating that they had been responsible for the *foibe* executions. Therefore, it was in the authorities' interest that evidence be collected in a systematic manner. The priest then declared himself prepared to speak and made the following statement.

1. The persons who were thrown into the pit at the beginning of May were executed at the express orders of the Military Tribunal of IV Army which acted on orders given by Gen. Peter Drapsin, whose HQ was at that time at Lipizza near Basovizza.

2. Don Malalan declared that all the persons who were thrown into the pit had been regularly tried, and that they had at least three witnesses against them.

3. All those Questura agents whom the Yugoslavs had been able to capture in Trieste were thrown into the pit.

4. Don Malalan expressed the opinion that they richly deserved the end they met. He also stated it was incorrect that all the victims had been cast into the pit alive, as the greater part of them had been shot in the proper manner before being thrown in.

5. On May 2, don Malalan went to Basovizza, where his brother was a 'commissar' and he was requested to be present at the execution of all those criminals whom it had been possible to collect from Trieste. He however refused.

6. Some days later he went to Corgnale and learned from the village priest, don Virgilio Sceck, what had been going on there. Don Sceck admitted to Malalan having been present at the throwing into the pit. He had even given religious succour to some of the condemned persons. This spiritual assistance which don Sceck meted out was of a peculiar character, as don Malalan relates, as when addressing an agent of the *Pubblica Sicurezza* from Trieste he told him: 'You have erred until now, you have amused yourself by torturing the Slavs, and now nothing remains but for you to commend your soul to God. The punishment now to be given to you has been fully deserved.'

7. Don Malalan assured Source that the authorities of IV Army have the complete list of all the persons 'legally condemned' and that

Luisa Morettin

when the moment arrives they will publish this list in order to prove that everything was carried out in a regular manner.

8. He stated further that as far as Signora Pettarossi, who lived in his parish, is concerned, it is possible that she may have been thrown into the pit, but that he personally maintains that she had been killed prior to May 2, as her body has never been found. He could throw no light on the disappearance of her husband and young daughter.

9. In any case, he concluded hastily, it is very difficult to be sure whether she was killed before or after May 2, because at that time there was a great deal of confusion.

10. Signora Pettarossi was suspected by the partisans of being a spy for the Germans. The only fact which could support this was that, due to her profession of postmistress, she was obliged to make frequent visits to Trieste.

11. Don Malalan insisted that the executions were carried out by regular troops of IV Army and not by local partisans in a spirit of vendetta.[379]

Three days later, on 10 August 1945, the same Allied source visited Corgnale. The priest of the village in the province of Trieste, later allocated to Yugoslavia, named don Sceck was labelled by the informer as 'A rabid anti-Italian,' who made the following statement about the executions at the pit of Basovizza.

1. That all the executions carried out by the officers of IV Army were perfectly in order.

2. On May 2 he went to Basovizza, as the priest of that village was not there, to officiate to the burial of some partisans.

3. While there he saw in a neighbouring field about 150 civilians who were recognisable by their faces as members of the Questura. The populace wanted to carry out summary justice upon them, but the officers of IV Army were against this.

4. These persons were questioned and tried in the presence of all the populace, who accused them. As soon as one of them was

---

[379] WO 204/12753, Appendix B, 18 August 1945.

A Journey into Darkness

questioned, four or five women rushed up to them and accused them of having murdered or tortured one of their relatives, or of having burned down their houses. The accused persons were buffeted and struck, and always admitted the crimes described to them. Nearly all of them were condemned to death. Those who were not condemned to death were left together with the others.

5. All the 150 men were shot by a group of partisans en masse. The partisans were armed with submachine guns, and afterwards, as there were no coffins, they were thrown into the Basovizza pit.

6. When asked by Source if he had been present at the shooting or had heard the shots, don Sceck answered that he had not been present nor had he heard the shots.

7. On May 3 don Sceck again went to Basovizza and saw in the same place about 250-300 persons. The greatest number of them was civilians. There were only about 40 German soldiers.

8. These persons also were killed by machine guns after a summary trial. They were most of them civilians arrested in Trieste during the first days of occupation.

9. Don Sceck states that they were nearly all members of the Questura.

10. He refutes the suggestion that he administered the Sacrament to any of them, as was stated by don Malalan of San Antonio in Bosco, as it 'was not worthwhile'.

11. Don Sceck states that the corpses of German soldiers and the dead bodies of horses were also thrown into the pit.[380]

The testimonies by don Malalan and don Sceck raise the little-explored issue of the role of religion in defining the local war culture. Although little is known about the attitude of pro-Yugoslav clerics toward Italians in Venezia Giulia during the Second World War, and particularly between 1943 and 1945, it was customary for clergymen to interact with their parishioners, either by advocating conciliatory approaches or with the spiritual language of anger that leads to violence and consciences are roused to action. Violence is made up not only of deeds, but also of words

---

[380] Ibid., Appendix C, 18 August 1945.

144   *Luisa Morettin*

and words do have consequences, even if at times it is not possible to show a causal link and for that reason they are often overlooked.

It is undeniable that the Catholic Church was an ongoing, unofficial channel of political communication, an intermediary between state and people, and a powerful factor in the cultural mobilisation of opinion.[381] As Dennison Rusinow noted, the influence of the Slav priesthood on local nationalism was a major factor in creating and moulding Slav nationalism and South Slav consciousness among Slovenes and Croats.[382] This had occurred since the time of Josip Strossmayer, the influential Croatian bishop and politician, who in the 1850s supported the union of all South Slavs.

Whilst the two pro-Slav priests were not materially responsible for the murders, their comments, which endorsed the killing of defenceless civilians, may have encouraged and contributed to the fomentation or intensification of the purges. Extremist Slav nationalists took control of the situation and their policy became one which was to eradicate Italians in the region. The two priests' views may also have mirrored Slav mainstream opinion, as gathered from evidence of an elderly Slav woman who, when discussing the executions, stated that in her opinion, 'It was a great pity to waste good clothes, and the Fascists should have been undressed before being thrown down.'[383]

There also exist examples in works of fiction and non-fiction that document how some Yugoslavs, who were typically dispossessed, suddenly revealed their hostility toward Italians, not necessarily because they had been mistreated, but because their Slav identity was in part shaped by envy for, and insecurity toward, prosperous landowners and more educated city dwellers, who in most cases were Italians. The arrival of Communism provided an excuse for them to put the record straight.[384]

---

[381] See Elio Apih, op. cit., p. 9, as well as Denis Mack Smith, *Modern Italy*, p. 131.

[382] Dennison Rusinow, op. cit., pp. 26-8.

[383] WO 204/431, Appendix A.

[384] *La miglior vita* (1977) by the distinguished Istrian writer Fulvio Tomizza; *La foiba grande* (1992) and *La malga di Sîr* (1996) by Carlo Sgorlon; *Bora* (2005) by Anna Maria Mori and Nelida Milani; *Chi ha paura dell'uomo nero?* (2004) by Graziella Fiorentin, represent well

A Journey into Darkness

What is important to highlight here is that the trial, which one of the priests refers to, is exceptional for what happened in Venezia Giulia, as nearly all witnesses speak of continual extrajudicial killings. In fact, with or without trial, it still made little difference to the outcome. These legal proceedings were essentially an artful *mise-en-scène*, a masquerade of legitimacy, reminiscent of the infamous 'Moscow show trials,' where humiliation, torture and self-accusation of an alleged and false crime preceded the inevitable death sentence. Witness reports reveal that during trials in Venezia Giulia, accusers were often mobilized from nearby villages and forced to bear witness, enabling 'authorities' to convince Slavs that their Italian neighbours were reckless pillagers or dangerous agents. If at times there was the possibility that some victims were indeed guilty of fascist crimes, the case of Mrs Pettarossi is one of many disturbing examples which illustrate how innocent civilians were executed with their families, including children and the elderly, for no particular reason at all. In short, above anything else there was not the power of law, but the law of power by partisans who played the role of judge, prosecutor and executioner at the same time. They found pleasure not just in killing their enemy, but took satisfaction at killing him in the cruellest way. By casting him dead, or alive, into a pit was invalidating his earthly existence, throwing him back into the bowels of the earth. Here, no one would know what happened to him, where he had been taken from or how he had vanished. The symbolism of such a form of violence had a spellbinding effect amongst survivors, who lived in continual terror and eventually, fearing for their lives, fled the region.

NOT ONLY ITALIANS

Many Italians responded to the Yugoslav violence by developing an almost exclusive sense of grievance, holding a distinct sense of the uniqueness of

---

the microcosm of border life with its complexities and the terror unleashed against class and political enemies.

146   *Luisa Morettin*

their predicament. But in fact, the wartime Anglo-American enquiries produced evidence to the contrary. Tito's ruthless operations to eliminate the former enemy were not confined to Italians, as other national and ethnic groups shared the same treatment and fate.

> In [the] Basovizza area a pit called the *Pozzo della miniera* was used by the Yugoslav partisans, particularly between the 3 and 7 of May 1945 for the disposal of Italians. ...
>
> The victims were ordered to jump across the pit (about twelve feet wide) and were told that their lives would be spared if they succeeded. Witnesses report that although some people did manage to jump over, they were later shot and thrown in.
>
> A Yugoslav Commissar is reported to have stated that more than five hundred living people had been thrown into the pit.
>
> Afterwards the bodies of about one hundred and fifty Germans who had been killed in the local fighting were thrown in, and also about fifteen dead horses. Explosives were then dropped into the pit.[385]

Violence usually commanded publicity in order to leave behind a sense of terror. If, on some occasions, the violent spectacle had no audience, all it required was the word to spread - for some peasants knew or some passers-by had heard something, which would then leave villagers intimidated. Others were also forced to cooperate in macabre rituals, which would then spread the terror further.[386] Regarding the latter, it was reported by an eyewitness, who found himself forced to transport wounded Germans in his lorry to the Opicina *foiba*, near Trieste. He later disclosed to the Allied authorities how this pit was used for the disposal of wounded German soldiers:

> The transportation was made many times. I could personally observe that these wounded Germans were certain to be brought to a field hospital. They did their best to be quick in coming down of the car, just to

---

[385] WO 204/431, Appendix A.
[386] Anna Maria Mori and Nelida Milani, op. cit., p. 118.

A Journey into Darkness

accelerate transfer operations in their new place. I saw on their faces many smiles, I saw their sighs of satisfaction believing to find assistance and comfort, confiding in international law. Suddenly their faces got terrified when the first of them were machine-gunned on the edge of the pit. The terrible massacre culminated partly with the falling in the pit due to shots and partly due to pushing and kicking by the murderers. I couldn't state if they were all Germans.[387]

Although many of these deeds were hidden from sight, locals later reported that on the edge of the *foiba* at Opicina, belts, blood spots and empty cartridge boxes were seen. In addition, after the killings an unusual, terrible smell was coming out of the mouth of the pit.[388]

An account of such murders can be found in the memoir written by journalist Anna Maria Mori and academic Nelida Milani, both from the city of Pola:

After the 8 of September [1943] Tito's comrades became the absolute rulers of Istria for a long period during which a few thousand people vanished. The places of their disappearance would be revealed by newspapers only some decades later, after the fall of the Berlin wall. But the locals had always known them, although they had never made word with anyone. Peasants had immediately identified them, one by one, because of the groans coming from the cracks in the rocks. They would tell that they could hear pleas and calls for help coming from the bowels of the earth. They were the sobs of the slow agony of those who were still alive and longed for life, despite the terror for their certain death, terror which ended with a death rattle.[389]

The British War Office dossier contains a document, together with pictures, of decomposed bodies, received from the Trieste Committee of National Liberation. It discloses how a group of Italians from the local fire brigade ventured to the bottom of pit No. 149, the imposing well in

---

[387] WO 204/431, Appendix B.
[388] Ibid.
[389] Anna Maria Mori and Nelida Milani, op. cit., p. 118.

Opicina, with a depth of 400 feet. It begins with a drop of approximately 337 feet and its mouth opens on the west edge of a *dolina*. After the ladders were sent down, two explorers landed at 200 feet onto a heap of stones. Although the characteristic smell of decomposing flesh was apparent, no corpse was found. However, descending in a small lateral cavern, the explorers saw amongst the stones a footless leg separated from the body. A few meters lower the first body appeared, and this was the only body found which was partially unburied. The head was unrecognisable, as the face was crushed; the bust showed visible tracks of hard blows and yet the body still wore a grey-green pullover and a coat. The body was soon found to be that of a German soldier of the Fourth Artillery. His identity disk bore the name of Stefan Langlechner, Fg. 33369.

The explorers continued in their search and soon started to dig a trench with their hands along the southern wall of the pit, and it was here they found other human remains consisting of vertebrae, wrists stripped of flesh and tied together by electric wire, and broken thighbones belonging to three different bodies.[390] Explorers took pictures of the corpses they managed to bring up from the pit and all of the images show how the victims had their hands tied to each other.

Although Italian and German soldiers were the main target of killings, it can also be seen that a homicidal fury further claimed the lives of many Slavs who were taken to concentration camps. According to British sources, approximately 25,000 *Domobranci*, the anti-communist Home Guard Officers, were interned in the Sabirni camp in Maksimira, near Zagreb, by August 1945, whilst in Cerquinizza, 500 Italians, Germans and Cossaks were imprisoned in a ruined building on a hillside. The scale of human suffering and the horror of living conditions can be deduced by a short description of an Allied source that compared the situation to that of German death camps, where inmates slept on the ground with no covering

---

[390] WO 204/431, Appendix B.

A Journey into Darkness　　　　　149

whatsoever, they were completely stripped of all personal possessions, and clothed covering only part of their bodies.[391]

Other witness reports confirm that the violence Tito's partisans referred to as the 'final clean-up' or 'the final countdown,' targeted many Slavs who became victims of vicious communist crimes. On 20 May 1945, local communists killed Anton Stergar, the well-respected former Mayor of the Slovenian town of Kamnik, during one of his daytime walks. The reason for his murder was down to the fact that after being imprisoned by the Germans in 1943, he was later released together with other prisoners, and the Communists believed him to be a fascist collaborator.[392]

Suspicions of collaboration with the German occupier were apparently the cause of death and confiscation of the assets of the aristocrat Herman Rehbrach, the wartime Mayor of Kamnik. The unjust sentence motivated the local population to start a petition to leniency, as during the war Rehbrach had used his German connections to save many partisans from German roundups and financially helped deprived Slav families in the municipality. As a result, Rehbrach had his sentence commuted to nine years of forced labour.[393]

A LUCKY ESCAPE

Given the nature of the *foibe* and the methods of the atrocities carried out, it was considered almost impossible to escape from a 'death by pit' or execution by firing squad, although there were some cases of fortuitous survival.

Vladimir Zinger, a Slovene from Ljubljana who had joined anti-partisan and anti-Communist forces, was one of the few lucky ones. He stated that, after his arrest on 15 January 1945, he was sent to the

---

[391] WO204/12754, 20 August 1945.
[392] Franc Perme, Anton Zitnik, Frank Nucic et al., *Slovenia 1941-1948-1952. Anche noi siamo morti per la patria*, (Grosuplje: Associazione per la sistemazione dei sepolcri tenuti nascosti, 2000), pp. 314-9.
[393] Ibid., pp. 322-3.

concentration camp of Teharje, in Slovenia, where partisan groups removed approximately 600 people from the camp every night. On 5 June 1945, Zinger's turn came and he was taken, tied in pairs, hands behind his back, wrists bound with telephone wire, beaten with rifles, and driven to the wood above Hrastnik by truck. Here, he was then stripped to underclothes and forced to stand facing a mass grave. All of the prisoners were shot in the back of their necks, and two partisans who fired simultaneously killed each pair tied together. Zinger fell and later woke in a grave, which must have contained approximately 2,000 victims, including women. His restraints were either broken by the fall or by a stray bullet, enabling him to get out and flee to Trieste on foot. The Allied Information Service officers who recorded his statement commented that Zinger appeared to be 'a perfectly honest peasant,' who bore 'a mark on the back of his neck and high on a cheek that would correspond to bullet marks and his wrists had marks similar to those that are made by telephone wire.'[394]

Vladimir Zinger's survival represents a very unusual case; however the Allied files report a similar, yet much more detailed story concerning a young man named Giovanni Radeticchio, an Italian soldier stationed at Marzana (Marčana), in the southern part of Istria, who luckily escaped 'death by pit.' He told of how, on 29 April 1945, he presented himself to the partisans, who had promised Italian soldiers to set them free if they handed over their weapons. However, after spending three days at his home near Pola, partisans took him away and incarcerated him, constantly moving him from one prison to another. Radeticchio and other prisoners were robbed of their personal belongings, clothes, and shoes and then were subject to the most commonly used form of torture: beating and being forced to keep tight wire or barbed wire around one's wrists. Radeticchio recalled:

> They brought us to Pozzo Littorio [Podlabin] near Albona. ... Then they tied us together by the wrists with wire and brought us to Fianona

---

[394] WO 204/431, Section IV.

A Journey into Darkness

[Plomin], barefoot and on foot. There we arrived at 10:00 or 11:00 o'clock. They left us to sleep on the ground, always tied together. My companion had his hand swollen by lack of circulation and was crying during the whole time we were on the way. The wire cut into his flesh. I tried to lose the wire but as they saw me do this, they tied the wire yet closer. The next day they put us in a cell, always tied together till the evening, when they gave us a little flour with warm water and then untied us for half an hour. ... They brought us in another room, where they asked for our names and then began to beat us. I was the last and as I entered the room ... [10 x 13 feet], I saw lying on the ground bags stained with blood and all my companions too lying on the ground or upon bags, bleeding and looking as if they were dead. On their backs and faces were marks of blows and hits.

There were five individuals who beat us, the one of them with an iron bar, a girl by means of a belt, another with a stick, and other two of whom one with kicks, and the other one with fists, thus five individuals were on one person. For an hour or more they beat us. I heard a man – he spoke Slovene – saying that they had to take us away from there and were in a hurry because they feared to be seen by the population.[395]

Radeticchio then described the march to the local *foiba*, in the surroundings of Fianona, and the way in which his companions were executed.

About 3 or 4 o'clock in the morning, when they finished beating us, they again tied our hands on the backs with wire and then tied us together by the arms. We were six men. During the march they beat us continuously and when we fell down they made us stand up by beating us with their guns or sticks. We arrived near the pit. One of them [...] asked us if we were glad to be thrown into the pit, which is beautiful and nice and there is water in it too, so we can take a bath. [...] They tied a stone with a wire. [...] Then they made us reach the pit, one after the other, and we had to jump in. I was the second; when I came near the pit, I was waiting a moment and soon one of them who was on a rock [50 feet] from the pit,

---

[395] WO 204/430.

152 *Luisa Morettin*

began to shoot with his machine gun, without aim, and he shot the wire
with which the stone was tied on my hands and I jumped in falling into
the water. My hands were still tied and I began to swim with my feet until
I reached the rock and there I remained hidden till I saw the other four
companions fall down.[396]

Not yet satisfied, partisans fired their pistols into the pit and threw
explosives, making sure no survivors were left behind.

I heard them say: 'Another time we shall pull them into the pit on this
spot' showing another point which they considered more suitable. I could
also understand that they would return at night time.

When they were gone, I tried to loosen the wire with which were tied
my hands and after one hour I succeeded. The wire was so tight that I lost
pieces of flesh. Then climbing little by little I came out of the pit and
decided to hide myself until it got dark.[397]

After saving himself, Radeticchio made his way home, ending his
nightmare.

I arrived at Pozzo Littorio (there was no other way to go home) and after
a march of five days and five nights, without food, I reached my home in
the night [...], hiding myself in the cellar. My father, as he entered the
cellar, did not recognise me and when he saw my back he began to weep.
He brought me in my room and there I remained one month assisted by
my family. [...] At last the partisans abandoned Pola and so after a month
I could present myself to the Allied authorities.[398]

Unfortunately not many stories have such a successful conclusion.
Radeticchio's account is important as it reveals the gruesome details of
torture and it gives evidence to the standard extermination procedures,
which were taking place in Venezia Giulia. His testimony also leaves a

---

[396] Ibid.
[397] Ibid.
[398] Ibid.

A Journey into Darkness 153

clear impression that this episode was part of a larger plan, one that was a systematic, considered and methodical execution carried out by Communist partisans against Italian soldiers and unarmed civilians.

Basovizza and Opicina were not the only chasms used as human dumping sites by Tito's partisans. The clandestine Istrian Exiles Group Committee, (the aim of which was to get the parts of Istria, which were predominantly Italian, returned to Italy), helped to gather information on existing pits and killings, which were then passed on to the Allied command. The Anglo-Americans commented that although reports of atrocities were written with an Italian bias, it was evident that all facts appeared to be true, also because they were confirmed by other sources.[399]

YUGOSLAV CONCENTRATION CAMPS

Under the Slav dominion we lived forty-five [sic] days of terror, they deported people day and night. Who knows where they are now.

Since the 1 of May till the 15 July I was at the concentration camp near Ljubljana. …

During the seventy-five days of imprisonment I was left only with my bones. … From one hundred and eighty [officers] of the *Finanza* [custom guard] twenty died of hunger. I live by a miracle.

I have been in Borovnica. … What a horror! It is a second Buchenwald! How I pitied them. You could see from far away a mass of naked flesh, lacerated, dirty, hungry.[400]

The outpourings of grief and disbelief are evident in these letter excerpts by the Civil Censorship Group, which were collected by Anglo-American sources. These reports cannot be confirmed, but by their unsolicited nature

---

[399] WO 204/431, no day, November 1945.
[400] WO 204/430.

154 *Luisa Morettin*

they are of significant value. The place these excerpts refer to is Borovnica, a settlement 15 miles from Ljubljana and the site of a concentration camp for Italian prisoners of war. In the same way as the word 'Kolyma' came to signify the hardships of the Soviet Gulag system, so Borovnica has become the camp that symbolises all other Slav camps and the harsh conditions prisoners were subjected to. It was a self-contained universe, a place to live, and a place to die.

Life at the camp was simply a slow execution. For prisoners, the elements of their detention, physical hardship and hard labour (mainly heavy construction work) were accompanied by having to endure the most frightful torments and violent beatings. They endured the humiliation of urinating and defecating in front of others in a small cell. Prisoners documented the long marches on foot, in any weather conditions, as well as the all-consuming and ever-obsessive hunger and thirst, the unbearable exhaustion, and the shame of being nearly naked. Resisting dehumanisation and the sense of worthlessness became difficult.

The grim experience at Borovnica was described similarly by hundreds of survivors who were moved between internment camps or from prison to prison on foot in extenuating marches, and in conditions calculated to kill prisoners whilst en route. Prisoners 'were beaten like animals. Whoever went away from the ranks was shot without mercy,' Eugenio Volpi, from Caltanissetta, witnessed.[401] If prisoners could not continue walking and fell, the guards whipped them and if they were unable to get up, then they would be shot. Whenever rules were infringed upon, the punishment was harsh and the fear of being tortured or killed was constant. Giuseppe Siccardi, from the province of Cuneo, recalled how a prisoner who arrived five minute late for roll call, was bound with his hands to a stake for hours.[402]

Hunger was a permanent state which the prisoners had to endure and led to a serious deterioration of their physical and mental health. It was one of the primary contributors to the mortality rate at Borovnica. A university

---

[401] Ibid.
[402] WO 204/12754, 20 August 1945.

student from Rome, Corrado Tiburtini, reported how prisoners went around 'looking like corpses, with their looks on the ground to search grass to still their hunger.'[403] However, it was a useless exercise: even if occasionally they found something to eat, they were not allowed to take it. Siccardi reported how a prisoner, seeing an edible herb outside the wire perimeter, stretched out his hand to pluck it and was immediately shot dead by the guard.[404] In the last days of their lives, those dying of starvation showed physical incapability, mixed with mental insanity caused by hunger. Angelo Vecchi, a prisoner, described an episode when an inmate, already in his final stage of starvation, became delirious:

> Prisoners were shot thoughtlessly if they tried to search for grass to eat.
> ... A friend of mine Giorgio Lionetti, from Rodi, had symptoms of madness caused by hunger; he came out from a barrack of the camp yelling. The partisans, amused, killed him with their pistols.[405]

One of the absurdities of the camp institution was the practice of sending sick prisoners to hospital. Indeed, its very existence contradicted the general principle on which concentration camps were founded: slow and painful death. The hospital in Škofja Loka, located 30 miles north of Borovnica, became particularly notorious amongst inmates. Stories of the terrible treatment there appear repeatedly in witness testimonies. When Armando Tosello fell sick, he was interned in Škofja Loka, which he described as:

> A hospital so to say, because the sufferings were the same as those in the concentration camp. Many ill ones [were] massed together in a room, closed in, obliged to do everything in there, which caused an irresistible bad smell. At the camp there died from two to three [individuals] per day. At the hospital from six to seven a day.[406]

---

[403] Ibid.
[404] Ibid.
[405] WO 204/430.
[406] Ibid.

Ivo Boglioni was reduced to a skeleton, suffering from exhaustion, and with large infected ulcerations resulting from torture. He was eventually hospitalised in Škofja Loka where patients 'had to sleep on the floor without blankets.'[407] He received medical treatment only every four days and yet still managed to survive.

In such extreme circumstances it became a Darwinian survival of the fittest. Each prisoner handled the burden of slavery in the camp differently, but a commonly developed method of survival was keeping to oneself. Romildo Tiengo, from Mestre, recalled, 'During those moments one cared only to remain standing in order not to be shot, nobody cared for the names.'[408] Another prisoner, Salvatore Bettini, remembered:

> Many prisoners, who were in the rank together with me, never came back to the camp. They have been certainly killed. How can one know their names? One had to try that hell in order to understand that one cared for other things than to reveal his name. [...] If one could, he tried not to reveal his name being afraid that there were false accusations in their regards.[409]

Torture was not necessarily used by Tito's partisans to coerce prisoners to give information, but often, it was gratuitous in nature and was used to extend the feeling of terror amongst all prisoners. On his release, Antonio Cau tried to make sense of or find some wider significance in the suffering he witnessed and endured. 'They did this for nothing, for hatred, for sadistic pleasure. ... Sometimes the yells of pain made us almost become mad, who were obliged to assist to the torture.' Cau continued:

> One night they advised us to look out because the guards had to be changed. ... It was the 15 of May [1945] ... I rose from the floor exhausted and heard yells and screams of pain coming from the yard. I went to the window and saw a horrible spectacle. They had placed in file

---

[407] Ibid.
[408] Ibid.
[409] Ibid.

A Journey into Darkness

hundreds of prisoners who one by one, from the front and from the back, were beaten with whips and rifle butts by the partisans. The victims, yelling from pain, tried to protect themselves with their arms from the rain of strokes which were falling on their shoulders, faces and heads. After a few hours the platoon of soldiers of Tito who had just finished this action came to our room. They were armed with ropes, telephone wire, whips and weapons. They gave the order to all to stand up. We did. They tied us and then they started to slap us, to hit us with the whips and the rifle butts. It was a scene which would have horrified even savages. I myself, weak from lack of food fell twice to the floor, fainting under this. While I was on the ground, the partisans kept on hitting me with their butts. Tied like criminals between yells, mockeries and beatings they pushed us in a cattle car and sent us to Postumia.[410]

It is clear that Borovnica was a sadistic playground and torture was a widespread practice. Captors and guards could be inventive in their choice of persecution, as Nicola Durante, from Catanzaro, witnessed:

One day I was seized, tied at a wall, hands on the back of the head, kept fast by a belt and with a sharp knife they cut my right cheek, visible to all now.

Some days later I was brought to the fireplace; I was laid down, hands tied on the back with a wire, and my right leg brought over the flames which burned the sole of my foot. The same was done to my left foot. With their fingers they took the burned skin from the wound. Then they forced me to go on foot back to my cell. The same was done to my companions. ... Then we were denuded and they poured boiling oil on us, whipping us. I have still the scars visible on my body.[411]

Another survivor recalled:

We were tortured by means of lit matches placed under the nostrils, burning our breasts, arms and feet and they seeing us suffer laughed

---

[410] Ibid.
[411] Ibid. This witness report is taken from the newspaper *Vita Nuova*, published on 7 July 1945.

158   *Luisa Morettin*

mockingly. How many returned with their gangrenous arms, because they were tied at the stake with a barbed wire tied around their muscles.[412]

Not everybody who made the journey from imprisonment in Borovnica to the nearest Allied refugee camp in Udine was so lucky to be fit enough to release a witness account or to go back home. There were those that the Anglo-American officers called 'the living dead' and epitomised the camp system. Leone Buson, from the province of Padua, was one of them. Suffering from dysentery, myocarditis and severe depression, he barely managed to say his name and that he was a soldier of the Italian artillery, sent to Borovnica by Tito's partisans, on 2 May 1945. [413] Likewise, owing to his debilitating physical state, Alberto Guarnaschelli was able to utter just a few words: 'I have been reduced like Jesus Christ [...] by the partisans of Tito. [...] I have not the strength to speak otherwise I would tell you things which would fill you with fear.'[414] He was 'a living corpse. It is horrible to look at him,'[415] was the comment of the Allied officer who tried to question Guarnaschelli. The same officer also tried to interrogate Ennio Sandri, yet was unsuccessful as he was comatose. A further witness report collected from a 22-year-old soldier, Marino Genovesi, from the province of Lucca, stated:

> I was taken prisoner by the partisans of Tito. They have treated me like a dog. Always walking for many days under the sun without a little bread and a drop of water. Who fell out of ranks to drink, was shot. They have beaten me. I suffered famine and thirst. And many ill treatments; if I could have the strength to tell it, nobody would believe it. I feel so tired. I feel I am about to die and I cannot say more.[416]

At 11:30 on 23 August 1945, Genovesi died due to enterocolitis, organ exhaustion and mitral insufficiency.

---

[412] Ibid, from Civil Censorship Group – Italy.
[413] WO 204/430.
[414] Ibid.
[415] Ibid.
[416] Ibid.

A Journey into Darkness

The same cruelty of Borovnica was the norm in camp complexes scattered throughout Yugoslavia, but their location and the names and numbers of Italian prisoners interned there were never officially disclosed by the Belgrade Government. However, from other sources it was understood that each region of Yugoslavia had its own camp. The main ones were located in Belgrade, Niš, Arandjelovac and Valjevo in Serbia; at Demir Kapia in Macedonia; Ljubljana, Borovnica, Kocevje and Novo Mesto in Slovenia; Zagreb, Sisak and Karlovac in Croatia; and Spalato, Lissa and Ragusa in Dalmatia.[417]

The camp prisoners were not exclusively soldiers, as in the case of Borovnica, but also civilians and priests and the latter were as vulnerable as anyone else. Father Fingerle and *don* Clonfeo Nais, for instance, recount the events, repeated in various forms by other prisoners, of the brutality they endured. In particular, they were aghast to see 'the hatred of the camp's guards' and recall how the rights of medical personnel and units, as devised by the first Geneva Convention in 1864, were simply disregarded by the partisans. Further, they noted how the Red Cross was not respected, as doctors and nurses 'were deprived of their medical equipment. A doctor and an assistant were killed because they stopped to assist a wounded person.'[418]

Unlike Fingerle and Nais, many other members of the clergy did not even make it to a concentration camp. Father Vittorio Perkan, a priest in Fiume, was murdered during mass; Father Angelo Tarticchio, a priest in Villa di Rovigno (Rovinjsko Selo), was tortured, murdered, and thrown into a bauxite quarry where he was later found with his genitals severed and stuffed into his mouth; Father Placido Sancin, the parish priest of San Dorligo della Valle, was kidnapped by the Slav partisans and vanished, never to return; Father Nicola Fantela was drowned in Ragusa with a stone tied around his neck.[419]

---

[417] ASMAE, AP-Jugoslavia 1946-50, b. 14, f. 1, par. 5, Comportamento delle forze armate jugoslave di occupazione nei riguardi della popolazione della Venezia Giulia e Dalmazia.

[418] WO 204/430.

[419] WO 204/431.

160   *Luisa Morettin*

Amongst Italian prisoners, many men and women had fought on the side of Yugoslav partisans helping the cause of the revolution. Yet often, they outlived their usefulness and were considered a liability. As a result, they were treated as an enemy of the people, as the following reveals:

> Thirty-seven Italians arrived yesterday night in Trieste coming from Yugoslavia where they have been fighting against the Germans, Ustaša and Chetniks as soldiers of Tito's army. At the end of the war they were disarmed, their uniforms and belongings stolen and sent to POWs concentration camp together with German and other prisoners of war.
>
> They have been released now being seriously ill.
>
> They have declared: 'No medical assistance in the camps. Cases of malaria growing every day. Daily ration consists of watery soup of beans and fifty gr. of maize bread. Forced work is so hard that cases of T.B. exhaustion reach terrific numbers.
>
> Prisoners with strong fever are obliged to work, and if they stop they are tied in the sun with their hands over their heads until they faint.[420]

On their way back home, the newly released prisoners came across concentration camps, which, they stated, had approximately the following number of Italian prisoners:

Demir Kapija, Macedonia camp	about 1,600 prisoners
Niš	about 1,000 prisoners
Bor	about 600 prisoners
Zemun, Belgrade	about 400 prisoners
Novi Vrbas	about 2,000 prisoners
Sebenico	about 280 prisoners
Spalato	about 280 prisoners
Ragusa	about 500 prisoners [421]

It is impossible to verify the precise figures and the exact nationality of the camps' population reported by the group of Italian survivors. However,

---

[420] Ibid, 12 November 1945.
[421] Ibid.

A Journey into Darkness 161

their testimony is still noteworthy as it provides a snapshot of the Yugoslav internment and labour camp system, of which scant information exists, unlike that of their German and Soviet Union equivalents.

The head camp of Zagreb Sabirni, was reserved only for civilians, and here, interned were around 10,000 men, mostly opponents of Tito's regime, collaborationists and a large number of high-ranking officials of the Ustaše party. From this camp, some of the prisoners were sent to join the military units, whilst the remainder were sent to work in Serbia, Slovenia and Siberia.[422]

It is known that 1,200 *bersaglieri* and 450 civilians and Italian civil servants were imprisoned at the camp of Prestane (Prestranek). Reports reveal how prisoners were hit, without provocation, with a multi-tailed whip made of electric wires bound together, barely fed and forced to live in shocking conditions.[423] What is striking about the Allied reports is their consistency regarding the inhumane treatment of prisoners: the only detail which changes, is the location of the camp.

SLAVE WORK: THE STORY OF ROSSI KOBAU AND COLOMBAI

A few Italian medical-orderly prisoners, who tried to protest against [their inhuman] treatment asking that the Geneva agreement be observed, were answered textually by the camp commandant, called the Hangman: 'There is no Red Cross for me, the only cross I know is this one' and he showed his pistol.[424]

Conditions concerning the treatment of prisoners of war were contained in the 1929 Geneva Convention, which was adhered to by many countries, including Yugoslavia. The international treaty outlined that prisoners of

---

[422] WO 204/12754, 20 August 1945.
[423] Ibid.
[424] WO 204/431, 12 November 1945.

162   *Luisa Morettin*

war were to be treated humanely by their captors, who must provide information about them, allowing representatives of neutral states to visit the prison camps. As the previous chapters have shown, all of those paragraphs were violated by the Belgrade Government. More specifically, Yugoslavia illegally detained prisoners of war who had previously been in the German *Lager* and were caught whilst in transit through Yugoslavia on their journey home.

According to British and American authorities and the director of Welfare and Displaced Persons Division of United Nations Relief and Rehabilitation Administration (UNNRA), the international relief agency for war victims, the Yugoslav authorities were refusing to return Italian deportees, pending the settlement of the question of repatriation of Yugoslavs and possibly the final settlement of the Trieste problem.[425] As to the first, in Italy at the beginning of 1947 there existed several British camps, which offered protection to around 30,000 anti-Tito fighters, comprised of Ustaša, Chetniks, and Zelenaši (a group of Montenegrin nationalists and separatists). Historian Costantino Di Sante stated how, in the city of Rome alone, there were 20,000 of such fighters who were politically engaged against the Communist government in Belgrade, and for this they received logistic and economic support from the Vatican and the Anglo-Americans.[426] The Belgrade government asked permission from the Allied forces to send a Yugoslav commission, further asking for the repatriation of those 'alleged Yugoslavs criminals,' yet this was in vain.

As to the second issue, undoubtedly the controversy over the prisoners was exacerbated by the dispute over ownership of Trieste, the recovery of which was instilled into partisans during their fighting days. The struggle for the coastal city was of primary importance in Tito's foreign policy, who on 1 April 1946 declared that Belgrade should concentrate, 'all [it] energies in order that Yugoslavia may realise her rights.' One of her rights

---

[425] FO 371/48951/R20220/15199/92, 20 November 1945.
[426] Costantino Di Sante, *Nei campi di Tito. Soldati, deportati e prigionieri di guerra italiani in Jugoslavia 1941-1952*, (Verona: Ombre Corte, 2007), pp. 142-3.

A Journey into Darkness 163

was indeed, 'Istria, the Slovene littoral with Trieste, the Slovene part of Carinthia, etc.'[427]

The unsuccessful return of Italian prisoners of war and deportees meant they could be used as a source of manpower: slave labourers, who would work on the extensive reconstruction plans in Yugoslavia after the conflict. These prisoners were held responsible of belonging to military units, which had destroyed the country and killed 1,600,000 young Yugoslavs,[428] thus their detention was now integrated into Yugoslavia's economy and terror network. They became a sort of new *Untermenschen*, who suffered indescribable physical and psychological damage in the many camps scattered throughout Yugoslavia. There are scant witness accounts by former prisoners of these camps, and only a few memoirs exist, compared to the testimonies of those in Nazi camps. However, as Aleksandr Solzhenitsyn wrote, 'To taste the sea all one needs is one gulp.'[429]

One such witness report comes from Lionello Rossi Kobau, whose ordeal as a slave labourer is quite common amongst prisoner accounts. After the surrender of his unit on 1 May 1945 in Idreska (Idrsko) near Caporetto, his unit, the *bersaglieri* corps, a light infantry unit of the Italian Army, were marched to a small village on the foothills of Mount Matajur. They then continued an arduous journey to the camps in Istria, Slovenia, Croatia, Slavonia, Vojvodina, Bosnia and Serbia, without much food and water. Occasional meals consisted of soup made with dry and fresh grass. Harsh punishment was delivered, not only by the slightest infringement of unspoken rules, but often as a result of the captors' whims, and Rossi Kobau's anecdotal evidence is abundant with descriptions of such violence. Yet one episode is particularly revealing. One morning, whilst the captives were being handed out their meagre meal, a guard, eager to continue with the journey, shot the hungry prisoners who were still

---

[427] Major Niall MacPherson, M.P., 'The Trieste Question,' *The Spectator*, 28 June 1946, pp. 5-6.

[428] Data provided by the United Nations War Crimes Commission in London, quoted in Costantino Di Sante, op. cit., p. 143.

[429] Aleksandr Solzhenitsyn, *The Gulag Archipelago 1918–1956*, (Boulder: Westview Press, 1997).

164 *Luisa Morettin*

awaiting their food. The first prisoner fell, his upper body resting inside the large pot containing the soup, where his blood dripped into the liquid meal. Despite the horror of this, such was the hunger of the prisoners that they still stretched out their arms to receive their daily ration.[430]

Rossi Kobau's memoir eloquently describes the extreme conditions of his work as a woodcutter in the mountain woods above Borovnica. Undernourished men, weighing on average between 45 to 65 pounds were forced to cut trees and carry chunks of wood, which weighed the same as them, up and down slippery slopes. During the winter, when temperatures reached 15 or sometimes 30 degrees below zero, the prisoners were still forced to work. Many of them had no shoes and tied rags around their feet to protect them from the freezing snow. They would perform many tasks, such as digging holes and erecting light and telephone poles as well as unloading cargos from railway cars: at all times a guard would be watching. On some occasions, guards would tie the logs to a prisoner's neck with iron wire, so if they fell, the weight of the chunks of wood would strangle them. If captives, weakened by starvation and freezing temperatures, were unable to carry whatever heavy cargo they were required to, they would be ferociously hit on their backs and heads by the guards' rifle butts. It was by this very means by which one of Rossi Kobau's close fellow prisoners, the 18 year old Silvano Antonini, died, his skull so crushed that his brain could be seen.

Entertainment for the guards was what Rossi Kobau called the 'cabaret'. After the day's work had ended, slave labourers were not allowed to go back to their barracks, but were forced to lie down in the snow, ice and mud. Then they were forced to immerse their heads in the cold water of a nearby brook, and then repeat the action of lying in the snow. This could go on for hours. Other examples of so-called pastime activities would include forcing detainees to eat moss and their own faeces. The consequences of the 'cabaret' were pneumonia, nephritis, pleurisy, or

---

[430] Lionello Rossi Kobau, *Prigioniero di Tito 1945-1946. Un bersagliere nei campi di concentramento jugoslavi,* (Milano: Mursia, 2001), p. 30.

typhoid, yet the sick were only admitted to the camp infirmary if their fever was high enough.

The broad picture of war contains stories such as Lionello Rossi Kobau's. Aldo Colombai's ordeal as a slave labourer is of a similar vein. In an interview with the author, Colombai, a prisoner from Naples, who was fortunate not to succumb to his brutal experience and to be released in 1947, evokes a dramatic, but not unusual story. Having been captured first by the Germans, then by the Yugoslavs, Colombai was in a position to compare the two types of captivity. He associated his time as a German prisoner to that of the first circle of Dante's *Inferno* and his captivity in Tito's camps to that of the last circle. 'The Nazi detention was certainly harsh,' he said, 'but we were not subject to forced labour. The Yugoslav cruelty was inconceivable. To them we were like fodder.'[431] Indeed, it was a very deep pit reserved in this man-made hell for Italians and for all of Tito's opponents, whether real or imagined.

According to Colombai, the prisoners of war were not just used to rebuild Yugoslavia, but their captors showcased them as spoils of war. They were a tangible sign of a glorious victory gained against all odds. Colombai's view of this was derived from his own experience. After he was liberated from the Nazi camp by Tito's troops in October 1944, he and other prisoners were not allowed to return home. Instead, they were offered a choice: either to join partisan troops or to work in what became known as the 'workers' battalions,' which in reality was simply forced labour. Such an alternative was not always offered as in the areas where the Italian occupation had been harsher, and along the Dalmatian coast, Italian prisoners were used solely for reconstruction work purposes. In the town of Spalato, for instance, thousands of Italians were compelled to work night and day, with no break; they were starved, dirty and the majority of them half-naked, which made partisans laugh while it gained them the sympathy of the local civilians.

---

[431] Luisa Morettin, 'Trattati come schiavi. Intervista ad Aldo Colombai, ex-prigioniero nei campi di concentramento jugoslavi,' *Fiume. Rivista di Studi Adriatici*, Jan-June 2013, 27, pp. 111-8.

After choosing to work rather than to join the partisans, Colombai was taken with a long line of prisoners, by foot, on a journey which lasted days. When the long queues of prisoners reached inhabited areas, villagers were alerted beforehand by the partisan guards and allowed to or spurred on to shout insults at the captives, beat them with clubs and throw stones at them. If prisoners backed away, they were hit by guards' rifle butts and forced to go back into the line. If charitable Yugoslav women tried to offer water and bread to the prisoners, a reminder of a little bit of humanity, they were kicked away. When someone collapsed because of the blows, bleeding feet, and extreme hunger and thirst, the other prisoners would stumble and fall over those in front of them, which eventually led the guards to shoot whomever was unable to stand.

Prisoners of war and abducted civilians were used primarily as a workforce on the railroads and for the construction industry, as well as in agriculture. Therefore jobs could range from transporting building materials to unloading barley and corn sacks from rail carriages. Colombai's role changed frequently: he worked in the construction work of a railway line, as a builder and as a dockhand. However, some jobs were worse than others. One of the dreaded tasks for detainees was to pull pontoons loaded with wood, along rivers, by using ropes that sawed into their shoulders: those who stopped to change the bloody rags covering their shoulders were furiously beaten by guards. It is extraordinary that anyone was capable of withstanding these conditions and keeping working.

Colombai described how a Sergeant Major of the *carabinieri* woke him and other prisoners in the middle of the night and ordered to take with them a, 'spoon and mess tins in order to unload the jam.' The general understanding amongst the prisoners was there was some food to be offloaded, part of which would be given as a compensation for their work. However, the prisoners were taken to a river and ordered to dig a 32 feet long ditch alongside it, technically moving the width of the river. They then were forced to camp for the night on a nearby field, hearing in the middle distance the clatter of machine-gun fire, lasting on and off until the following evening. The prisoners were then forced to throw the bodies of the victims into the ditch, cover them with soil and move back the riverbed

A Journey into Darkness 167

to its original position. The river thus became the grave for hundreds of victims.[432]

THE DEATH TOLL

The fits of barbaric intoxication and the violent excesses carried out by Tito's partisans are indicative of the unparalleled democratisation of violence unleashed by the war throughout Central, Eastern and South-Eastern Europe, and of the ideological polarisation of contending factions. Yugoslavia, specifically, was a battleground where internal and ideologically motivated vengeance imposed a scale of brutality and reprisal so deprived of all sense of proportion, that one would have to look back to the Thirty Years War to find similar levels of destruction and barbarity.

The Allied investigation established that many of the pits scattered throughout the Istrian peninsula were used as mass graves during the Yugoslav occupation of Trieste and surrounding areas, thus giving us a broader picture of the geographical expanse of the atrocities. In addition to the previously examined sources, two eyewitnesses declared that many thousands of people were thrown into the Bertarelli pit, which at the bottom has an underground stream passing through supplying the village of Pinguente (Buzet). Due to the decomposing bodies, the water from the stream was polluted.[433]

At the Casserova pit, near Obrovo, where 6,000 bodies were reportedly thrown, the mouth of the pit had to be closed with explosives, as the stench emanating from it was so bad. Further witness accounts revealed that at the *foiba* in Scadaiscina many people were forced to jump into the pit and some victims had their eyes gouged out with the excuse that they would not be afraid to jump if they could not see.[434]

---

[432] Ibid.
[433] WO 204/431, Appendix B.
[434] Ibid.

168   *Luisa Morettin*

In Racia, near Lanischie (Lanišće), several thousands of people were reported to have been thrown into the local pit, including Allied aircrew shot down by Germans. Many bodies were said to have been disposed of in the Gollac *foiba* that was later closed by explosives. Other death pits recorded by Allied documents are at Corgnale, Valle di Rosandra, Baccia, Castelnuovo d'Arsa (Rakalj), Porta Meresego,[435] San Servolo, Matteria, Antignana (Tinjan), Checchi (Heki), Comino, S. Domenica d'Albona (Sveta Nedelja), Tarnova della Selva, in the hamlet of Cobbia (municipality of San Daniele del Carso), and in the vicinity of Fianona and Aidussina.

At Gargaro (Grgar), the local pit was the grave to 700 people and eyewitnesses declared to have heard the cries of the victims during the massacre.[436]

Such reports elicit the question of the death toll in Venezia Giulia, Istria and Dalmatia in the period of 1943-45 at the hands of Tito's troops. During and after the Yugoslav killing campaigns many tried to estimate the number of casualties. In certain cases, due to an environment which has long been defined by the instrumentalisation and manipulation of historical claims, the number of victims was augmented or diminished according to the ideological inclination of the claimants.

The first objective method was to count the bodies retrieved from the pits, and later use the number of people who disappeared against who was found. However, figures were inevitably vague, varying from hundreds to possibly thousands.[437] Whilst some historians such as Paul Garde suggest that in Slovenia alone approximately 20,000-30,000 people died,[438] others such as Raoul Pupo and Roberto Spazzali claim the total number to be in the region of a few thousand victims.[439] Pupo and Spazzali based their claim on how, in 1943, 217 bodies were exhumed from pits in southern Istria, but the overall number of the disappeared was in the region of 500

---

[435] Ibid.
[436] WO 204/12753.
[437] Kati Pizzi, *A City in Search of an Author*, (London: Sheffield Academic Press, 2001), p. 1.
[438] Paul Garde, *Vie et mort de la Yugoslavie*, (Paris: Fayard, 1992).
[439] Raoul Pupo and Roberto Spazzali, op. cit., pp. 26-31.

A Journey into Darkness   169

people. In 1944, approximately 200 people were arrested and deported from Zara, whilst in 1945 approximately 500 individuals disappeared from Fiume. It is more complex to establish the casualties in the areas of Trieste and Gorizia, but Pupo and Spazzali record the numbers respectively at 601 and 332.[440] Both historians, however, admit that such figures are approximate.

Mass graves are still being discovered such as the grave in the Ajdov Field (Grobišče Ajdovsko polje) in the Slovenian village of Ustje where, in March 2002, 72 skeletons were disinterred. They were later identified as the remains of 57 Italian soldiers and 15 Germans.[441] Likewise, in 2018 the remains of eight Italians were resumed from a mass grave in Castua (Kastav), near Fiume:[442] among them the body of *Senatore* Riccardo Gigante, who disappeared together with *Senatore* Icilio Bacci on 3 May 1945, when Tito's troops entered Fiume.[443] More recently, a mass grave was discovered at Ossero (Osor) on the island of Cherso: the bones of 27 people, believed to belong to Italian sailors of the *Decima Mas* (10th Assault Vehicle Flotilla), were excavated from the site.[444]

Therefore, the number of those who died because of Yugoslav atrocities is extremely difficult to ascertain. There are several limitations that prevent to accurately estimate the extent of human losses. These limitations included the fact that it was not possible to explore pits, which Tito's troops controlled and then were allocated to Yugoslavia. Further, often the families of the victims did not even report the death or disappearance of their relatives out of fear of reprisal from the local Communist partisans. Similarly, many civil servants, who were kidnapped and then vanished, came from mainland Italy and lived alone in Venezia Giulia and Dalmatia and as a result they went unclaimed. In addition, prisoners who returned from Yugoslav concentration camps sometimes did

---

[440] Ibid., pp. 26-8.

[441] Fausto Biloslavo, 'La foiba nascosta per 60 anni,' *Il Giornale*, 11 February 2018.

[442] Giovanni Vale, 'Tornano alla luce a Castua i cadaveri di italiani uccisi dagli jugoslavi,' *Il Piccolo*, 12 July 2018.

[443] Conference 'Ricordo dei Senatori di Fiume Riccardo Gigante ed Icilio Bacci,' Senato della Repubblica, Istituto di Santa Maria in Aquiro, Rome, 3 May 2019.

[444] 'Cherso, esumati i resti di 27 caduti della Seconda guerra,' *Il Piccolo*, 17 May 2019.

not report themselves to the Allied or Italian authorities, either because they did not know they were unaccounted for or because of their proven Fascist past. Allied reports provide witness testimonies to affirm the number of victims of the Yugoslav violence, yet it is unwise to agree that witnesses were able to verify the exact number of victims, as they are still unverifiable. In the case of concentration camps, it is not known if the camp administration kept track of the arrivals and deaths of its inmates, yet it is plausible to believe the importance at this time was not to record numbers, but to keep the prisoners, whilst alive, and their death a secret. Finally, prisoners who were taken from their homes were executed and buried in unmarked mass graves scattered in the countryside, which adds to the difficulty to draw accurate conclusions as to the death toll.

Counting the number of victims is a historical necessity, but in the case of the *foibe* crimes it is an almost impossible exercise. The statistical approach became a bone of contention, but numbers are flawed and will never be complete. Regardless of the numerical log of deaths, there is clear evidence suggesting virulent violence did not derive from popular fantasy, nor was it the work of Fascist reactionaries. What matters is that although at the end of the Second World War Tito was hailed as a hero for Yugoslavia, he proceeded to govern his country for 35 years in the same authoritarian way and with the same violent methods as those of the oppressors he had so courageously defeated. Despite the antagonistic ideas, which set them apart, Italian Fascism and Yugoslav Communism shared the same hostility to liberal democracy, the same dishonourable crimes, and the same dictatorial outlook that took root in people's minds. As historian Karel Bartošek wrote, 'Rarely in the course of history had the arrival of a new regime been preceded by a bloodbath on the scale of the one seen in Yugoslavia. ... A series of ethnic, religious, ideological, and civil wars tore the country apart. ... The genocide and purges ensured that

A Journey into Darkness 171

at the moment of liberation, Tito and the Communist Party had hardly any political rivals left.'[445]

UNDERSTANDING YUGOSLAV ATROCITIES

The analysis of the documents which describe Yugoslav atrocities raise some questions. First and foremost, what reason decided a person's arrest or execution in Venezia Giulia? As previously noted, victims were usually Fascist Party officials, *carabinieri*, the Italian military police force, *Guardia di Finanza* officers, who were tasked with border related security and financial crimes, and *podestà*, Mayors with full executive and legislative powers. Yet, there were also teachers, doctors, solicitors, midwives, veterinarians, tax collectors, shop owners, and postal officers who were either arrested, killed or both.[446] In short, representatives of the Italian State, persons of education, economic means, or influence were targeted, summarily shot or deported to concentration camps. Italian landowners and industrialists should also be added to this list, as the political fight of liberation from fascism became entwined with the partisan class hatred and class struggle. The clergy was no exception either, as monks and priests could influence their flock and had followers, especially amongst the most ordinary and less educated people, who could not be reached by Communist propaganda. The members of these categories were a symbol of the detested Italian invader. A state that had long believed it was a great power, that had claimed its cultural and historical superiority to 'backward Slavs' and yet had a totalitarian leader who first oppressed the Slav minority in Venezia Giulia, and later conquered Yugoslavia, ordering unspeakable atrocities to be meted out on Slavs. The army of such a 'civilised' state had ruthlessly invaded, raided, looted, tortured and killed

---

[445] Karel Bartošek, 'Central and Southeastern Europe,' in Stéphane Courtois, Nicolas Werth, et al., *The Black Book of Communism. Crimes, Terror, Repression*, (Cambridge, Massachussets: Harvard University Press, 1999), pp. 397-8.

[446] Raoul Pupo and Roberto Spazzali, op. cit., pp. 10-11.

172 *Luisa Morettin*

the people of Yugoslavia.[447] It was now the time to address the individual and historical wrongs suffered by Slavs.

As the Communist cadre contended and some left-wing supporters still do, especially in the milieu of the *Associazione Nazionale Partigiani d'Italia* (ANPI),[448] after the fall of fascism revenge was an important motivation behind the violence against Italians. They argue that a long-standing grudge leading to retaliation was the inevitable result of prior Italian dominance, injustice, and oppression. The first wave of violence in 1943 is explained as a spontaneous peasant revolt (*jacquerie*), which punished Fascists and freed Slavs from their hated masters. The *jacquerie* component also meant criminal-like individuals and opportunists were lured into the killing of Italians with the perspective of loot, wholesale violence, and the possibility of sorting out personal issues and old resentments. From the interviews and witness accounts, it emerges that among the perpetrators, there were also those who thrived on the identity and status, which the new political situation afforded them, who enjoyed, and were even emboldened by what can be defined as 'a licence to kill'. At first sight then, the killings were a 'settling of accounts,' expected in such situations.

Left-wing supporters interpret the second period of violence in Zara in 1944, as well as the third in Venezia Giulia in May-June 1945, as justice. Justice in the aftermath of the conflict was a subjective and painful affair in Italy as well as in Europe, and Venezia Giulia was therefore no exception. It was supposed to be 'a just revenge' on people involved with the Fascist regime. After all, victims do not have to participate physically in a crime to be historically or politically co-responsible for it. Instead, rather irrespective of individual persona, everyone is tarred with the same brush.

---

[447] Galeazzo Ciano, op. cit., 17 July 1941, p. 534.

[448] The association was founded by participants of the Italian resistance and is still alive thanks to the activity of its antifascist members. Some of these deny the foibe killings. See Natascia Celeghin, 'Rovigo, ANPI choc: "Le foibe sono un'invenzione storica." Salvini: "Fate schifo." I vertici nazionali si dissociano,' www.corrieredelveneto.corriere.it, accessed 10 February 2019.

However, in Venezia Giulia it was not simply the 'hunt for Fascists' that was taking place in the rest of Italy. There was more to it. Whilst it cannot be excluded that spontaneous pay offs may have been behind many local killings, for instance as a result of disputes between neighbours or an unrequited love, at least three general arguments justify a different, more complex interpretation, which has more to do with a Communist sanctioned plan of killing.

The first argument relates to the victims' category. Indeed, attentive readings of witness accounts purport that the victims were not only Italian Fascists, Germans, Chetniks, and Ustaše, but in fact the list for elimination was widened to include others. Although the Partisan leadership denied it, on the grounds they were the fruit of enemy propaganda,[449] the list included unarmed civilians, who were wealthy, or anglophiles, masons, members of the Croatian Peasant Party, democratic rivals or fellow partisans who placed national interests above the supranational interests. In short, liquidations included the arbitrarily chosen category of 'enemies of the people,' that is to say enemies of the Communist Party of Yugoslavia, a category of whomever did not or was believed would not support Tito's revolutionary goals. The shift from targeting the war enemy, i.e., Fascist soldiers, officials, and proven collaborators, to tackling people without apparent connections to the Italian regime, may be interpreted as a sign that the elimination of political opponents was becoming a more important objective for Tito's short- and long-term policy in order to take over Yugoslavia.

The second reason which defies the interpretation of the killings as 'spontaneous' is the sense of the 'assembly-line' design of the murders. There are many elements, which testify to the interpretation that the violent events were pre-planned. Indeed, it cannot be dismissed that persecution required preparation, organisation, delegation of power, and division of tasks and labour. Therefore, death lists were being drawn up in preparation

---

[449] Zdenko Radelić, 'The Communist Party of Yugoslavia and the Abolition of the Multi-party System: The Case of Croatia,' in Ognjenović, Gorana and Jozelić, Jasna, (eds.) *Revolutionary Totalitarianism, Pragmatic Socialism, Transition,* Vol. 1, (Basingstoke: Palgrave Macmilan, 2016), p. 22.

174 *Luisa Morettin*

for the killings. The Allied sources reveal all arrests followed the same tactics, rituals and logistics, something that would have been unthinkable in spontaneous attacks. Arrests were presented as ordinary checks or an informal questioning, so the false air of normality would serve to disarm many victims, yet what awaited them was often detention and death. It was usually at night that Communist partisans would 'visit' their victims, when people were hiding in their homes. Tito's troops swarmed the houses, pounded on doors with the butts of their rifles, shouted, dragged their victims from their homes to their deaths, into awaiting lorries, known as the 'death coaches.' Some of those arrested would return, but the majority did not. According to a well-devised script, they were interrogated, occasionally would go through a farcical people's tribunal, which gave a verdict inevitably sentencing them to death. Very often, summary extra judiciary verdicts were administered. Even if the date and place of the specific executions were often shrouded in mystery, in the distance, villagers could hear the cries of terror, screaming, begging and the bursts of gunfire coming from prison yards or from the open countryside.

Another recurring feature was that those deemed for execution were tied in pairs with wire around their wrists, and then taken in groups to a *foiba*, a quarry or, by boat, to high sea and thrown into it. This well rehearsed violent choreography took place according to the same patterns during all three of the previously identified stages of the Yugoslav killing campaign. In no sense, therefore, were the murders the result of spontaneous retribution.

Third, but no less important evidence was the use of sustained terror as a specific, political instrument to spread a psychosis amongst Italians, who saw themselves as 'fair game' to brutal violence. Whilst Tito's partisans in Venezia Giulia and Dalmatia were carrying out the policy of shock and awe, a sense of insecurity was in the air – an acute, chronic fear, which had been strategically instilled. It was fear of loss of liberty and deportation, fear of pain, fear of one's own or a relative's death. Such gnawing, lingering terror was attributed to the impossibility of knowing how to save oneself, the uncertainty of who the next batch of victims would be, and what would happen to them. Fear would materialise as verbal intimidation

A Journey into Darkness 175

or informal questioning, which might be a prelude to the disappearance of the person; extortion or the rape of women with the humiliation, which it brought to them and their families; a sudden onslaught leading to a manhunt and immediate arrest and torture; or, more devastating than anything else, the unspeakable horror of a prospective death by pit. It was the spectre of such harm that wreaked havoc on the psyche of the populace, as the certainty that everyone will die eventually is not the same as the apprehension of an early death because of indiscriminate violence.

Death was both suggested and hidden; there were whispered stories, which spread amongst local inhabitants like an invisible poison, as acute fright increased with such tales and the objective realisation that the stories were based on truth and people did vanish. Such wholesale terror was made worse by the evident difficulty in comprehending the logic used by partisans in deciding whom to kill. Alceo Ranzato, a solicitor from the province of Ferrara, who at the time was a child living in Fiume, illustrates the point. In 1945, five members of his family, three uncles and two cousins, disappeared never to return. Ranzato explained:

> They were not involved in politics, but I assume that one of them was found 'guilty' of having worked for a short while as a waiter at the *Circolo Ufficiali*, [the Italian Officers' Club]. Another one's crime was to be a civil servant in the local municipality. ... We think they must have been thrown into a pit because their bodies were never found, but in fact nobody knows for sure. We looked for them, but not at the Yugoslav command as it was extremely dangerous to say you were a relative of a disappeared individual, or to be linked in some other way to people who had been taken away. It was not advisable to show interest in them as you might become the next victim.[450]

The account of the punishment of Fascists did not fit with the actual political background of the victims, as many of them were not involved with the past regime, and very often simply to get a job, Italians would have had to become members of the Fascist Party.

---

[450] Interview with the author, Ferrara, Italy, 27 December 2012.

In contrast with the secrecy of the executions, about which there was utter silence, the communication of fear spread the not too subtle message that Tito's forces had control over life and death. This is something which left a deep impression on locals. Punishment in Venezia Giulia was a spectacle and an act of terror did not necessarily have to result in large-scale deaths to be effective and reach its intended 'pedagogical aim.' Indeed, as the circle of potential victims was wide and violent incidents occurred within a limited space of time, as terror eroded trust and divided communities, Italians in Venezia Giulia and Dalmatia felt there was no real defence against the unpredictable murders.

The unpredictability element, which determined the fate of Alceo Ranzato's family, occurs many times in witness reports. It is unknown, for instance, what the motive was for the arrest of Romano Meneghello from Trieste, employed at *Banca d'Italia* (Bank of Italy). During the war, he had been an infantry officer in the 2nd Army Corps in the Balkans. After Italy's capitulation, he did not join the Republican Fascist Part nor did he cooperate with the Nazi-Fascists. On the contrary, from July 1944 he took an active part in the clandestine fight against the Germans and at the end of April he was in charge as Commander of the brigade 'Venezia Giulia.' In spite of his proven anti-Fascist record, on 24 May 1945, at four o'clock in the morning, approximately twenty Yugoslav regular soldiers arrested Meneghello in front of his frightened parents. After the arrest, the public prosecutor declared that Meneghello had to consider himself prisoner of war.[451]

In other circumstances, the motives of arrests were whimsical if the case of Mario Bonara from Trieste is considered. Unlike Meneghello, Bonara had never served in the military because he was unfit for service. He did not belong to the Republican Fascist Party nor had he cooperated with the Nazi-Fascist organisations. Still, he was taken away on 4 May 1945 by regular Yugoslav troops. It was believed Bonara was arrested because he had a permit to carry weapons as part of his job within a bank, which had been formerly handed to him by Italian authorities and further

---

[451] WO 204/430.

A Journey into Darkness

confirmed by a German permission. According to the statement of a prisoner who returned from Yugoslavia, both Meneghello and Bonara were detained in Ljubljana in a former lunatic asylum adapted as a prison.[452]

Fearing for their lives, many townspeople and villagers fled the region. That was the case of Margherita Cettini, from Fiume, who left her city and arrived at the refugee camp of Udine on 24 August 1945. She spoke extensively of her fear to remain in Fiume due to the atrocities and forced deportations committed by partisans against civilians, many of whom she personally knew. Finding it unbearable to continue living there, Cettini said that she would search for a place in Venice or somewhere else to live in.[453] This decision to migrate was replicated in households across Venezia Giulia and Dalmatia, which were scarred by the dynamics of terror.

Upon his arrival at the AMG refugee camp in Udine on 6 September 1945, Fioravante Billotta declared he had left Venezia Giulia for Rome, adding:

> In normal conditions of time and place I could make a complete statement on the violence, difficulties and atrocities committed by the partisans of Tito, which would horrify each civil person. At present I am not able to do it. I am scared. Among those people who are coming and going from Yugoslavia there are many emissaries of Tito. There are some in this camp who observe everything is going on and go to report. ... If you knew how savage, ferocious and vindictive the Yugoslavs are, you could understand what prudence in me is. ... They go around into the houses bringing lists and forcing the citizens to sign that Istria, Venezia Giulia, Trieste and Dalmatia have to belong to Yugoslavia. In spite of coercions, threatening and impositions, they could obtain but few signatures. ... You must know that still today it happens that people disappear mysteriously or that citizens are persecuted, imprisoned and deported. They are so ferocious and inhuman that even the Croats think to abandon the Yugoslav territory; you may see indeed that in the next days many Croatian families and especially militaries will leave from there. ... In

---

[452] Ibid.
[453] Ibid.

178   *Luisa Morettin*

addition to the *foibe* they also use the trenches built by Germans to hide corpses.[454]

Terror and death played a central role in shaping the new society in Venezia Giulia. Marshal Tito and his closest collaborators had the objective to spread the Communist catechism as widely as possible, taking advantage of the fact that memories of fascist oppression prevailed among the population. The ideological impulses and fear-based strategies used by Communist partisans are documented in an interview given to *Panorama* by Milovan Djilas, a Lieutenant close to Tito and a leading figure in the Yugoslav Communist Party during and after the Second World War. Long after becoming a dissident, Djilas admitted that he and Edward Kardelj, another Yugoslav Communist leader, were given the task to spread terror and organise anti-Italian propaganda in order to show Allied forces that those territories in Venezia Giulia were Yugoslav. They were to encourage Italians to leave the country by any means possible.[455] In one of his books Djilas wrote: 'It seemed to me that ideology and reality were the same. The more total our ideological fervour was, the greater the success of our actions.'[456] However, the ideological fervour of some, meant death for others. The message to the Italians of Venezia Giulia was that their presence was untenable. There is further evidence that the flight of Italians was the main aim of pro-Tito's Communists, as the terrorist bomb attack at Vergarolla Beach in Pola, which killed 65 people in August 1946, clearly demonstrates.[457]

By creating depopulated areas, which were easier to control and to retain, the Slavs could then claim them knowing that appropriation of property would soon be legal. Stalin himself famously shared his philosophy with a visiting Yugoslav delegation early in 1945, suggesting that facts on the ground would be the new law. 'This war is not as in the

---

[454] Ibid.

[455] Alvaro Ranzoni, 'Se interviene anche l'Islam', (interview with Milovan Djilas), *Panorama*, 21 July 1991.

[456] Milovan Djilas, *Wartime*, op. cit., p. 342.

[457] Gaetano Dato, *Vergarolla 18 agosto 1946. Gli enigmi di una strage tra conflitto mondiale e guerra fredda*, (Gorizia: Libreria Editrice Goriziana, 2014).

A Journey into Darkness

past,' Stalin said. 'Whoever occupies a territory imposes on it his own social system. Everyone imposes his own system as far as his army has power to do so. It cannot be otherwise.'[458]

With their ability to alter the methods of social relations, terror, violence, and death marked a major turning point in the modern history in the area of the Italian north-eastern border. Raised levels of anxiety irreparably transformed urban society in such a way that voluntary exile became a reality for thousands. The ultimate purpose of such policy of terror was not only to cause migration from Venezia Giulia, as revealed by Luigi Nicolicchia's statement.

> Even today persecutions, strong hand intimidations and threatening continue towards those who do not sympathise for Yugoslavia. Towards the Italians, fascists or not, the Slavs show a ferocious hate. Inhabitants are very upset and scared, but not only the Italian ones. There are many Croats and Slavs who would abandon these dangerous regions. The guards of Tito are continuing to visit the houses and threaten citizens to sign a plebiscite in favour of Yugoslavia.[459]

The plebiscite mentioned by Nicolicchia was the direct result of Yugoslavia's plan to take Venezia Giulia. Arrests, physical brutality, executions and mass deportations of Italians in Venezia Giulia were meant to eliminate all their influence and their resistance in anticipation of a referendum, which given the circumstances, could hardly fail to be favourable to Yugoslavia.[460] Such methods were the last step in the Yugoslav policy of territorial expansion in the area that followed the fight against Axis occupation. Supporters of the annexation of Venezia Giulia did not attempt to conceal their policy of intimidating people into signing a petition. An Allied source reported how a barber named Bisiacchi, who lived and worked in Trieste, was stopped one day by two men on the street.

---

[458] David W. Ellwood, *Rebuilding Europe: Western Europe, America and Postwar Reconstruction*, (New York: Routledge, 1992), p. 5.

[459] WO 204/430.

[460] CAB 121/602, F/Italy/11, Vol.1, 12 May 1945.

180   *Luisa Morettin*

They invited him to step into a doorway telling him they had something to show him. 'They handed him a pen and a Yugoslav petition form. When the barber refused to sign, one of the two men pointed a pistol at him. After he signed, they told him to go away and say nothing about it if he wished to remain alive.'[461]

The municipality of Pinguente (Buzet) offers a most typical story. The President of the Regional Committee, Giuseppe Sestan, assembled the town committee on 25 August 1945, forcing people to sign the annexation petition in what was defined as the 'voluntary plebiscite in Pinguente.' When the committee itself called his attention to the unreasonableness of such an action, Sestan accused them of being 'An obstacle in the way of the popular movement' and declared that all those who would not accept the vote would be regarded as 'fascists and against the will of the people.' Nobody dared to argue, knowing how grave the accusation was in which he or she could fall.

The source further explains how people went from house to house asking for a signature, a process they accompanied with the words of: 'Who is not with us, is against us,' 'If you are thrown into a *foiba*, who is going to take you out?,' 'We came to see you so that you may not have any repentance and say you have not been warned.' Sestan also went to see those who had refused to sign and further warned them: 'I will not be responsible for what the people will do with you.'

It was not simply ordinary citizens who were made to feel continual unease, but members of the Town Committee were also targeted and told that they were 'at the head of the opposition and therefore susceptible of the most severe punishment.' Rumours began to circulate suggesting that somewhere in the countryside somebody had been taken from their home, another was to be arrested, and six people were missing from the town. The head of each family was called to the town's committee meeting and recounted with the stories of how the population of Pinguente were being threatened. They were then asked to sign in favour of Tito, in order to save

---

[461] WO 204/431.

A Journey into Darkness

181

any of them who were possible suspects. As of the evening of 29 August 1945, the signatures of almost everyone in the area were taken.[462]

Similar scenes took place throughout Venezia Giulia. The clandestine Istrian Exiles Group Committee informed the Allies that after 11 September 1945, in the municipalities of Pisino, Gerreto, Pedena (Pićan), Gallignana, Vines and Albona (Labin), those Italians who refused to sign the form of adherence to Yugoslavia were imprisoned. In Rovigno (Rovinj) workers had been forced to sign the Yugoslav petition under threat they would lose their jobs. Many of them, on returning home after signing, broke down and wept. In Buie (Buje) it was recorded how Tito's supporters, by arming themselves with machine guns, had managed to extract a few signatures in favour of Yugoslavia from the populace, particularly in the surrounding districts. However, the city itself was described as 'a rock of Italianity.'[463]

The Yugoslav policy of forced signatories to its petition resorted to intimidation and violence and to any other measures in order to reach the required number of signatures. Indeed, the Allied evidence reports the case where a reliable source, having reviewed the names on five completed petition forms, listed 53 names as fakes. The names had been checked with the *anagrafe* (civil registry) in Trieste, which confirmed that no persons corresponding to the names and addresses on the list were on the Trieste register; only two names corresponded to real citizens, Michele Scafridi and Gaspare Buccellato, both living in Trieste, but they stated their signatures had been forged as they had not signed the petition.[464]

Of crucial significance to understand the *foibe* killings, and demystify the myth of the *jacquerie* or justice against Fascists, are some key dates in the history of the construction of Communist Yugoslavia. They reveal the existence of an additional, more relevant element showing Tito's very precise strategy of territorial aggrandisement.

---

[462] Ibid.
[463] Ibid. Report by Istrian Exiles Group Committee, 11 September 1945.
[464] WO 204/431

In Pisino, on 13 September 1943, the People's Liberation Committee and in Otočac, on 20 September 1943, the *Zemaljsko antifašističko vijeće narodnog oslobođenja Hrvatske*, ZAVNOH (State Anti-fascist Council for the National Liberation of Croatia), proclaimed the annexation to Yugoslavia of all previous Italian areas: Istria, Fiume, Zara, and Dalmatia. A similar decree was issued on 16 September 1943 by the Slovenian Liberation Front with the territories included in the provinces of Trieste and Gorizia. On 29 and 30 November 1943, the councillors of the *Antifašističko veće narodnog oslobođenja Jugoslavije*, AVNOJ (Anti-fascist Council for the National Liberation of Yugoslavia), gathered in Jajce, Bosnia. They assumed greater legislative and executive functions and elected a central National Liberation Committee, which virtually became a provisional government, declaring Marshal Josip Broz Tito their Prime Minister. The Council also renewed the territorial claims to Venezia Giulia put forward in September 1942 by the Slovene and Croat assemblies. As a result, the annexation of Venezia Giulia was considered as a given[465] and each local Liberation Movement had the duty to defend those lands in every possible way, if necessary by force. Therefore, acquisition of Venezia Giulia and Trieste was one of the main aims of the AVNOJ Congress in November 1943.[466]

Later, Tito's speech in Ljubljana in May 1945 leaves no doubt as to his intention to lay claim to the whole territory, thus rectifying what he called, 'the injustices committed' after the Great War. He further declared: 'There is a new Yugoslavia today. ... This Yugoslavia is not an object for barter and bargaining.'[467] Marshal Tito's speech was directed not only to the Western Allies but to Soviet Russia, the support of which was only half-hearted, not only out of their fear of a conflict with Allied forces, but also in order not to jeopardise the election result of the Italian Communist Party (PCI) by antagonising Italian nationalists.

---

[465] Bogdan C. Novak, op. cit., pp. 91-3.

[466] Duncan Wilson, *Tito's Yugoslavia*, (Cambridge: Cambridge University Press, 1979), p. 34.

[467] Stephen Clissold, *Yugoslavia and the Soviet Union 1939-1973. A Documentary Survey*, (London: Oxford University Press, 1975), pp. 165-6.

A Journey into Darkness
183

The murderous campaigns in Venezia Giulia were driven by the aim of creating a Communist regime in the region, thanks to a close co-operation between the Italian Communist Party (PCI) and its Yugoslav counterpart. An Italian partisan named 'Vanni,' battle name of Giovanni Padoan, the political chief of IX Slovenian Corps, which was directly under the leadership of Marshal Tito, explained how the lists of 'enemies of the people' were written by Italian Communists, who since 1944, had recorded the names of those who were to be taken away as soon as it was convenient. For instance, when the town of Gorizia was liberated, Tito's troops had a detailed list of over 1,000 'enemies of the people' who were to be arrested. In order to speed up and facilitate arrests and deportations, local Communist collaborators would guide Tito's partisans to the homes or work premises of the victims. In the words of historian Marco Pirina: 'The PCI was not interested if the arrested were Fascists or anti-Fascists: the discriminating factor was whether people were against the revolutionary fight and the annexation of Italian territory to Yugoslavia.'[468]

The Communists had assumed power in Yugoslavia under trying circumstances, in the middle of a world conflict and in the middle of a civil war, which had set them against the Chetniks. They were beset by hostile Western powers who would aid them during the Second World War, but would oppose them at the first opportunity at the end of the conflict. Tito and his troops had revolutionary goals in mind and to achieve them they had to act swiftly and kill their enemies, when possible, or outwit them, when physical elimination was not an option.

The Communist violence towards real or perceived threats was not unique to Venezia Giulia and Dalmatia, but was a blueprint for the happenings in the rest of the Yugoslav territory from 1944 until 1953. During this period, thousands of individuals were killed; in Serbia alone, the figure reached 50,000.[469] Also in Austrian Carinthia murder became a central feature, when the violence in the village of Bleiburg became the

---

[468] Marco Pirina, *Il confine orientale negli atti del PCI e PCJ*, (Gorizia: Edizioni ANVGD, 2009), pp. 58, 130.
[469] Gorana, Ognjenović and Jasna Jozelic (eds.), op. cit., pp. 2-3.

184   *Luisa Morettin*

shorthand for all partisan massacres of collaborationists and anti-Communists around the Austrian border in 1945.[470] This was an event, which would continue to cast a shadow over contemporary Croatian politics, and to a lesser extent Slovenian and Austrian politics to this day. As in Venezia Giulia and Dalmatia, Tito advanced territorial aspirations toward the Austrian Carinthia.

When in 1945 the defeat of the Axis forces was a certainty, it became clear that the race for Trieste was mandatory if Yugoslavia was to recover the lands lost to Italy at the end of the First World War, and if partisans wanted to impose a Communist rule in Yugoslavia. To achieve this required the undertaking of two tasks: the thrust toward the West and the elimination not just of Fascists, but also of all 'enemies of the people.' When, in the third week of May 1945, Stalin ordered Tito to withdraw his troops from Trieste and Carinthia in order to avoid a clash with the Anglo-Americans, the Yugoslav leader acquiesced; he had to reduce his claims in Venezia Giulia and abandon those in Austrian Carinthia. Still, this was too late for the victims of his revolutionary and territorial ambitions.

As a result of the arrangement between Tito and General William Morgan the so-called Morgan Line was drawn. It was a temporary boundary that divided Venezia Giulia into two zones, 'Zone A' under Allied military administration and 'Zone B' under the administration of Yugoslavia. On 11-12 June, the Yugoslavs left Trieste and were replaced by Allied troops. In spite of that, a trickling of kidnappings from Zone A to Zone B would continue well into 1946 and 1947.

Finding such political violence disturbing, the elderly Conservative Christian Democrat leader Alcide De Gasperi, later confided to Luigi Sturzo, founder of the *Partito Popolare Italiano* (Italian People's Party), that 'the unity of Communists, their courage, their organisation, their means, make them a block that has the same power as old-school fascism.'[471]

---

[470] Jozo Tomasevich, op. cit., pp. 763-4.
[471] Letter of Alcide De Gasperi, April 1946, in De Gasperi, Vol II, p. 44. Quoted in Keith Lowe, *Savage Continent. Europe in the Aftermath of World War II*, (London: Viking, 2012), p. 279.

Source: Public domain.

Figure 1. The Narodni Dom (National Hall) of the Slavs in Trieste burnt down by Fascists on 13 July 1920.

Source: Wikimedia.

Figure 2. The Italian concentration camp at Gonars, near Udine. It was the first proper civilian camp, especially used for Slovenian political prisoners.

Source: Public domain.

Figure 3. The Italian concentration camp on the island of Arbe.

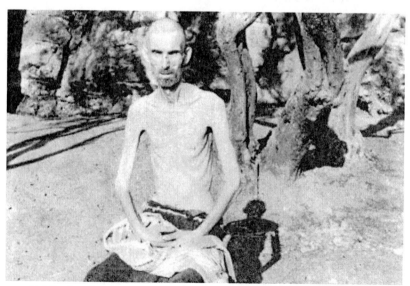

Source: Public domain.

Figure 4. A prisoner at the Italian concentration camp on the island of Arbe.

Source: Wikimedia.

Figure 5. Bodies of prisoners at Arbe.

Source: Archivio-Museo Storico di Fiume, Rome.

Figure 6. Entrance to the *foiba* Kevina Jama, in Croatia.

Source: Archivio-Museo Storico di Fiume, Rome.

Figure 7. Entrance to the *foiba* Plutone, near Trieste, Italy.

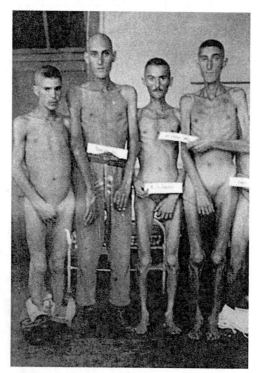

Source: Public Record Office, London.

Figure 8. Survivors from a Yugoslav concentration camp.

A Journey into Darkness

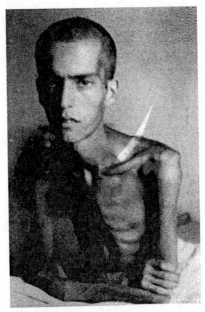

Source: Public Record Office, London.

Figure 9. A survivor from a Yugoslav concentration camp.

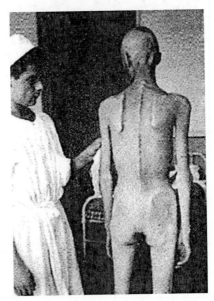

Source: Public Record Office, London.

Figure 10. A living skeleton.

Source: Archivio-Museo Storico di Fiume, Rome.

Figure 11. An Italian soldier's helmet found on a heap of human bones, stones and rubble at the bottom of the *foiba* Kevina Jama, Croatia.

Source: Archivio-Museo Storico di Fiume, Rome.

Figure 12. In Gropada, near Trieste, a firefighter discovers bodies at the bottom of the 146 feet deep local *foiba*.

A Journey into Darkness

Source: Archivio-Museo Storico di Fiume, Rome.

Figure 13. Victims exhumed from a *foiba* in 1943.

Chapter 5

THE BOUNDARY ISSUE

> *This war is not as in the past;*
> *whoever occupies the territory*
> *also imposes on it his own social system.*
> *Everyone imposes his own system*
> *as far as his army has power to do so.*

> Milovan Djilas
> *Conversations with Stalin*

BEHIND CLOSED DOORS

The tactics of spreading fear among the inhabitants of Venezia Giulia was part of Tito's project to create depopulated areas and win the plebiscite. Yet, the intention to claim Venezia Giulia had been there well before Tito's plans, as the Yugoslav government had pursued sovereignty over the Italian region as early as January 1941, when the Yugoslav Ambassador to Moscow, Milan Gavrilovič, had approached his British counterpart, Sir Stafford Cripps. Gavrilovič suggested that his compatriots, particularly

194 *Luisa Morettin*

pro-German Croats, might be strongly influenced to join the war effort on the side of London if the British Government would convey to Prince Regent Paul (at the time still sticking to his country's neutrality), that Britain would not make a separate peace treaty with Italy at Yugoslavia's expense. This was a latent fear in Belgrade, which wanted Britain to recognise the claims Yugoslavia had to Istria as far as Gorizia and to the Italian islands off the Yugoslav coast.[472]

At a time when, after the fall of France in June 1940 and before America's entry into the war in December 1941, Britain was left alone to face the Axis powers, Gavrilovič's proposal unsurprisingly elicited interest amongst British officials. However, diplomats at the Foreign Office took a cautious stance, as Sir Philip Nichols stated that the British government would not 'embark upon any policy of territorial bribery in advance of events.'[473] Yet, it was not just a matter of bribery. The British government had resolutely decided against any further treaties such as the 1915 Treaty of London, which had caused them great embarrassment at the Paris Peace Conference as it had been made secretly between the parties involved.[474]

Nevertheless, in order to be 'armed at all times,' Nichols found it useful to know the case that the Yugoslavs were able to produce in support of frontier rectifications. With this in mind, Professor Arnold Toynbee, the head of the FRPS, the Foreign Research and Press Section of Chatham House at Balliol College, was instructed by the Foreign Office to prepare a report into the merits of a possible Italo-Yugoslav border revision.[475] Scrutiny of the document gives insight into the steps taken by British diplomats and politicians concerning the complex issue surrounding the Italo-Yugoslav frontier, and indirectly, the crimes against Italians.

The detailed FRPS memorandum, submitted on 5 February 1941, reported that, based on the principle of nationality, the Yugoslav government was able to present claims to some of the Italian lands, as the division of territory, which had been carried out by the Treaties of Rapallo

---

[472] FO 371/30205/R 589/73/92, 24 January 1941.
[473] Ibid., 29 January 1941.
[474] Ibid., 26 January 1941.
[475] Ibid., 29 January 1941.

and Rome, had 'violated the principle of nationality to the disadvantage of Yugoslavia.' These two former treaties confirmed Italy's possession of lands, which in 1910, were inhabited by approximately 318,000 Italians and 488,000 Yugoslavs. Yugoslavia received territories populated by approximately 3,000 Italians and 268,000 Yugoslavs. An exception to this was seen in the predominantly Italian western coast of Istria, the island of Lussino, Fiume, Zara, Gorizia, Gradisca, Monfalcone and Trieste, where 'the business ... was mainly in Italian and German hands'. As to nationality numbers, the Austro-Hungarian census figures of 1910 were considered approximately accurate. Robert Laffan, the writer of the Foreign Office report, felt the Italian census of 1921 'accentuated the Italian character of the districts given as Italian in 1910.'

The ethnic claim, according to the FRPS researchers, was enhanced by the harsh measures Italy had taken since World War I to denationalise the Yugoslavs living within Italian territory. Specific attention was devoted to the suppression of civil liberties and the document identified in detail three stages of the treatment of the Yugoslav minority in Venezia Giulia: a) 1918-1923 b) 1923-1929 c) 1929 – [*blank in the original*].

a) The Italian government accorded to its Yugoslavs most of the rights attributed elsewhere to minorities by treaty; but failed to protect them from mob violence. Of 531 Yugoslav primary schools, 149 were suppressed. Of seven Yugoslav secondary schools, four were suppressed. Yugoslavs enjoyed the use of their own language in dealing with legal tribunals and their economic and cultural organisations survived. Five Slovene and two Croat deputies were elected to Parliament in 1921, despite terrorization in Istria, which elicited protests from the Italian Bishop of Trieste and Pope Benedict XV. On the other hand many Yugoslav priests were expelled from the country and several communities of religious were suppressed; and the Yugoslav clergy and publishing offices were the special object of unofficial terrorisation.

b) Italian policy changed after 1922. All Slav place names gave way to Italian in official publications, maps, timetables, postcards, etc. Decrees of 1926 and 1927 ordered the Italianisation of family names officially held to be the corruption of Italian originals. In 192[illegible] ... Slav Christian names were forbidden. Between 1923 and 1930 all Yugoslav primary and secondary schools were suppressed. In 1925 Yugoslavs were deprived of the use of their language in legal procedure. With the nomination of Italian officials as mayors, even village affairs had to be conducted in Italian. Of 300 Yugoslav cultural and welfare associations all were suppressed in 1927-8. Under the Fascist regime there have been no Yugoslav deputies in Parliament. Thus the Yugoslavs were left with no expression of their nationality, except in matters of religion thanks to the stubborn support which they received from Mgr. Sedej, the Slovene Archbishop of Gorizia, and of Mgr. Fogar, the Italian Bishop of Trieste.

c) By the Concordat of 1929 the Holy See sacrificed the Yugoslavs of Italy. Henceforth every parish priest had to be an Italian subject and to speak Italian. The catechism was to be taught in Italian. The Slavonic liturgy (which had survived among the Croats) was suppressed. Neither the Slovene nor the Croat language could be used in church. The last Yugoslav religious house, that of the Lasarists near Trieste, was suppressed in 1935.

By stressing how successful the Italian authorities had been in suppressing the national sentiments and character of the Yugoslavs in Venezia Giulia, the FRPS report felt that 'the injuries done to Yugoslavs call for remedy.' Another substantial section of the memorandum was dedicated to the reasons why Italy had insisted on 'a settlement so ethnically unjust to the Yugoslavs.' It listed a few elements, amongst them, the nationalist 'ill-informed tradition, widespread in Italy, that Gorizia-Gradisca, Istria and Fiume (not to mention Dalmatia) were historically and ethnically Italian,' and the economic desire to obtain the quicksilver mines of Idria (Idrija), the second richest in the world.

Although it seemed simple to revise the frontier on ethnic lines, it did in fact present particular problems. First, a strategic issue existed as it would bring Yugoslavia dangerously near to Trieste and 'render the position of the Italian part of Istria precarious in the event of an Italo-Yugoslav war.' Second, the valley of the upper Isonzo in 1921 was predominately Slovene and economically centred on Gorizia which was a city densely populated by Italians. Gorizia might, on economic grounds, be attributed to Yugoslavia; in the case of Fiume, if the border revisions were

The Boundary Issue

carried out, the city would be isolated within Yugoslav territory. This same concept would be relevant for the remote Italian enclave of Zara, which would find itself without railway connections or any trade with its hinterlands. In this case, both cities could be allocated to Yugoslavia. Third, of the islands, the only one with an Italian majority in 1910 was Lussino; but life on the island was closely bound with that of the island of Cherso, which was physically joined by a bridge. According to the FRPS memorandum, Lussino might also be attributed to the sovereignty of Belgrade.[476]

The memorandum was unquestionably in favour of a revision of the existing Italo-Yugoslav frontier in Istria, opinion further supported by two other FRPS reports, which outlined in greater detail the 1910 statistics for the population of the disputed territories[477] and included an ethnological overview of Venezia Giulia in the period after 1918.[478] On that basis, Foreign Office diplomats agreed that if they were 'to hold out this bait [i.e., Venezia Giulia] to the Yugoslavs,' they had first to obtain Cabinet approval.[479]

A Cabinet meeting was duly called for the following day and, on 27 February 1941, the Cabinet approved a provisional authority to be sent to Anthony Eden, the Secretary of State, suggesting to Prince Paul the possibility of the revision of the Italo-Yugoslav border in Istria. The general conviction of British politicians, the Foreign Office and War Office, was that in doing so the matter was extremely vague as Britain was not embarking upon territorial revision or promising anything, but simply 'studying with sympathy the case for revision.'[480] The permanent Under-Secretary for Foreign Affairs, Alexander Cadogan, wrote to Winston Churchill the following day: 'I suggest that at this stage it is perhaps hardly necessary to take the Americans into our confidence as on this telegram Mr

---

[476] FO 371/30240/R 960/960/92, 5 February 1941.
[477] FO 371/30240/R 1736/960/92, 26 February 1941.
[478] FO 371/30240/R 2314/960/92, 3 March 1941.
[479] FO 371/30240/R 960/960/92, 26 February 1941.
[480] FO 371/30240/R 1949/1949/G, 2 March 1941.

Eden will not commit us to anything definite.'[481] Indeed the Foreign Office felt that even if 'His Majesty's Government have hitherto adopted the general rule that during the war they cannot discuss any territorial changes, ... the decision of the Yugoslav government at the present juncture is of such importance that it would be worthwhile to disregard this rule on this occasion if by so doing we could induce Yugoslavia to intervene forcibly on behalf of Greece,'[482] which had been invaded by Italy in October 1940. The report, which had initially been carried out as a preliminary examination for information purposes, eventually sealed the boundary line between Italy and Yugoslavia.

Despite the favourable attitude, the ambiguity which the British authorities displayed generated anxiety amongst their Yugoslav counterparts. Momčilo Ninčić, the Royal Yugoslav Minister for Foreign Affairs in exile, wrote a memorandum to the Foreign Office to advocate the case for Yugoslavia, setting forth his views regarding frontiers and international relations in post war Europe after an Allied victory.[483] The Prime Minister's Office also received an annexation request of Venezia Giulia from Medvscek, the President of the Yugoslav Refugees Committee in Buenos Aires.[484] Another request was presented by Dr Chok, the leader of the Slovenes and Croats under Italian rule,[485] to George William Rendel, the British Minister to Yugoslavia. Their persistence was such that Rendel commented: 'The Slovenes ... are strongly irredentist and keep on producing documents about their claims against Italy.'[486]

In June and July 1942, King Peter visited Canada and the United States in order to generate awareness and support for the Yugoslavs, but he obtained no promises that would pre-judge the peace negotiations at the end of the conflict or depart from the principles of the Atlantic Charter.

---

[481] FO 371/30205/R 1770/73/92, 28 February 1941.
[482] FO 371/30240/R 1949/960/92, Memorandum by the Foreign Office, 1 March 1941.
[483] FO 371/33446/R 35/35, 27 December 1941.
[484] FO 371/30240/R 10769/960/92, 21 December 1941.
[485] FO 371/33446/R 918/35/92, 5 February 1942.
[486] FO 371/33446/R 1985/35/92, 23 March 1942.

The Boundary Issue

199

The British government soon became aware of the danger of making any assurances, however vague they were, when Dušan Simović, the Prime Minister of the government in exile made his first radio broadcast to Yugoslavia on 27 June 1941, one week after arriving in Britain. He stated that 'with the victory of the Great Democracies, all those regions inhabited by the Yugoslavs will be united with the Fatherland: Istria, Trieste, Gorizia, Zara, and all other Yugoslav ethnic territories.' He then detailed how the British and Americans had made assurances to the territorial aggrandisement, causing a diplomatic incident. The broadcast immediately generated protests from Italians in America and in particular from Count Carlo Sforza, the active leader of Italian antifascism in exile and later Foreign Minister of Italy, who wrote to the *New York Times* and to Lord Edward Halifax, the British Ambassador to the United States. The latter distanced the London government from what were publicly labelled as 'the personal views of the Yugoslav minister,' but behind closed doors the Foreign Office had to reassure the Yugoslavs 'in the vaguest possible terms,' making sure that this time they needed to keep the assurances to themselves.[487]

Eventually, the British assurances to consider border revisions was not to be enough to convince the Prince Regent Paul to either enter the war allied with Britain or to keep Yugoslav neutrality. On the contrary, on 25 March 1941, the Belgrade Government signed the Axis Tripartite Pact, but two days later Yugoslav military figures forcibly removed Prince Regent Paul, declaring Prince Peter II of age and King of Yugoslavia. Hitler's response to this was swift and brutal: on 6 April 1941, the Luftwaffe launched Operation *Bestrafung*, the bombing of Belgrade and many Yugoslav airfields, which contributed to the Yugoslav surrender ten days later.

The Axis attack certainly foiled the Anglo-Yugoslav talks of frontier revisions, but did not stop them entirely. However much the British

---

[487] Stevan K. Pavlowitch, 'Momčilo Ninčić and the European Policy of the Yugoslav Government in Exile, 1941-1943,' II, *The Slavonic and East European Review*, Vol. 62, No. 4 (Oct. 1984), pp. 531-3.

200 *Luisa Morettin*

Government wanted to forget the issue, on 16 December 1941, whilst discussing the terms and conditions of the Anglo-Soviet Treaty – which would become effective on 26 May 1942, Stalin expressed to Anthony Eden his desire to discuss his ideas of the future map of Europe in a secret protocol, annexed to the proposed political treaty. He submitted thirteen points for the Foreign Office to consider and they were all frontier-related amendments. Amongst them was Stalin's plan for Yugoslavia, which amounted to an extension of the Yugoslav frontiers at the expense of Italy 'so far as the islands were concerned and certain coastal towns'[488] with no consideration for the economic, administrative and strategic aspects that the suggested changes would involve.

The Foreign Office's previous view that all questions of territorial frontiers must be left to the decision of the Peace Conference was now based on a further aspect, which had emerged during the conflict: the internal fragmentation of Yugoslavia due to the divisive parochialism endemic in the region. Hence the British decision:

> We should not pledge ourselves to restore pre-war Yugoslavia, since the centrifugal forces in Yugoslavia may be so strong as to make it impossible to reconstruct a unitary Yugoslav State. It is possible that the Yugoslav problem will have to be solved by splitting up Yugoslavia into Serb, Croat and Slovene States, which would be bound together within [a] Balkan Confederation but which internally would be more or less autonomous, though possibly owing allegiance to the same King.[489]

What was really new to Britain was that Yugoslavia's border claims were now backed by the Soviet Union, a great land power seeking to advance its empire in the Balkan no-man's land and get free access to the Mediterranean, as Stalin made clear during a visit to Berlin in 1940. Suspicions regarding the close relationship between the two Communist leaders, and the dangers associated with any solution of the problem of

---

[488] FO 371/32880/N 2182/5/98, 23 April 1942.
[489] Ibid.

The Boundary Issue

201

Venezia Giulia, would be confirmed two years later. Despite Tito's proclaims of a future agreement with the Yugoslav monarchic government in exile, the Anglo-Americans would discover that on 18 September 1944 Tito had secretly abandoned the British protected hideout in Lissa and headed to Moscow to re-establish contact with Stalin. It seemed that the Grand Alliance was turning to a pretence for all involved.

OLD PROMISES AS NEW COMMITMENTS

Since the invasion of Yugoslavia a brutal local resistance, fanned by the subversive activities of the British Special Operations Executive (SOE), confronted the Italian occupying forces. British official policy had supported the Chetniks until June 1943, when the SOE started supporting also Tito's troops. The royalists of Mihailović were suspected of collusion with the enemy in order to fight the communist partisans who, in the eyes of the SOE Cairo, were fighting the Germans more effectively than the Chetniks.[490] This change was the result of British requirements from the Yugoslav resistance movements, as devised by the Casablanca Conference, which planned an attack on Sicily and the preparation of the final national uprisings to coincide with the arrival of the Allied armies.

In March 1943, the Allies had not decided whether to treat Italy with reasonable leniency in the hope she would surrender and cooperate with the Anglo-Americans in the new European order. A Foreign Office brief, given to the Secretary of State, expressed that regardless of the long-term policy decided, the only certainty was that the German and Italian territories gained from dividing Yugoslavia were to be unrecognised by the British government.

In some cases various considerations made the re-establishment of the Italian control 'virtually impossible.' As to Venezia Giulia, the Foreign

---

[490] David Stafford, *Britain and European Resistance, 1940-1945. A Survey of the Special Operations Executive, with Documents*, (London: Macmillan, 1980), pp. 119-21. Winston Churchill, *The Second World War. Assault from the Air*, Vol. 10, op. cit., pp. 120-5.

Office reminded the British government that it had assumed definite commitments, which it should honour. Although the Foreign Office did not attempt to determine the exact areas which it might be desirable to remove from Italian sovereignty nor had the future of Trieste been decided upon, it appeared 'probable that, in addition to the revision of the mainland frontier, the Slav islands in the Adriatic and Zara should be ceded by Italy.'[491]

Yugoslavia periodically established contact with British senior diplomats and, on 4 June 1943, Yugoslav Prime Minister Slobodan Jovanović, called on Sir Alexander Cadogan, the Permanent Under-Secretary for Foreign Affairs, to get reassurances regarding Allied intentions with regard to the Italo-Yugoslav border. In the course of the conversation, Jovanović mentioned that with Italy as a great power, there was a considerable risk that she could play a not always benevolent part in the Balkans. On the ethnographic questions raised by Jovanović about Italian areas inhabited by alien populations, Cadogan replied by reporting the decision of the Casablanca Conference on the subject of unconditional surrender, reassuring the Yugoslav Prime Minister that the London government had no contact with any section or party in Italy itself.[492]

On 20 August 1943, soon after the fall of Mussolini and shortly before the Italian Armistice, the Foreign Office learnt from the British Embassy in Washington that President Franklin D. Roosevelt had intervened in the Italo-Yugoslav border question. He was 'strongly of the opinion that Trieste, Fiume, and Pola should constitute three outlets for countries in the interior, and be free ports for all countries.' The President also suggested that towns should have a territory of ten miles long and fifteen miles wide and should include an international administration under an Italian, a Yugoslav and perhaps an American and a British representative.[493] An internal draft illustrated the Foreign Office's criticism of the American proposal. The comment of the British diplomat Sir Orme Sargent was

---

[491] FO 371/37281/R 2132/2132/22, 8 March 1943.
[492] FO 371/37281/R 4958/2132/22, 4 June 1943.
[493] FO 371/37276/R 8489/362/22, 20 August 1943.

ironic: 'Are we going to stud Europe with Danzigs? [...] It was one of the worst arrangements of the Treaty of Versailles. I suggest that it might be a good idea if the Library were to produce a memorandum on Danzig showing that the idea of free cities may be a good one in transatlantic theory, but a damn bad one in European practice.'[494] Even sharper was the view of P. Rose, diplomat at the Foreign Office: 'Like all similar papers [by the American President], this one suffers badly from ignorance of the future international background.' It was seemingly impossible to assess the workability of an international solution without having any idea of whether there was going to be a revised League of Nations after the war, what powers it would possess and what forces it would have at its disposal. Roosevelt's plan to fabricate a new Danzig was unanimously rejected by British diplomats, who believed international commissions only incited international rivalry and deception. If there was to be a revitalised League of Nations, its authority would be weakened by its time taken up in settling petty squabbles 'such as the number of post boxes to which the Polish postal administration were entitled in Danzig.'[495] However, there was a difference between the arrangements for Danzig and Roosevelt's plans for the Adriatic ports. Whereas Danzig was given self-government as a city-state, the American President was proposing each of the three ports should be governed by an international commission, which implied that the United States would accept permanent responsibility for maintaining the post-war settlement in at least one area of Eastern Europe. A possible option, Arnold Toynbee suggested, was that the ports should be in the territory and under the sovereignty of a larger state, and the necessary outlet for the countries of the interior should be secured by giving them free port facilities, such as those Yugoslavia enjoyed at Salonica under Greek sovereignty there. 'The alternative,' he argued, 'had the advantages of avoiding the geographical and administrative awkwardness of small enclaves, but the political drawback of creating an irredenta.'[496] Given that limitation, the

---

[494] Ibid.
[495] Ibid., 4 October 1943.
[496] Ibid., 26 August 1943.

204 *Luisa Morettin*

conclusions of the Foreign Office memorandum was for Fiume to go to Yugoslavia, whereas Trieste and Pola were to remain part of Italy.

On 4 September 1943, the FRSP department, examining the future of Trieste, Pola and Fiume in detail from economic, ethnic and strategic perspectives produced another lengthy memorandum. As historian John Whittam has argued, all the discussions and memoranda, highlighting the impossibility to reconcile conflicting claims to the capital city of Venezia Giulia, are likely to have been at the origin of the creation of a Free Territory of Trieste in 1947.[497]

In the meantime Britain, impressed with the strength of partisan troops, withdrew official support from Mihailović and conferred it to Tito. Since the Italian Armistice, thanks to Tito's dynamic policies, good organisation and strict discipline; partisan forces were now the leading resistance movement in Yugoslavia. Consequently, they obtained maximum aid from the Allies, who had considered Yugoslav issues and the procedure for the liberation of Venezia Giulia at the Teheran Conference (November – December 1943). At the strategy conference, the Anglo-Americans decided the technicalities for Operation Overlord, the codename for the Battle of Normandy, in conjunction with a landing in southern France. President Roosevelt suggested 'a right-handed movement from the north of Italy, using the Istrian peninsula and the Ljubljana Gap, towards Vienna.'[498] The suggestion, enthusiastically backed by Churchill, would expedite securing Trieste as the essential supply point for future occupation zones in Austria.

On 5 June 1944 Rome was in Allied hands and the following day the D-Day landings began. With Africa cleared, German gains in Russia reversed, the Polish borders reached and Italy fighting on the Allied side, Hitler was doomed. There was a general sense of relief that all efforts during the previous four years were now paying off and the tide was turning in the favour of the Allied forces. Despite this, the road ahead was still full of difficulties, as during the following months Tito would refuse to

---

[497] J. R. Whittam, 'Drawing the Line: Britain and the Emergence of the Trieste Question. January 1941 – May 1945,' *The English Historical Review*, Vol. 106, No 419, (April 1991), pp. 346-70.

[498] Winston Churchill, *The Second World War. Assault from the Air*, Vol. 10, p. 18.

The Boundary Issue

co-operate with King Peter, and the unavoidable clash between Churchill's short-term military expediency and long-term political interest would emerge.

In early May 1944, Churchill had written to Eden about 'the brute issues between us and the Soviet government, which are developing in Italy, in Rumania, in Bulgaria, in Yugoslavia and above all in Greece. Are we going to acquiesce in the Communisation of the Balkans and perhaps of Italy?'[499] The advance of the Soviet Army into Eastern and Central Europe during the summer of 1944 made it necessary for the Anglo-Americans to reach a political agreement with the Soviet Union and to start talks with Tito. At stake was Europe's post-war configuration, and Churchill decided to go to Italy, where – as he would later recall – 'many questions could be more easily settled on the spot than by correspondence.'[500]

On 12 and 13 August 1944, Churchill met with Marshal Tito to discuss the Balkan strategy and a possible Allied landing on the Istrian peninsula, in order to weaken German defences and provide supplies by sea. Churchill explained that the Allies planned to establish an Allied Military Government (AMG) to secure lines of communication through Ljubljana-Maribor-Graz. With this in mind, Tito agreed that Yugoslav forces would join the Allies. From this, it was evident the Yugoslav leader wanted to be associated with the future of Venezia Giulia.

The meeting also covered the much-anticipated territorial issue. 'The status of Istria,' Churchill told Tito, 'which still remained Italian, could not be prejudged ... The United States government was against territorial changes in time of war, and we ought not to discourage the Italians more than could be helped because they were now making a useful contribution to the war.'[501] Tito understood the Allied plan was to strengthen General Alexander's influence in the Mediterranean theatre as much as possible and agreed to assist allied troops on their way to Austria through Venezia Giulia. He could not, however, accept an Italian civil administration, as his

---

[499] FO 371/43636 P.M.'s Personal Minutes M. 487/4 and 498/4, 4 May 1944.
[500] Winston Churchill, *The Second World War. The Tide of Victory*, Vol. 11, p. 78.
[501] Ibid., p. 81.

206 *Luisa Morettin*

National Liberation Movement already controlled many of those areas.[502] Churchill was disappointed with the outcome of the meeting and feared after the war Tito might use the weapons provided by the Allies to impose a Communist rule in Yugoslavia.[503]

Churchill later met Generals Henry Wilson and Harold Alexander, and Admiral Andrew Cunningham in order to assess the situation on the Italian front, where General Alexander was to continue the offensive until winter conditions would bring large scale operations to a standstill.

In those August days, Admiral Ellery W. Stone, the Acting Chief Commissioner of the Allied Control Commission, received a confidential telegram from Marquis Giovanni Visconti Venosta, the Italian Undersecretary for Foreign Affairs. Although Tito had claimed his long-term plan for Yugoslavia was the establishment of a democratic federation, not communist rule,[504] Italy feared a repetition of the violent crimes carried out by partisans against Italians in 1943. Venosta wrote: 'Conflicts may break out between armed bands [of partisans] and peaceful citizens, causing bloodshed in the towns and villages of a region that already has been sorely tried,'[505] asking the Allied forces to take 'whatever measures may be deemed suitable ... in useful time.' Stone reassured Venosta,[506] but realistically, there was not much the Allies could do, apart from insist that until a peace treaty was drawn up, it was the duty of the AMG to function in all territories under Italian sovereignty at the time of the outbreak of war.[507] There were alternative courses, which could be followed, including for the Anglo-Americans to accept, as a provisional arrangement, the Yugoslav military government over those Italian territories, which Tito's troops already occupied. Another option was to negotiate with Tito of some arbitrary boundary line accepted for reasons of practical convenience, but without any commitment regarding the future frontier.

---

[502] Ibid., p. 82.

[503] Walter R. Roberts, *Tito, Mihailović and the Allies, 1941-1945*, (New Brunswick: Rutgers University Press, 1973), p. 247.

[504] WO 204/9796.

[505] Ibid., 15 August 1944.

[506] Ibid., 19 August 1944.

[507] Ibid., 28 July 1944.

The Boundary Issue

However, the Supreme Allied Command supported the policies of the Italian government led by Ivanoe Bonomi, who pledged to maintain national unity until the liberation of Italy was complete. In case any part of Venezia Giulia was occupied by Tito's forces, before the arrival of the Allied Armies in Italy (AAI), control for the purpose of military administration and government should be passed to AAI on the arrival of Allied troops.[508]

Tito's plans were different, however, and became transparent by the autumn of 1944. After the joint Partisan-Red Army Belgrade offensive (September-November 1944), which ended the German occupation of Serbia, Tito's troops gradually drove the Axis forces north-westwards, through Serbia and Croatia, gaining significant ground. Their plan was to reach Venezia Giulia in the interval between the withdrawal of German forces and the arrival of the Allies, building up an administration and claiming the area for Yugoslavia.[509]As they were determined not to renounce to it, the Anglo-Americans would have to accept the situation as a *fait accompli*.

STRATEGIC DIVERGENCES

Two main factors were delaying the AAI in their Italian Campaign, a campaign which could see a conquest of northern Italy, or at least a landing in Istria, which could have opened the way to Vienna, taken Venezia Giulia away from Tito's control and avoided the bloodshed of the *foibe* crimes. The first factor was the question of Allied capability to break through Marshal Albert Kesselring's Gothic Line, the major line of German defence; and the second, the dependence on American support to

---

[508] Ibid., 26 October 1944.
[509] C. R. S. Harris, *Allied Military Administration of Italy, 1943-1945*, (London: HMSO, 1957), pp. 271-2.

enable an amphibious assault to occur along the Istrian Peninsula, either as a direct assault or as an advance from the Dalmatian coast.[510]

In February 1945, at the Crimea Conference, in a note handed to Edward Stettinius and Vyacheslav Molotov, respectively the American and Soviet Foreign Minister, Anthony Eden expressed the urgent need for a clear declaration of policy regarding Venezia Giulia. He called the region 'a potential powder magazine' and tried to draw his colleagues' attention to the fact that as the war drew to a close, it was likely there would be clashes between Yugoslavs and Italians. The Allies, Eden wrote, 'must prevent these outbursts to the best of our ability. … Even if under extreme pressure he [Tito] was forced to accept Allied (British) Military Government, his partisans would remain in arms throughout the district, and it would be a miracle if sooner or later they did not obstruct our Military administration.'[511] To that end, Eden wanted the Big Three to agree to a provisional line of demarcation between the area to be controlled by Tito, and the area over which Anglo-Americans would establish their Allied Military Government, a unanimous decision that willingly or not, the partisan forces would have to accept and respect. The Foreign Office and War Office's concerns were because Tito had made it clear that he would not agree to the proposal of establishing an AMG in Venezia Giulia, as in other parts of liberated Italy. His secret visit to Stalin in September 1944 did not portend cooperation either.

However, at Yalta no occasion arose to discuss the subject and neither Stettinius nor Molotov replied to Eden's note. That would carry serious consequences. Eden discussed the question further with Harold Macmillan, the minister resident at the Allied headquarters in the Mediterranean, and Field Marshal Harold Alexander. He proposed that Alexander should try, during his forthcoming visit to Belgrade, to reiterate to Tito what had already been discussed with him in the summer of 1944, therefore securing the desired facilities: control of the railway from Trieste to the Austrian

---

[510] PREM 3/275/3, 8 October 1944.
[511] CAB 87/69, APW (45) 31, Annex A, 12 March 1945.

frontier and the territory up to that line.[512] The Allied and Post-War Committee, which met on 15 March 1945, agreed this would be a beneficial move.

However, later that day, Washington telegraphed London giving strict instructions: the whole of Venezia Giulia, including Zara and the Adriatic islands, should be occupied and governed by British troops, without Yugoslav intervention, which could not be approved 'since Yugoslavia is party to the dispute and its participation in AMG in full partnership would doubtless serve to prejudge the final disposition of this territory.'[513] The United States also added they could not furnish the British with additional military personnel to administer AMG or civil affairs in Venezia Giulia.

The Allied administration of Zara and the islands could be 'no more than a polite fiction,' according to the Foreign Office, as the Yugoslavs were already in possession of those areas and were governing them. Despite that, British diplomats believed that keeping up the pretence concerning the *de jure,* as opposed to the *de facto* administration, may be a negotiation strategy, which could be used with Tito. At this stage, aware of the likelihood they could lose the race for Trieste, the Anglo-Americans understood they had to make the best deal open to them.

At the beginning of May 1945 the military and political situation was progressing quickly and every hour brought a change of news. Hitler and Mussolini were reported dead. On 2 May Berlin fell to the Russians. In a fierce race with the 8th Army, Tito's troops penetrated the pre-war Yugoslav frontier into southern Austria and Venezia Giulia. They occupied most of Istria and entered Trieste on Tuesday 1 May 1945, one day before the New Zealand 2nd Division under 13 Corps arrived, taking the surrender of the German garrison. On 3 May, Fiume fell to the Yugoslavs. The race for Trieste continued as New Zealand troops held the dock areas, whilst Tito's partisans occupied the city centre.

These events resulted in an overlap of the operational areas of SACMED, the Supreme Allied Command Mediterranean, and Tito's

---

[512] FO 371/50788/U 1081/51/70, 16 February 1945.
[513] FO 371/50788/U 1855/G, 15 March 1945.

210   *Luisa Morettin*

armies. Tito's resolve to keep Venezia Giulia was hardening in the light of his units' successes, which caused a frenzied exchange of telegrams amongst all the parties involved, searching for some solution to the seemingly insoluble problem of Venezia Giulia.

The Americans and British discussed whether it was suitable to involve the Soviet government on the immediate operational phase and in the policy for Allied administration of the whole province. The British were reluctant to explore the American proposal to contact Moscow, so it would not prevent Field Marshal Alexander from arriving at any direct arrangements with Tito.[514] The Foreign Office cabled Washington stating that whilst it would have been of the greatest assistance if the Soviet government could be prevailed upon to support the Anglo-Americans in ordering Tito to evacuate the province, there was no likelihood whatsoever of their doing so. British diplomats thought 'Tito would not have acted as he has or taken the truculent line shown ... unless he was sure of Stalin's support.'[515]

However, the Chiefs of Staff Committee expressed the view that provided they obtained free and unrestricted use of the ports of Trieste and Pola and the railway line Trieste-Tarvisio, as promised by Tito, they could not say that the Marshal's proposals did not meet the Anglo-American military requirements.[516]

The British Ambassador to Italy, Sir Noel Charles, was very much perturbed about the situation in Trieste, fearing it would be the downfall for the Italian government, as the leader of the Italian Communists Palmiro Togliatti had expressed his support for Tito's territorial claims. Macmillan shared his concerns, as 'neither British nor American troops will care for a new campaign in order to save Trieste for the "Eyeties." On the other hand, to give in completely may be a sort of Slav Munich.'[517]

It was not until Victory in Europe Day, on 8 May 1945, that General William Morgan, Chief of Staff to Field Marshal Alexander, was sent to

---

[514] FO 371/50790/U 3377/51/G, 5 May 1945.
[515] FO 371/50790/U 3346/51/G, 4 May 1945.
[516] FO 371/50790/U 3355/51/G 70, 2 May 1945.
[517] Harold Macmillan, op. cit., 9 May 1945, p. 753.

The Boundary Issue

Belgrade to propose the final terms of a purely military agreement to the Yugoslav partisans, which foresaw giving Tito control of the area west of a suitable demarcation line. Tito declined to accept Allied proposals by stating it was unfair that Yugoslav troops should not be allowed to remain in the territory they had conquered by force. Then resorting to victimhood, he complained that 'there were evidently three different classes of allies and Yugoslavia came in the third class and did not enjoy the same rights as other Allied powers.'[518] The partisans' leader then suggested Anglo-American forces recognise both the *de facto* and *de jure* Yugoslav sovereignty east of the Isonzo River, which was well into Italian territory. In exchange, Alexander would receive use rights of Trieste and the lines of communication into Austria. For the Anglo-Americans, the developments were unsatisfactory, as Tito's counter-proposal implied he wanted to be installed in the capital city of Venezia Giulia and only allow Alexander user's rights.

In the meantime, as Macmillan wrote in his diary on 14 May 1945, the partisans implemented 'the so-called Yugoslav administration, of thieving, raping and killing,' in Venezia Giulia, and in part, if not in all of the Austrian province of Carinthia, to which they laid claim. The similarities of Tito's occupation of the two regions were striking and seem to reveal an agreed and coordinated *modus operandi*.

> Here again, the Yugoslavs (under Tito's orders) are a source of trouble and anxiety. ... With the same idea as in Venezia Giulia – that possession is nine-tenths of the law – they have raced us into Austria. ... [They] are bringing in considerable numbers – partly regulars and partly irregular forces – and repeating the Venezia Giulia tactics. We put up A.M.G. notices. They pull ours down and put up their own. They requisition and loot and arrest so-called Nazis and Fascists. We have to look on, more or less helplessly, since our plan is *not* to use force and *not* to promote an incident.[519]

---

[518] CAB 121/602 F/Italy/11, Vol. 1, 393B, 15 May 1945.
[519] Harold Macmillan, op. cit., 13 May 1945, p. 757.

212   *Luisa Morettin*

The British ambassador in Rome informed the Foreign Office the Italian press contained daily reports of increasing acts of violence by Yugoslavs against Italians in Venezia Giulia. Sir Charles pointed out that all arrests and executions were 'being done almost under the noses of Allied troops. [That] inevitabl[y] saddles us with a certain responsibility and places the Allies (and especially ourselves as it is the British troops who are involved) in a most embarrassing situation towards the Italian government and people both now and in the future.'[520]

Macmillan was wearied by the fact the Chief of Staff was unable to exercise any authority by use of force, but had to 'sit by and watch the Yugoslavs set up a local government of their own, … conscript villagers, requisition food and … ma[k]e AMG unworkable in certain areas west of the river [Isonzo]. The British soldier can only lean up against them (like the London policeman) and there are many more of them than of us.'[521]

From the military point of view, the Allied situation was not strong. Between 15 and 11 May 1945, Yugoslav forces were increasing in number in the Gorizia-Trieste-Monfalcone area, and it was estimated approximately 34,000 Yugoslav regular army troops were gathered between Trieste and the Isonzo River. In addition, a force estimated at 14,000, under the IX Slovene Corps, was in the area around Gemona, Cividale and Udine. Further, in western Istria there were around 5,000 irregular troops of the Garibaldi Division, a division composed of Italian partisans that were fighting under the command of the Yugoslav army. British troops east of the Isonzo were so positioned that they could defend themselves, but under the circumstances it was impossible to regulate the movement of Yugoslav troops as partisan forces were positioned on parallel lines, preventing the complete security of Allied lines of communications.[522]

British forces occupied the port of Trieste, but not the surrounding hills. Even in the port, the Yugoslav sentries were seen and in many cases,

---

[520] CAB 121/602 F/Italy/11, Vol. 1, 333, 12 May 1945.
[521] Harold Macmillan, op. cit., 12 May 1945, p. 755.
[522] CAB 121/602 F/Italy/11, Vol. 1, 385, 15 May 1945.

The Boundary Issue

213

side-by-side with British sentries: 'In effect.' Macmillan wrote to the Foreign Office, 'the Yugoslavs occupy and govern the town.'[523] General Edwin Harding, who was in command of the 13th Corps in Monfalcone, pointed out that in Venezia Giulia the British and Yugoslav armies were completely mixed, up to the point that in some cases, British and Yugoslav personnel were found billeted in the same house. Forcing out the Yugoslavs in their present numbers would entail a significant operation. In addition to the Yugoslavs, British troops had to deal with nearly 400,000 surrendered Germans, who had to be taken somewhere, fed and given camps.[524] Such was the Allied military situation whilst diplomatic negotiations continued.

By mid-May 1945 the lack of food in Venezia Giulia was becoming a very serious problem. The provinces of Trieste and Gorizia were largely dependent on the Po Valley for supplies and in the province of Udine Yugoslav raiding parties had seized large quantities of food. Under such circumstances relief could not be provided by Allied forces, as conditions were not considered stable enough for UNRRA to undertake distribution, and no facilities existed for the introduction and distribution of civilian supplies by Tito's administration. Handover to partisan forces was the only alternative, but Field Marshal Alexander believed if that happened, supplies would be diverted to Tito's army.[525]

Meanwhile, the Yugoslav press campaign for Trieste was led by newspapers such as *Borba* (Serbo-Croatian word for 'struggle') that on 14 May 1945 announced the civil administration in Trieste was 'firm in the hands of the National Liberation Committee composed of Slovene and Italian anti-Fascists whose programme was the purging of Fascist and pro-Fascist elements,'[526] a euphemism to describe the indiscriminate and random killings in Venezia Giulia. There was also a tendency in the Yugoslav press to shift the main weight of criticism from Italian

---

[523] Ibid., 14 May 1945.
[524] Harold Macmillan, op. cit., 13 May 1945, p. 757.
[525] CAB 121/602 F/Italy/11, Vol. 1, 350, 13 May 1945.
[526] Ibid., 350A, 14 May 1945.

214 *Luisa Morettin*

'imperialists' to the British, allegedly backing them.[527] Since the capture of Trieste, there had been no official public statements made, yet on 16 May 1945 one of Tito's close political advisers made the first statement: on that day, the press published a long exposé by Edvard Kardelj. The Communist activist repeated the thesis that solely Yugoslav military forces liberated Istria and *Primorska* (the Slovene Littoral) and as such, Belgrade had the right to occupy those areas.[528]

The 'Tito problem,' as named by the Anglo-Americans, was incredibly delicate and difficult. On 27 April 1945, Churchill had raised the Trieste question to the new President Harry Truman after Roosevelt's death on 12 April 1945. The Prime Minister highlighted the late President had always attached great importance to Trieste and immediately found 'robust and encouraging' support from Truman, who agreed there was no need to ask the Russians beforehand about operations in Venezia Giulia.[529] Both the American State Department and Truman were violently anti-Tito and demanded strong action from the Allied troops in Venezia Giulia. At that moment, a plan for an eastward drive seemed a necessary course of action. Truman wrote to Churchill:

> The present issue was not a question of taking sides in a dispute between Italy and Yugoslavia or becoming involved in Balkan politics, but of deciding whether Britain and America were going to allow their Allies to engage in uncontrolled land-grabbing or tactics which were all to reminiscent of Hitler and Japan. Yugoslav occupation of Trieste would have more far-reaching consequences than the immediate territory involved.[530]

However, the British Foreign Secretary believed that in fact the Americans were uncertain about the next steps if Tito did not respond to Anglo-American demands, whilst reconciling themselves to the fact that as the

---

[527] Ibid., 393C, 18 May 1945.
[528] Ibid., 360A, 16 May 1945.
[529] Winston Churchill, *The Second World War. Triumph and Tragedy*, Vol. 12, cit., pp. 200-201.
[530] CAB 121/602 F/Italy/11, Vol. 1, 14 May 1945.

The Boundary Issue   215

last resource force would be used.[531] If Moscow decided to back Tito, the resources needed by Allied forces would be beyond those available in the Mediterranean theatre of operations.

Despite the encouraging telegram Truman sent to Churchill on 12 May 1945, four days later the United States backtracked from pursuing a firm policy. President Truman wrote to the British Prime Minister, stating that 'unless Tito should attack ... I am unable and unwilling to involve this country in a war with the Yugoslavs unless they should attack us.'[532]

From Washington, Anthony Eden sent a telegram to Churchill, detailing the changing moods of American officials, who probably got worried by Field Marshal Harold Alexander's military considerations: after years of praise of Tito by the BBC and the British press, it was not easy to now ask troops suddenly to embark on operations on a considerable scale against Yugoslavia.

This change in American intention upset Churchill, who wrote: 'It seems probable that a somewhat violent internal reaction at Washington followed the new President's bold telegram to me. The argument 'don't let us get tied up in Europe' had always been formidable.'[533] Churchill believed the President 'was oppressed by the prejudices of his military advisers. ... Our American friends were comforted in their obstinacy by the reflection that at any rate we have stopped entangling us in the Balkans.'[534] The Americans thought that Britain's Mediterranean and Adriatic strategy was self-serving and aimed at preserving a European balance of power and the interests of the British Empire at the expenses of winning the war quickly.[535] The disagreement displayed that the Grand Alliance was a marriage of convenience, where national rather than 'Allied' perspectives prevailed, and that Venezia Giulia's fate was doomed. Macmillan recalled in his war diaries:

---

[531] Ibid., 373, 394, 14 May 1945.
[532] Ibid., 373, 398, 16 May 1945.
[533] Winston Churchill, *The Second World War. Triumph and Tragedy*, Vol. 12, p. 202.
[534] Winston Churchill, *The Second World War. Assault from the Air*, Vol. 10, p. 19.
[535] Mark A. Stoler, *The Politics of the Second Front. American Military Planning and Diplomacy in Coalition Warfare, 1941-1943*, (Westport: Greenwood Press, 1977), pp. 79-82.

216   *Luisa Morettin*

The President says he cannot make war against the Yugoslavs unless they 'attack' our troops. But as they are in possession and keep moving in more forces, of course they will not 'attack' us. The point is that unless we can push them out by force, there is no way of ejecting them.[536]

Churchill was convinced that the partisans would push hard, however even if Tito was backed by the Soviet Union, he would not dare to make a move against Anglo-American forces in Trieste.

In the meantime, the local situation in Venezia Giulia worsened. Churchill described how 'Our men were obliged to look on without power to intervene at actions which offended their sense of justice, and felt that they are condoning wrongdoing.'[537] 'As a result,' Field-Marshal Alexander sent a telegram explaining how the 'feeling against Yugoslavia is now strong, and is getting stronger. It is now certain that any solution by which we shared an area with Yugoslav troops or partisans or permitted Yugoslav administration to function would not work.'[538] Yet without American support, Churchill felt his hands were tied.

What had further prevented a potential Allied action to liberate Venezia Giulia ahead of Tito's arrival, or at least prevented British forces from using strong action against Tito, was the experience of *Dekemvriana,* the December 1944 events. Armed confrontations had broken out between the Greek Government and the Greek Communist EAM-ELAS and KKE groups, in which British troops got involved. As Germans forces withdrew from the western side of the Peloponnese, ELAS entered the town of Pyrgos and killed several hundred of their political opponents.[539] Communist troops had taken most of the police stations in Athens, killing the officers, when Churchill decided to take a 'more direct control of the affair.' Allied troops did not leave the capital and the Piraeus, as ordered by General Ronald M. Scobie, the Allied Commander-in-Chief designate in Greece, but on Churchill's instructions Scobie and his 5,000 troops were

---

[536] Harold Macmillan, op. cit., 16 May 1945, p. 760.
[537] Winston Churchill, *The Second World War. Triumph and Tragedy*, Vol. 12, p. 202.
[538] Ibid., p. 202.
[539] Llewellyn Woodward, *British Foreign Policy in the Second World War*, Vol III, p. 411.

The Boundary Issue

217

to open fire against Communist forces. In the British Prime Minister's words: 'The mob violence by which the Communists sought to conquer the city and present themselves to the world as the Government demanded by the Greek people could only be met by firearms. There was no time for the Cabinet to be called.'[540]

Describing the actions of ELAS, the distinguished historian Sir Llewellyn Woodward pointed out: 'If the Greek left-wing parties had produced a leader as powerful as Marshal Tito, the history of British policy towards Greece might have ended, as in Yugoslavia, in an unwilling acceptance of a Communist regime imposed by the usual Communist methods on a population which was, for the most part, non-Communist. [...] At all events, as things were, the British government were able, and indeed compelled, in Greece to carry through their policy to the end. They had to use force in order to reach this end.'[541] If Churchill and his advisers felt the situation in Athens required a strong hand, and withdrawing could mean a massacre in the capital as well as an establishment of an extreme left-wing government, the interference of British forces in the Greek civil war was met with Roosevelt's opposition, an experience that the British were cautious to repeat in the future.

Indeed, the British intervention caused a stir in the House of Commons, whilst British papers, such as the *The Times* and *The Manchester Guardian,* disapproved of Churchill's reactionary policy. The vast majority of the American press also violently condemned the British intervention. The reaction to the six week battle for Athens from Communist rule damaged the reputation of British forces, who received world-wide condemnation.

That Britain was very careful not to repeat the Greek experience in Venezia Giulia is evident in several official papers, and some diaries of British officials. As early as January 1945 the Post Hostilities Planning Committee discussed directions received by the Foreign Office, with regard to disputed territories in the Mediterranean theatre of operations.

---

[540] Winston Churchill, *The Second World War. Triumph and Tragedy*, Vol. 12, p. 255.
[541] Llewellyn Woodward, op. cit., Vol. III, p. 383.

218 *Luisa Morettin*

The Foreign Office consider it desirable, in the light of recent experiences in Greece, to review existing plans for the establishment of Allied Military Government. And use of British troops in disputed areas in the Mediterranean theatre where there is risk of clashes with Allied Partisans or local population.[542]

Before giving an answer to the Foreign Office, the Committee suggested asking the Supreme Allied Commander if he still considered it essential to insist on AMG in Venezia-Giulia, or if he would be satisfied to agree with Tito on an Allied military control those areas needed to safeguard the communication lines.

The British desire to avoid what Churchill called 'the Greek torment'[543] is further confirmed by evidence in the war diaries of Macmillan, who complained about the Americans' 'very pedantic attitude,' thinking that British forces must occupy and govern all Venezia Giulia until a peace conference could settle its future. As mentioned above, the plan was unrealistic since the Yugoslavs were in control with a civil and military organisation and ready to fight to hold onto it. 'Unless we are very careful, it will be another Greece … as usual no instructions from the U.S. and U.K. Governments, only vacillation or silence,'[544] Macmillan remarked. Two days later, he noted how British forces abandoned any attempt to set up an AMG even in those areas where Allied troops were: 'All very like Greece!'[545]

Eventually, neither the planned Allied landing in Istria nor a full withdrawal of Tito's troops from Venezia Giulia materialised. Although absent from Churchill's war account, historian C. R. S. Harris reports that President Truman approved Fleet-Admiral William Leahy to ask for Soviet assistance in the complex negotiations.[546] It is unknown what Stalin's role in this delicate matter was, but perhaps because of Soviet intervention, Tito agreed to meet the essential Allied requirements and the boundary line,

---

[542] FO 31/50787/U 141/51/G, 8 January 1945.
[543] Winston Churchill, *The Second World War. Assault from the Air*, Vol. 10, p. 184.
[544] Harold Macmillan, op. cit., 5 and 6 May 1945, p. 751.
[545] Ibid., 7 May 1945, p. 751.
[546] C. R. S. Harris, op. cit., p. 340.

The Boundary Issue

which would become known as the Morgan Line. On 10 June 1945, The Belgrade Agreement was signed. The demarcation divided the Julian March into two zones, Zone A under Allied military administration and Zone B under the administration of the Yugoslav People's Army. Tito's troops withdrew from the new Zone A of Venezia Giulia on 12 June 1945.

Two days later, the Italian Committee of National Liberation in Trieste sent an alarmed telegram about the Basovizza killings to the Allied Forces located in Italy. During the so-called 'Forty days' of Yugoslav occupation, gruesome acts of violence against Italians were widespread:

> In the name of civility we plead that light is shed on these many crimes. The details that we are referring to relate only to the atrocities committed in Basovizza which are similar to those reported in Istria in September 1943 and probably they are not isolated episodes of cruelty.
>
> On 2, 3, 4 and 5 May several hundreds of inhabitants were taken to Basovizza to the disused mine-shaft and thrown into the pit which is 240 meters deep. Later approximately 120 bodies of German soldiers, killed during the fight of the following days, were thrown on top of the Italians. The decomposed carcasses of horses were thrown in last of all.[547]

This triggered an Allied investigation into partisan atrocities in Venezia Giulia, where the end of the Second World War did not conclude with celebration as seen in the rest of the liberated countries.

---

[547] Document dated 14 June 1945 in WO 204/12753, Summary, 4 August 1945.

Chapter 6

ANATOMY OF A RETICENCE

It is forbidden to kill;
therefore all murderers are punished
unless they kill in large numbers.

Voltaire
Philosophical Dictionary

INVITATIONS

Killings and kidnappings were not the only form of violence perpetrated by Tito's troops in Venezia Giulia. Whilst diplomatic and military echelons were dealing with sensitive border negotiations, the British Embassy in Belgrade had collected further information. These included a poster from Gorizia dated 1 May 1945, copies of the Fiume newspaper *La Voce del Popolo* dated 5 and 15 May 1945, and a printer's proof of a mobilisation order in Trieste dated 14 May 1945. They revealed the Yugoslavs had enforced illegal conscriptions of large numbers of Italian nationals, especially in Fiume, Trieste, and Gorizia, into the ranks of the Yugoslav Army. Threats of heavy punishment were directed at all those who failed

222 Luisa Morettin

to respond to the summons, as they would have been considered deserters, and as such, handed over to the Military Court.[548] On this basis in October 1945, the British Embassy sent a complaint to Tito's government. The British War Office felt it was likely the Yugoslav intention to conscript the men of Venezia Giulia for military service was connected to the deportations of Italians. For obvious reasons, forced conscription was not implemented officially and on several occasions it was achieved by going house-to-house and threatening those who resisted. Further, in provincial towns and villages, town criers proclaimed mobilisation.[549]

Compulsory enlistment was nothing new. As early as 8 September 1943 Tito's troops had created a wide network of voluntary recruitment for Italian soldiers both in Southern Italy and abroad, like for instance in the Allied prison camp in Algiers.

The drive to enlist Italian soldiers in the partisan units falls into the contest of the emotional turmoil following the Italian Armistice. After 8 September 1943, whilst some soldiers held onto their fascist ideals and fought for the Republic of Salò, for others the real motherland worth serving and fighting for was 'that of the poor devils who ha[d] paid for the sins of others with their lives.'[550]

In order to enlist as many Italian combatants as possible, partisans promised them generous food rations, new jobs, the possibility of fighting in areas close to home, and even an advance payment of one thousand lira upon enrolment. However, the contract for conscription, written in Serbo-Croat, was in fact a document with which Italians surrendered their citizenship. Until they were on Italian soil, their treatment by partisans was good, but as soon as they were sent to fight in Yugoslavia, Italian soldiers were treated like slaves: mistreated, underfed, and sent to fight with unsuitable equipment. Although it is true there was poverty throughout Europe, Italians were further mistreated and robbed by Communist

---

[548] FO 371/48951/R18438/15199/92, 18 October 1945. WO 204/2297, 7 and 17 July 1945.
[549] WO 204/12753, May-June 1945.
[550] Nuto Revelli, 'La ritirata di Russia,' in Mario Isnenghi (ed.), *I luoghi della memoria*, p. 374.

Anatomy of a Reticence 223

partisans of their shoes, watches and clothes and given smaller food rations than their fellow combatants.

When, in 1943, the Italian authorities reported to the Allied officials the illegal military conscriptions, the answer they received was disappointing: simply notifying them that 'the case and allegations had been noted and submitted to the relevant authorities to take action upon, reserving the right to obtain further information.'[551] The Anglo-Americans failed to act quickly in this humanitarian emergency and did not heed the urgency required in such a state of war. Such a slow use of diplomatic channels would become a *leitmotiv* in the Allied attitude toward the Yugoslavs and Belgrade would take advantage.

The recruitment of the inhabitants of an occupied area was a breach of international law and as such, in 1945 the British Government asked for an effective explanation, showing a more assertive attitude than the one used in 1943 when they were informed of the illegal conscriptions for the first time. The answer from Belgrade arrived a few days later, categorically denying the Yugoslav call-up of the inhabitants of Fiume, Gorizia, Pola and the Slovene littoral. It went on to state that 'Yugoslav units during the war helped the people of Venezia Giulia in their struggle against the enemy, and that these units, composed mainly of local population, invited the people of the districts to join them.' Similarly, both during the war and after the liberation of the area, some local Yugoslav commanders issued 'invitations' to local people to join the fight, as it was considered that the struggle against fascism was not yet over.[552]

The Yugoslav response used a conciliatory tone, whilst trying to minimise the severity of the incident. It stated: 'On learning that some of their local commanders did not understand the changed status of Venezia Giulia since its liberation, and in order to avoid doing anything which would prejudice a just and peaceful settlement of the area,' on 15 May, the Yugoslav government issued the following order: 'In the area of Trieste, Istria, Fiume and other districts of Venezia Giulia not to make any

---

[551] Paola Romano, op. cit., pp. 41-7.
[552] FO 371/48951/R18353/15199/92, 25 October 1945.

conscription. If volunteers present[ed] themselves to our [Yugoslav] army, you [commanders] may exceptionally receive them and enlist them into our [Yugoslav] army.'[553]

According to John R. Colville, a Foreign Office diplomat, it was 'a lame explanation' as he pointed out in a handwritten comment. Undeniably, the evidence disclosed was that the Yugoslav government had used very precise conscription orders and threats of severe punishment, rather than innocent 'invitations.' The truth behind the episode was so evident that Maurice Williams, another Foreign Office diplomat closely involved with Yugoslav policy between 1945 and 1947, did not see much point in pursuing the correspondence with Belgrade.

The British Embassy in Yugoslavia declared itself unable to accept the Belgrade's assertion that the conscription orders issued by local Yugoslav commanders were merely invitations to volunteer. Using the words 'call-up' and 'general mobilisation,' and exacting punishments for those who ignored the order, could not be regarded as coming within the most extended meaning of the word 'invitation.' However, the Embassy noted, counter orders were issued and it was believed the local Yugoslav commanders would, in future, refrain from going above any instruction.[554] Nevertheless, no mention was made to the fate of those who had already been illegally conscripted.

THE BLAME GAME

The sea of unspeakable accounts coming from Venezia Giulia prompted the Allied Forces Headquarters to initiate a Special Commission of Enquiry into the arrests and executions alleged to have been carried out by the Yugoslavs. The result of the investigation is a report dated 18 August 1945, covering the period from the arrival of Tito's troop's into the region and its capital city Trieste on 1 May until their retreat on 12 June 1945.

---

[553] Ibid.
[554] FO 371/48951/21051/15199/92, 28 November 1945.

Anatomy of a Reticence

Although it was – and still is – impossible to know the exact number of crimes and their location, the document reveals that the worst excesses of violence occurred outside places of urban settlements, but the forced removal of civilians and returning soldiers, by way of either arrests or kidnappings, took place mainly in towns and villages. The figures show how the genie of evil had been let out of the bottle.

According to Anglo-American sources, in the province of Trieste alone, 18,000 people were arrested, of which 8,000 were subsequently released; of the remainder, Allied informants believed 4,000 were executed and 6,000 were in detention. From the province of Gorizia 5,000 of those arrested were unaccounted for, whilst in Istria, the figure of those missing was estimated at 50,000. In addition, after Tito's withdrawal, the Yugoslavs kidnapped an unknown number of people from Allied occupied territory. [555]

The whole of Friuli-Venezia Giulia was awash with rumours, mingled with reliable news that terrible deeds were happening east of the Morgan line. *Primorski Dnevnik*, a Yugoslav newspaper started by partisans in Trieste, denied reports of deaths by pit near Trieste. An article published on 5 August branded the piece of news as 'calculated calumny,' intended to escalate tension in Italo- Yugoslav and Anglo-Yugoslav relations. However, Italo-Slovene friendship had much deeper roots, which could not be affected, the Communist journalist claimed.[556] The tones, as British officials noted, were not confrontational and polemic as it was typical of the *Primorski Dnevnik*, implying that with regards to the Venezia Giulia incidents Communist partisans were more sinning, than sinned against.

Another example of denial came from the pages of the Italian Communist newspaper, *L'Unità*. Despite the unpopularity inside Italy of the PCI (Italian Communist Party) concerning the Venezia Giulia events, the paper reported the alleged 'indignation of the whole Trieste press' in hearing the provocative 'tall story' about the Basovizza atrocities, which was originally published by the 'reactionary Roman paper *Libera Stampa*.'

---

[555] WO 204/12753, 18 August 1945.
[556] Ibid., 5 August 1945.

226

Luisa Morettin

The fabrications, continued *L'Unità,* smacked of the accusations made by Goebbels against the Soviets concerning the Katyn Forest massacre.[557] It was here that, on 11 April 1943, the bodies of 4,231 Polish officers were found in a mass grave in the forest of Katyn, located 12 miles west of Smolensk, in Russia.

What was the attitude of the leader of the PCI, Palmiro Togliatti, to Venezia Giulia's wartime nightmare? Documents cast an unflattering light upon his views. In mid-October 1944, a secret meeting took place in Rome amongst Togliatti and the Yugoslav leaders Edvard Kardelj, Andrija Hebrang and Milovan Djilas. Togliatti fully agreed with the Yugoslav territorial claims toward Italian territory and with the absorption of Italian partisan groups present in Venezia Giulia into Tito's army. Togliatti asked that the content of this agreement not be made known to Italians in order not to provoke a negative reaction, but his request was not taken into account. On 19 October 1944, Togliatti wrote to a close collaborator, Vincenzo Bianco, ordering him to use a more favourable attitude to Yugoslav claims. He specified: 'We must support the occupation of Venezia Giulia by Tito's troops in all possible ways [...] and especially the city of Trieste.'[558] Togliatti's attitude had immediate repercussions in the way the partisan war was being fought along the Italian north-eastern border. Partisans displaying pro-Italian feelings were eliminated, the CLN (the Committee of National Liberation) in Venezia Giulia was delegitimised, a pro-Yugoslav propaganda invested the whole Julian region whilst Italian Communist partisans who obeyed orders, entered into and depended on the IX Yugoslav Korpus. Later, they were displaced around the Istrian Peninsula and their groups split up within pro-Tito's fighters, so that they could not lay claim to having liberated the Julian region.

Earlier in January 1943, Vincenzo Bianco, who during the war was in charge of prisoners' work, tactfully wrote to Togliatti asking to make sure that Italian war prisoners in the Soviet Union would not die en masse, as

---

[557] Ibid., 17 August 1945.
[558] Elena Aga-Rossi and Victor Zaslavsky, *Togliatti e Stalin. Il PCI e la politica estera staliniana negli archivi di Mosca,* (Bologna: Il Mulino, 2007), pp. 135-69.

Anatomy of a Reticence

had already happened; otherwise, upon their return to Italy survivors would have discredited the Soviet Communist party. Togliatti replied very coldly that he had nothing to say in favour of the invading armies; Stalin had defined the Communist standpoint, and if a number of prisoners would die because of deprivation, it was simply a result of the poisonous fascist ideology. He also wrote: 'The fact that for thousands and thousands of families Mussolini's war, and his campaign against Russia, will end up in tragedy and personal bereavement is the best and most efficient antidote [against Fascism]. It is difficult, actually impossible, to distinguish between those who are responsible of polity and those who are not. [...] In the objective difficulties that can mean death for many of them, I cannot see anything else but the concrete expression of that kind of justice that Hegel thought is intrinsic in history.'[559]

In Britain, the Foreign Office entrusted the British Embassy in Belgrade to ask the Yugoslav Ministry of Foreign Affairs[560] to account for the killings at Basovizza and the deaths at the karstic pits scattered throughout Venezia Giulia. Further, he was to ask as to the whereabouts and prompt return of 2,472 Italian citizens[561] deported by the Yugoslavs to concentration camps from west of the Morgan line during Tito's occupation. The British authorities assumed that the veil of secrecy over the incidents would be lifted, as they were a serious contravention of clause 6 of the Belgrade Agreement. The treaty, signed on 9 June 1945, clearly stated that the Yugoslav government should return residents they had arrested or deported, and make restitution of property they had confiscated or removed. It was also thought that east of the Morgan line similar incidents had been and were still taking place after the end of the war, and Yugoslav military authorities were replacing Italians with

---

[559] Ibid. For further details see Leonid Gibianskij, 'L'Unione Sovietica, la Jugoslavia e Trieste', in Giampaolo Valdevit (a cura di), *La crisi di Trieste. Maggio-giugno 1945. Una revisione critica,* (Trieste: IRSMLFVG, 1995), pp. 39-78.
[560] FO 371/48951/R18659/15199/92, 23 October 1945.
[561] Ibid.

228 *Luisa Morettin*

Yugoslav citizens. However, the Allied government had no effective control over the activities of the Yugoslav government in that area.[562]

Renato Prunas, the Italian Minister of Foreign Affairs, as well as families from Venezia Giulia, brought the problem of Italian deportees to the fore by writing numerous petitions to Sir Noel Charles, the British Ambassador in Rome. This was in the hope that diplomatic pressure could secure the return of Italians to their country, but events showed that it was all to no avail.

In an effort to end the controversial issue regarding the deportation and killing of Italians, Marshal Tito refuted the accusations during an interview with the Allied press. Although not a decent nor reliable response to the Anglo-American demands for clarification, it is worth reporting in full.

The Italian Government has demanded of the Yugoslav Government through certain organs, the return of 4,000 Italians who, it is alleged, were removed from Venezia Giulia. What is this all about? When agreement was made with Field Marshal Alexander regarding Trieste it was stated in Allied demands that Yugoslavs should return some internees who it is alleged had been taken away. We refused this firmly for we know nothing of such internees and have no internees. We had only the prisoners whom we took in the war, many of which we have already allowed to return to Italy. In my opinion it is a great scandal that people in one country should demand something which is absolutely impossible to fulfil – something which does not exist. That in Venezia Giulia where partisan war was waged plenty of Fascists were killed is true, as a whole Yugoslav army corps was in action there. That plenty of them were killed for example when we took Venezia Giulia is also true for there they were fighting together with the Germans. And now we are asked to return all these dead men, who will return to us the hundreds of thousands who were killed in Lika, Dalmatia and Montenegro and other parts of Yugoslavia? When we draw up that list it will be an enormous book. This demand therefore represents an indemnification. We can see in such representations nothing more than an attempt to spite the Yugoslavs, even after the war such

---

[562] FO 371/48951/R18234/15199/92, 26 October 1945.

Anatomy of a Reticence

229

elements do not contribute to the improvement but to the worsening of relations.[563]

The British interpretation was rather different. 'It was expected,' commented Colville, 'that the Yugoslavs would deny the existence of those deported Italians and unless the Italians can produce proof of deportation instead of mere lists of names, there is really nothing we [Western Allies] can do. Such proof is unlikely to be forthcoming since the men in question are alleged to have been deported during the Yugoslav occupation of Venezia Giulia last May. ... The only hope, from the Italian point of view, seems to me, to be an inspection of the Yugoslav concentration camps by the International Red Cross. This might reveal that the unfortunate deportees do in fact exist.'[564]

By discrediting his enemies and tarring them with the crimes of the past, Tito's reasoning rested on the legal principle of *tu quoque*: you did it too. Italian Fascists had waged an aggressive war with brutal attacks against civilians; therefore, society had to be purged 'of all imperialist and Fascist elements.' This was what the Slovenian Communist leader, Edvard Kardelj, ordered as early as September 1944: all Italian partisans were to come under the orders of the Slovenian IX Corps; those individuals who would not accept the Yugoslav Communist political line would be unconditionally liquidated.[565] In addition, Tito's aim of describing Yugoslav actions as retributive was so they would be more acceptable, since Fascists had brought violence upon themselves.

More specifically, according to the telegram that Ralph Stevenson, the British ambassador in Yugoslavia, received from the Yugoslav Ministry of Foreign Affairs on 7 December 1945 the list of deportees was not a violation of Article 6 of the Belgrade Agreement. Rather, it was an attempt by certain Italians to mislead the world public opinion and an 'unheard of

---

[563] FO 371/48951/R19667/15199/92, Marshal Tito's statement to the Allied press, 17 November 1945.

[564] FO 371/48951/R19667/15199/92.

[565] Roberto Gualtieri, *Togliatti e la politica estera italiana dalla resistenza al trattato di pace 1943-1947*, (Roma: Editori Riuniti, 1995), p. 240.

230   *Luisa Morettin*

method of political agitation,' which had been started against the federative people of the Republic of Yugoslavia by those same Italians. The telegram continued to list names and chose examples of the following thirteen categories of people who did not come within the terms of reference of the Belgrade Agreement.[566]

a) People, who according to the list itself, reside in Yugoslav part of Venezia Giulia

b) Yugoslav citizens coming from Yugoslavia proper

c) Germans who were in Venezia Giulia as soldiers or collaborators

d) Italians born in or coming from Italy proper

e) Regular soldiers of Italian army

f) Soldiers of the so-called independent state of Croatia, i.e., Domobranci of quisling Pavelic

g) Those of had disappeared before the entry of Yugoslav troops into Venezia Giulia

h) Persons, the date [of] whose alleged deportation is not mentioned, who may therefore be 'missing'

i) Persons whose names appear twice in the list

j) Persons who according to information at hand are still moving freely about in zone A of Venezia Giulia

k) Persons who served as republican soldiers of the new Italian Republic [of Salò] or with SS troops, some of whom have already been sentenced by tribunals

l) Prisoners of war who have already been handed over to Allied authorities

m) Persons who were still on August 1 [1945] in [the] concentration camp at Buchenwald waiting repatriation.[567]

According to the Yugoslav note, all people in the list who did not fall into the above categories were, without exception, to be classified either as Fascists, who fell or disappeared in the course of partisan struggles, or as war criminals, who were disposed of by ordinary people at the time of their

---

[566] FO 371/48951/R20984/15199/92, 12 December 1945. The full document can be found in FO 371/48951/R21301/15199/92.

[567] Ibid.

Anatomy of a Reticence

231

liberation. The Yugoslav Ministry also mentioned by name a number of police officers, Fascist and Nazi spies, 'sneaks,' and criminals. The Yugoslav government, the Belgrade telegram specified, could not be responsible for the fate of such people, expressing the great regret that His Majesty's Government put so much trust in those who fought on the side of Nazism and Fascism in the most difficult period of the war.

If initially the Italian claims, according to which Marshal Tito had ordered, or at least approved, the kidnapping and murder of Italians, seemed odd, over time the Allies' understanding of Tito grew, as did the understanding of Yugoslav atrocities against Italian nationals. Although Belgrade's response is questionable, it succeeded in showing the unreliability of the list. The Allied Military Government office had received over eight thousand complaints,[568] which probably explains the inaccuracies immediately picked up by the Yugoslav officials. Furthermore, the list should have taken into account such elements as that some deportees had died in transit to Yugoslavia; consequently, no record of their entrance to Yugoslavia existed; the indexing showed many duplications; other people from the list may have returned home without informing the Allied authorities, either because they were unaware of being reported as missing or because they were indeed involved with the Fascist regime and preferred to go unchecked; finally, some deportees should have been regarded as prisoners of war.

Even so, the Foreign Office found the Yugoslav argument unconvincing, as did Sir Noel Charles in Rome. The list, not compiled by Italians, but from a variety of sources available to officers of the Allied Commission who, in the words of Charles, 'worked very hard to try to make it as accurate as possible,' was admittedly not entirely precise. As a result, the Yugoslavs had made the most of it; by picking small holes in the list, (some 200 names were singled out for comment out of a total list of 2,472 individuals). The Foreign Office was persuaded that the 'Yugoslavs [were] seeking to put up a smoke screen to cover their principal wickedness which [was] that, in defiance of all known laws of humanity,

---

[568] WO 204/10834, 30 March 1946.

232 *Luisa Morettin*

they [had] deported citizens of another state and [were] preventing their return to their homes.'[569] The British authorities were also convinced that if it was true that some of those persons perhaps had disappeared for other reasons, there were so many people missing from Venezia Giulia that it was not unreasonable to suppose the Yugoslavs had removed them, as they were the only ones interested in doing so and gaining from it.

The Yugoslav note also brought up the amorphous category 'Fascist,' which comprised soldiers serving with Fascist Republican forces (the so-called *Repubblichini* from the Republic of Salò), police, civil administrators, and Italian officials, small-time supporters of the regime and ordinary civilians with no political involvement. In the case of *Repubblichini* soldiers, they should have been treated as ordinary prisoners of war; if not, they were presumably living as civilians and should have been treated as such. If they were fascist, then they should have stood trial before proper courts set up for that purpose by Italian local authorities, and not Yugoslav courts, which were notoriously prejudiced against all Italians, whether fascist or not. The British Ambassador in Italy further pointed out to the British government that numerous Allied officers could testify that the bulk of deportations took place after the cessation of hostilities in Italy. Moreover, the Allies thought, there was 'every reason to believe that deportations from zone B were still going on in pursuance of Yugoslav policy of changing the ethnic character of the area;'[570] they also felt they were morally responsible for zone B and Yugoslavia had no right to expect that they should close their eyes to what went on there.

The American Embassy in Belgrade asked for the repatriation of illegally deported Italians. They specified to the Yugoslav Ministry of Foreign Affairs that even if the list contained some inaccuracies, (such as names of persons returned to Venezia Giulia since the roll was prepared), there was evidence that the total number of Italian nationals forcibly removed from the area was considerably greater than the number listed.[571]

---

[569] FO 371/59525/R1027/1027/92, 18 January 1946.
[570] WO 204/10834.
[571] Ibid., 24 October 1945.

The response received was similar in tone and content to the one the British Embassy had received.[572] Although Sir Charles was a strong advocate of the Italian cause and the Anglo-American advisors were well aware of the forcible deportations, still they had no tangible results. A different strategy had to be pursued.

DIPLOMATIC ILLUSIONS

Other diplomatic officials, such as Mr Babler and Major Waddams, respectively the Swiss and British Consul in Ljubljana, confirmed the existence of concentration camps. The latter reported the cases of those interned first in Dachau, Germany, and then in the Yugoslav camps. Upon release, they described the conditions in the camps 'so terrible that Dachau was just child's play.'[573]

Italians were in no position to take effective counter-measures to the disappearance of their nationals from Zone A. Further, the Yugoslav Government's attitude was reminiscent of people 'who seem to think they have sole monopoly of truth' leading Sir Charles to suggest, in accordance with the Foreign Office, that Belgrade should accept an international commission to ascertain whom they held in their concentration camps.[574] If the Yugoslav government refused them entry, it would be possible to expose Tito to the world, as supporter of mob violence and secret police systems.

Diplomatic pressure on the Yugoslavs and an International Red Cross inspection, although theoretically a good move, were overly optimistic, as a later episode would prove. Again, a full and detailed description of such an incident as reported by Marshal J. Truax, the American Red Cross representative in Trieste, is necessary as emblematic of the nature and extent of Yugoslav cooperation.

---

[572] Ibid., 8 December 1945.
[573] WO 204/431.
[574] FO 371/48951/R18438/15199/92, 18 October 1945.

234   *Luisa Morettin*

After obtaining all necessary permits to cross the Morgan Line, and thanks to a letter from the director of the Repatriation Division of the Yugoslav Red Cross in Trieste, Truax spent the 22 and 23 August 1945 in Yugoslavia. Together with Mr Enderle, of the International Red Cross, he was to meet Mr Silbar, the President of the Slovenian Red Cross (SRC) in Ljubljana. The purpose of the meeting was to help with the Allied inquiry into the repatriation of Italians. Truax and Enderle were accompanied to some meetings by Mr Babler, the Swiss Consul who showed a great deal of bravery, as it was dangerous for him to be seen in company of the two Red Cross representatives: some Swiss citizens living in the area had already been subject to arrests, imprisonment, and confiscation of their properties.[575]

Mr Enderle presented the letter to Mr Silbar, asking if arrangements could be made for him to visit the concentration camps, bring in food and medicines if needed, and help organise the repatriation of Italian civilians. The president of the SRC explained he could not authorise this, but would arrange for Mr Enderle to meet the commanding officer of the Yugoslav IV Army who was in Ljubljana. He also said that all requests for information on prisoners would have to be referred to Belgrade for action. The commander of the IV Army received Mr Enderle graciously and informed his guest that there was no problem concerning civilian internees in camps: indeed, the only camps in existence were for prisoners of war, since concentration camps for civilians had never been in operation by the Yugoslav authorities. In the light of such a blatant denial, it seemed nothing could be done to answer Mr Truax and Mr Enderle's requests.

Yet Mr Enderle did not give up and arrangements were made for him to talk to the Yugoslav Minister of Internal Affairs. Since the Minister was in Belgrade, the two Red Cross representatives were received by the Chief of the Cabinet for Internal Affairs, a man described by Mr Truax as 'very hard and shrewd,' probably, 'one of the leaders of the party in control and undoubtedly very intelligent and ruthless as well.' After displaying surprise that the Allies had such complete records and particularly that they had the

---

[575] WO 204/431.

Anatomy of a Reticence   235

names of concentrations camps and the prisoners, the Chief of the Cabinet promised he would wire Belgrade, to enable Mr Enderle to receive permission from the government so that he may undertake his plans within the camps. However, Belgrade answered the following day stating that Mr Enderle was to clear through Geneva and obtain the approval of the Yugoslav Minister there before he could be permitted to visit the camps.[576]

At the final meeting that the two Red Cross officials had with Mr Silbar, the president of the Slovene Red Cross feigned ignorance of the camps and of the civilians interned there. However, he diligently took the information, whilst promising to check with the authorities, and do all he could to effect the release of the individuals named.[577] The narrative was always the same: tactics of procrastination and affable duplicity led to the consistent refusal of access to the camps. The Belgrade government clearly had time on its side and the issue of the camps was a way to enforce the waiting game for the other parties. Mr Silbar further added insult to injury in the meeting: besides feigning no knowledge about Italian prisoners, he took the chance to claim that the Allies were not handling properly the Yugoslavs returning from Austria, Italy and Germany: allegedly they were not given enough to eat and, in Germany, they were being retained in camps.[578]

This charade ended the International Red Cross' search for Italians who they believed were illegally detained in Yugoslavia. The Yugoslavs were stonewalling and the Allied authorities knew it. The report of the failed mission concluded that 'Nothing [could] be done until the Yugoslav Government decided to act, and they [would] only act when it [was] for their advantage or because of pressure from the top. The country [was] still at war, they [had] no intentions of giving up any of their claims and [were] willing to fight whenever the time seem[ed] ripe.' It was felt that 'the Communists in control of Yugoslavia [were] certain that Russia [was]

---

[576] Ibid.
[577] Ibid.
[578] Ibid.

backing them and that they [could] do what they like[d] with the knowledge that they [had] a powerful ally.'[579]

As well as showing that international authorisations and permits were useless, the episode made the Allied authorities aware it was even more difficult to intervene than initially thought. According to Mr Truax, Yugoslav Communists did not have the backing of more than twelve per cent of the population, but with the control of OZNA and the military, they had little to fear as there was no organised opposition.

Mr Truax reported to Major John W. Ballew, a Chief Welfare and Displaced Persons officer, that he saw more soldiers and armed men in Ljubljana than since the end of the war. He also added some personal observations on his experience.

They cast a perceptive eye on the times of great stress and danger and on the plight of ordinary people in Communist Yugoslavia. 'I am damned glad to be out of Ljubljana and back to Trieste,' Truax said, 'I got my fill of communists and secret police. Everywhere I went there were secret police on guard and in the hotel where I stayed they were always sure to follow us to our meals, eat near our tables, follow us to the coffee shop, to meetings we attended, and no doubt listened to our conversations in the hotel rooms we occupied.'[580]

If no good came out of the visit from the International Red Cross, at least it was hoped that the deportees would not be hurt further. As the Chief of Welfare and Displaced Persons, Major Waddams, said, 'All that can happen is for them to die and they are doing that now.'[581] He plausibly suggested the prisoners should be given up for dead. And very few could disagree.

---

[579] Ibid.
[580] Ibid.
[581] Ibid.

Anatomy of a Reticence

RETURNING TO THE FRAY

The situation of deported Italians did not finish with the end of the war, as seen from the intense exchange of correspondence between Rome, London, Washington, and their respective embassies in 1946 and 1947. It was a time of repatriation for other prisoners of war, but there were still no news surrounding the Italian *desaparecidos*.

On 5 January 1946 Antonio Cifaldi, the Italian Undersecretary of State, requested a list of Italian civilians interned in Yugoslavia from Colonel James Regis, the President of the Allied Sub Commission POW, stressing the state of great anxiety in which the families of those internees lived.[582] Cifaldi's request was motivated by the numerous cases, already reported, of Italians removed from Venezia Giulia, and by new charges pressed against Yugoslavia. In February 1946, whilst in the rest of Italy the post-war future and reconstruction were the priority, Venezia Giulia was in the midst of a brutal, bloodstained period in its history, which formed an unbroken red line of continuity with the war. The evidence of past and new violence, especially kidnappings, continued being received, as the following examples describe. A letter that Antonio De Rubertis, an Italian surgeon made prisoner by Tito's troops in May 1945, managed to send clandestinely to his elderly mother at the beginning of 1946, urged her to make the necessary application for his return to Italy – depicting the forced detention suffered by many.[583] As late as April 1946, the British Embassy in Rome received further evidence, in the form of a list of names of ten Italian police officers of *Guardia di Pubblica Sicurezza* who had been deported from Venezia Giulia and Dalmatia.[584]

The following incidents clearly show that kidnappings of Italians and potential Slovene opponents continued well into 1947. On 3 September 1947, the British Political Advisor in Trieste reported that Andrej Ursic, a prominent Slovene Democratic Party and editor of *Democracja*, a Slovene

---

[582] WO 204/10834, 5 January 1946.
[583] Ibid., 16 February 1946.
[584] FO 371/59525/R 5877/1027/92, 10 April 1946.

238 *Luisa Morettin*

Democratic weekly published in Gorizia, was kidnapped from Robic, a village in Zone A, in the early hours of 1 September 1947. The report continued stating he was ambushed whilst he was driving his motorcycle and the nearby civil police patrol heard screams, but on arrival they had found only smashed glass and footprints leading into a field.[585]

A few weeks later, a jeep disappeared when travelling between Monrupino and Orle with five members of the Free Territory Civil Police. The men were visiting civil police posts in the Free Territory boundary to arrange wireless communications; however, they most likely crossed the provisional boundary by accident. They were subsequently taken into Yugoslav custody. As in previous cases, in spite of the many repeated requests for the prisoners' release, the Yugoslav Military Mission neither gave a satisfactory explanation of the events, nor did it release the arrested men. Substantiated reports show that witnesses went from Opicina, in Zone A to Sesana in Yugoslavia, whether voluntarily or under coercion it was unclear, in order to testify against the five prisoners. One of them, Vice-Inspector Baschiera, was sentenced to a term of imprisonment by a 'People's Court.' According to the Allied informant, another member of the group had been subjected to ill treatment under interrogation.[586] Thanks to the personal intervention of General Airey, the new Allied Commander of Zone A, and in conjunction with an energetic diplomatic action by the American and British ambassadors in Belgrade, the episode ended well, as the five men were released on 30 September 1947. Not the same can be said, however, for thousands of similar incidents which ended with complete silence.

At the beginning of 1946, Mr Homer M. Byington Jr, the Deputy U.S. political adviser, informed the Allied Commander in Chief in the Mediterranean Theatre that the Department of State approved showing the Yugoslav note, containing the thirteen categories of deportees, to the Italian government. The only condition was that it should not be publicised until the Department of State had an opportunity to study the results of the

---

[585] FO 371/67412/R 12120/128/92, 3 September 1947.
[586] FO 371/67412/R 13023/128/92, 20 September 1947.

Anatomy of a Reticence   239

investigation on the points raised by the Yugoslav government.[587] In the meantime, Rome was asked to examine the contested list with the names of 2,472 Italians.

The Italian reply reflected the fact that the list, drafted by the Allied Commission, did not correspond to the one presented by Italy to Anglo-American officials. It was then difficult to check the allegations from Belgrade. Notwithstanding, the Italian Ministry of Foreign Affairs expressed some general reservations to the reasons given by the Yugoslav government for the return of Italian deportees and reiterated its detailed accusations against Belgrade:

a) In accordance with article 6 of the Agreement signed in June 1945 between the Allied Command and Marshal Tito concerning the delimitation of Venezia Giulia into two zones ... the Yugoslav government took the pledge of returning all persons resident of the former zone who might have been arrested or deported while it was under Yugoslav occupation, with the exception of those having prior to 1939, the Yugoslav citizenship. By this commitment the Yugoslav government implicitly admitted that the Yugoslav forces had actually arrested or deported a number of Italian residents while occupying the so-called zone A. Nevertheless, according to statements delivered officially by Yugoslav spokesmen, it appears that the implications of arrests and deportations of people residing in zone A by Yugoslav Authorities are flatly denied. We cannot fail to observe that statements as such are in open contradiction with the commitment contained in article 6. Worth of notice is the assertion, having indeed no substantial grounds, that all persons that have disappeared are simply to be classified either as persons who perished in the course of partisan struggles or as persons who were killed at the moment of liberation by the insurgent local population.

b) The Yugoslav government ... do not deny however that they are holding a large number of Italians, such as soldiers of the Italian regular Army, Italians born in or coming from other provinces of Italy, former internees of the Buchenwald camp, and members of the

---

[587] WO 204/10834, 16 January 1946.

Fascist Republican Army or persons enlisted with the German Army. However, there does not appear to be juridical grounds in the Yugoslav claim for detaining such groups of Italian subjects. There is on the contrary a precise bond on the part of the Yugoslav government to return each one of them, in the first place because the Yugoslav government has no charges against them and secondly because these persons are responsible only towards the Italian authorities for their activities.

c) Moreover ... inhabitants living in a part of the national territory being under military occupation of another country ... their case should fall under the international regulations and agreements concerning military occupations, namely under the regulations attached to the Hague Convention of 18 October 1907. According to these regulations, the occupying military forces are bound not only to respect the lives of the inhabitants (art. 46), but also to refrain from restrictive measures towards them that could not be justified by the conduct of war of by special occupation motives. War being over since a long time and the dread that peaceful Italian citizens might menace the occupying forces decidedly not to be expected, the arrest and deportation of these people cannot be considered but an unlawful procedure fully involving the responsibility of the Yugoslav government.

d) ... As the terms of the Italian Armistice are applying to "the entire Italian territory" to which so far belongs the whole of Venezia Giulia, the Yugoslav military occupation for the area delimited by the 9 June 1945 Agreement between the Allied Command and Marshal Tito originates from an authorisation of the United Nations and falls under their responsibility according to articles 18 and 38 of the Armistice supplementary conditions.

Therefore, while the Allied government cannot ignore those occupation methods, which the Yugoslav authorities are carrying on in the territory assigned to them, on the other hand the Yugoslav government is responsible towards them as well as towards Italy for its conduct during the former occupation of zone A according to the terms of the 9 June 1945 agreement.[588]

---

[588] Ibid., 18 April 1946.

Following the evasive and unsatisfactory replies by the Yugoslav government, and Italy's renewed protests against Tito's violations in principle rather than the details of the case, the Allied Command set out to re-check the original list. Therefore, the 13th Corps submitted a revised roll of alleged deportees containing 4,338 names, a considerable increase on the number originally listed[589] divided as follows, depending on the area from where they had disappeared:[590]

I.	BELIEVED DEPORTED IN MAY/JUNE 1945				
	A.	TRIESTE	Vol. I	....	942
	B.	"	Vol. II	....	552 1494
	C.	GORIZIA	Vol. I	....	1225
	D.	"	Vol. II	....	38 1263
	E.	POLA	Vol. I	....	486
	F.	"	Vol. II	....	354 840
	G.	Believed died in captivity			44
		Believed repatriated or returned of their own resources			697
		TOTAL NUMBER BELIEVED DEPORTED IN MAY/JUNE 1945			4338
II.	BELIEVED DEPORTED PRIOR TO 1945 BUT SINCE 1939				
	All areas 1942-43-44				169
		GRAND TOTAL			4507
		Less repatriates etc. and those who died			741
III.	REMAINING TO BE REPATRIATED				3766

A frantic exchange of telegrams and memoranda between the various British and American advisors followed. They discussed the best way to proceed with the Belgrade government, in view of the Yugoslav persistent obstructiveness and reticence. Both Homer M. Byington and Philip Broad, from the Office of the British Political Adviser to the Supreme Allied Commander, drew the attention of the Combined Chiefs of Staff to the entire situation, requesting further representations to be made by Britain

---

[589] Ibid., 23 May 1946.
[590] Ibid., 1 June 1946.

242 *Luisa Morettin*

and America toward the return of those deportees.[591] It was felt that SACMED had certain responsibilities, since it was in command of the area where the incidents occurred. However, Brigadier General Archelaus Lewis Hamblen, the American Assistant Chief of Staff, believed that the matter, now placed in diplomatic channels, should not revert to a military status because of diplomatic failures. It should rather be 'considered a matter for diplomatic determination.'[592] Such a view was shared by the Supreme Allied Commander, who urged the resubmission of the list to the Yugoslav Government, pressing either the immediate return of the detainees or an acceptable explanation for their detention.[593] Even if the authorities disagreed about the way forward, all took for granted that the Yugoslavs would again deny the existence of Italian deportees.

Due to the previous unsuccessful diplomatic efforts, William Hayter and Colville suggested to Viscount Samuel Hood, of the British delegation for the Paris Peace Conference, that the matter could be conveniently raised in Paris in order to 'fling [it] in the teeth of [Soviet Minister] Molotov if his attitude over the Trieste [boundary] question justifie[d] it.' In doing so, the news would undoubtedly reach the Yugoslavs through the Russians and, from the point of view of the Italian prisoners, that could be more effective than any number of formal representations by the British and American authorities in Belgrade.[594]

Although the Peace Conference started on 29 July 1946, as of the 31 August the opportunity to tackle the issue of the deportation of Italians had not yet arisen. The Foreign Office decided to send a joint Anglo-American letter to the Yugoslav government, together with the revised list of almost 4,000 names, in the hope to expedite the matter.[595] Nevertheless, nobody was under the illusion as to the practical effect of further diplomatic representations to the Yugoslavs. The British authorities wanted to keep the letter on record, which could subsequently serve as the foundation for

---

[591] Ibid., 14 May 1946.
[592] Ibid., 23 May 1946.
[593] CAB 122/881, 30 May 1946.
[594] FO 371/59525/R9329/1027/92, 28 June and 14 August 1946.
[595] CAB 122/881, 31 August 1946.

Anatomy of a Reticence 243

anything they may find useful or necessary to say during the Peace Conference.[596] However, this was not to happen.

WALLS OF SILENCE

For British and American authorities, there was the question of whether to make the issue public or not. If it was made public, the British Embassy in Belgrade strongly recommended that military authorities in Trieste shuld be ready to produce proof through the largest possible number of convincing witnesses and, if possible, any deportees or prisoners of war who had returned from Yugoslavia.[597]

The issue had already been raised in Rome in 1945, but then the objection had been made that the British Press would not have published 'such material about our gallant ally Yugoslavia.' It is clear that the contribution of the Yugoslav forces to the common cause against the Axis had created a powerful picture of trust in Tito's troops. Communism liked to pride itself on its political integrity, and by the end of the war Tito and Yugoslavia had been 'portrayed as the soul of democratic protagonism,' as David McK. Key, the Chargé in Italy wrote to the Secretary of State back in 1945.[598] It was the very same portrayal, which prevented attempts to challenge the British public's entrenched mind-sets with news of illegal deportations, unspeakably harsh enslavement, and barbaric murders. This was considered the kind of 'utterly horrifying and unconvincing material which the British Press [were] always unwilling to handle,' as it was classified as 'unsaleable news.'

As with previous matters, the issue of publication became the object of an exchange of views between Foreign Office officers in 1947. Frederick Archibald Warner, a British diplomat, could 'see no reason why publicity

---

[596] FO 371/59525/R 2651/1027/92, 23 August 1946.

[597] WO 204/10834, 6 September 1946.

[598] FRUS, Diplomatic Papers, 1945, Europe, Volume IV, 740.00119 Control (Italy)/11-1445, 14 November 1945, viewed in https://history.state.gov/historicaldocuments/frus1945v04/d1 134, accessed 14 June 2016.

244 *Luisa Morettin*

should not be given to those extremely wicked deportations. While it serves no particularly useful purpose,' he continued, 'the public should have an opportunity to know how the Yugoslavs carried out their occupation of Venezia Giulia.' Publicity on those 'outrages would be admirable,' agreed Brown. However, at the same time, Warner advised that since the MP Philip Noel-Baker had made his visit to Belgrade, the Foreign Office should not have chosen that moment to throw 'any particularly strong stink-bombs at the Yugoslavs.'[599]

The British Embassy in Rome endorsed the publication postponement. It highlighted the uncertainties and 'repercussions it might have on the creation of the Free Territory, or on the implementation of Article 45 of the Italian Treaty, about the surrender of war criminals, etc.;' in all the circumstances it was 'preferable ... to wait until the trouble start over the delivery of war criminals, etc., by Italy to Yugoslavia.

Publicity [at that stage] could of course provide a retort to Yugoslav charges of bad faith by the British and United States over the surrender of quislings. ... The question of deportees from Zone A [was] however clearly one to be treated on its own merits.' According to Henry A. Hankey, from the British Embassy, it would have been best to avoid doing anything to link it in the public mind with the question of quislings and refugees. That would have been 'playing into the Yugoslavs' hands since, once they [were] dealing direct with the Italian government over the return of the refugees, they [would] no doubt try to use Italian deportees and prisoners of war in Yugoslavia as a bargaining counter. The longer they [could] be prevented from doing it the better.'[600]

In the meantime, the Association of Relatives of Deportees to Yugoslavia and their vice-president, Mr Pecorari, wrote another appeal to Admiral Ellery Stone, Acting Chief Commissioner of the Allied Commission for Italy. Pecorari had previously solicited the Anglo-Americans, the Italian and Yugoslav governments, the Vatican, the International Red Cross, and the Slovenian Red Cross, but always in vain.

---

[599] FO 371/67412/R 7497/128/92, (no day) June 1947.
[600] Ibid., 22 May 1947.

Anatomy of a Reticence

245

Even the requests addressed to the Commission of Experts, which went to Venezia Giulia, remained without reply.[601] On 2 April 1947 the British Embassy in Belgrade initially suggested to its counterpart in Rome that since Italians and Yugoslavs were by then in direct diplomatic relations with each other, it would have been preferable for them to deal with the deportee question on their own. However, it was realised that since Rome was not party to the Belgrade Agreement of June 1945, on which previous claims for the return of the Italians deported were based, it was still desirable for the Allies to act as intermediaries.[602]

On 17 April 1947 Colonel Alfred C. Bowman, a senior American civil affairs officer, sent a note to the Assistant Chief of Staff at the Headquarters of the AMG Venezia Giulia. In this he reported that the Allied inability, interpreted as unwillingness, to take any concrete action on the subject of the Italian deportees, was one of the most acute sources of local criticism of Allied administration by the bereaved families. Even if Bowman recognised that the Allies could not be held responsible for the return of the Italian deportees, nevertheless the families of the deported citizens had no one else to turn to or blame. Therefore, it would be a 'most fortunate development if, during the latter stage of [that] operation, the Headquarters could make a worthwhile intelligent statement of some sort as to the fate of [those] people and the prospects of their return.'[603]

The Vatican shared the Italian feelings of helplessness caused by the prolonged detention of Italian citizens and had appealed for help through Allied diplomatic channels on several occasions since the Yugoslav occupation. On 24 May 1946, the Under Secretary of State at the Holy See, Monsignor Domenico Tardini, sent another heartfelt plea, denouncing the already well-known killings and deportations and the stringent censorship regarding any aspect of life in Venezia Giulia. Furthermore he deplored the lack of religious freedom, the illegal change of family legislation and the terror and anguish in which the Italian population, and part of the Slav

---

[601] FO 371/59525/R 15455/1027/92, (no day) September 1946.
[602] FO 371/67412/R 4804/128/92, 2 April 1947.
[603] WO 204/10834, 17 April 1947.

246 *Luisa Morettin*

population, lived. Leaving many of them compelled to flee their 'houses from which the Yugoslav authorities [were] accustomed to carry away the furnishing and supplies. ... Wherever the Yugoslav administration had been installed,' bemoaned Tardini, 'every sign of liberty had disappeared.'[604]

Therefore, well into 1947 the essential question of the deportees remained unanswered. Many months of enquiry had produced a good amount of circumstantial detail, yet no real satisfaction came from the Yugoslav authorities. The personnel of the ex-*Questura* (Italian police station) in Fiume were yet another telling example. Despite extensive enquires made over a long period by Allied authorities, they seemed to have vanished. In addition, the Allied Welfare Division had corresponded at length with various Yugoslav agencies that at all times denied any knowledge of missing persons. Major James E. Long confirmed to the Allied Headquarters that amongst the corpses, which had been recovered from *foibe* in that area, several had been identified as being individuals 'deported' in May 1945, however they did not include any of those listed in the Allied enquiry.[605]

The Anglo-American authorities were under no illusion that any deportees were still alive. As a telegram from the British Embassy in Belgrade to London reveals, the Yugoslav practice was to usually return deported persons or POW, only if they had not already been so badly treated that release was inadvisable; negotiations were then carried out by members of the Communist parties in the concerned countries so they could obtain the credit for the releases.[606]

However, a further effort was made on 9 July 1947, when the British Embassy in Belgrade sent the Yugoslav Ministry of Foreign Affairs another list of deported persons, whose names had not been included in the ones previously compiled. As before, the British requested Belgrade to make a careful investigation into the fate of the deportees, asking their

---

[604] FO 371/59525/R 8970/1027/92, 24 May 1946.
[605] WO 204/10834, 6 June 1947.
[606] FO 371/67412/R 14906/128/92, 8 November 1947.

Anatomy of a Reticence

247

return home.[607] As before, no reply was received from the Yugoslav state officials.

Apart from moral reasons, the continuous Allied protest against the Belgrade government was motivated by the fact that the Anglo-Americans were responsible to the Security Council for the wellbeing of the deportees, who were original citizens of their zone of the Free Territory. Since the matter could be discussed in the course of the dispute regarding the allocation of Trieste, the Western Allies felt it necessary to show they had strived to convince the Yugoslavs, by proper means, to return the Italian prisoners deported by Yugoslav Military representatives.[608] Diplomatic correspondence further shows how, in October 1947, the Italian Legation questioned the issue of deportees directly with the Yugoslav government, yet was again met with no success. The Italians then proceeded, for the purpose of record, to send separate follow-ups on each individual case to the Yugoslav Foreign Office, with an eye to the question being aired at the United Nations level.[609] When it came to submitting energetic protests to Belgrade concerning the unwarranted detention and instances of maltreatment of Allied military personnel, the American Ambassador in Yugoslavia from July 1947, Cavendish W. Cannon, was so experienced to predict that Italian efforts 'would lead to no practical result.'[610] In spite of that, he suggested the British Political Adviser that the State Department considered it desirable to include the subject in the joint periodical report to the Security Council on the administration of the British/United States zone.[611]

Three weeks later, Major J. A. Kellett from the Welfare and Displaced Persons Division, provided the Headquarters of the Allied Military Government with another list of 342 Italian civilians and nine Italians, having membership of military or quasi-military formations, who had been

---

[607] FO 371/67412/R 10055/128/92, 9 July 1947.

[608] FO 371/67412/R 14906/128/92, 15 November 1947.

[609] FO 371/67412/R 15354/128/92, 30 October 1947.

[610] FRUS, 1947, Eastern Europe; The Soviet Union, Volume IV, 740.00119 Control (Italy)/9-1147: Telegram, 11 September 1947, viewed in https://history.state.gov/historicaldocuments/frus1947v04/d72, accessed 13 June 2016.

[611] FO 371/67412/R 15354/128/92, 30 October 1947.

248   *Luisa Morettin*

deported. However, whereas the previous lists of deportees were for Zone A, the one dated 24 November 1947, related to persons residing in what had become the Free Territory of Trieste.[612]

In December 1947, Sir Charles Peake, the new British Ambassador in Belgrade, had second thoughts about involving the Security Council in the deportees matter. He feared that the slightest hint of possible reference to the Council would have been 'sufficient to persuade the Yugoslavs to get in first with some complaint of their own.' This would have driven the Yugoslavs to some counter-measures, such as accusing the Allied authorities of protecting Fascists in Trieste. Peake also felt 'it was undesirable that the Yugoslavs should always [have] been allowed to claim the position of injured party.'[613] General Terence Airey, Commander and Military Governor of the Anglo-American Zone, Trieste, agreed with Peake's suggestion, fearing that making any reference to the deportees issue before the Security Council would provoke a demand from the Yugoslavs for the return from their zones of persons they regarded as their political opponents.[614] The British and American authorities found it safer for the matter not to reach the highest echelons of diplomacy and preferred to instruct General Airey to send appropriate communications to the Yugoslav Liaison authorities in Trieste, concerning the list of 24 November 1947. The goal was not to challenge the Belgrade government regarding a humanitarian crisis, but rather for the Western Allies to have on record that the joint Anglo-American administration had attempted on several occasions to 'obtain the return of the deportees by addressing themselves to the Yugoslav authorities through the proper channels.'[615]

---

[612] FO 371/67412/R 16240/128/92, 24 November 1947.
[613] FO 371/67412/R 16320/128/92, 11 December 1947.
[614] FO 371/67412/R 16357/128/92, 13 December 1947.
[615] FO 371/67412/R 16578/128/92, 16 December 1947.

CONCLUSION

In war time
the first casualty
is truth.

Doris Lessing
Prisons We Choose to Live Inside

In those years only the dead smiled,
Glad to be at rest.[616]

Anna Akhmatova's famous verses from *Requiem* seem to be a proper way to conclude this story the beginnings of which lie far back in time, and whose echo is still strong today as historical memories of communist atrocities still haunt people in Venezia Giulia.

In the peace and quietness of an archival room, it is easy to become desensitised when reading the hundreds of official papers describing the horrific torture and murders. Each of those who lived through the atrocities

---

[616] Anna Akhmatova, *Poems*, (New York: Alfred A. Knopf, 2006), p. 185.

250 *Luisa Morettin*

bore a name, yet when they died, they were lucky if they became even a number. For many, as in the case of the deportees to Yugoslavia and those who were killed anonymously in a *foiba* or in the sea, it was as if they had never existed and were forgotten. As historian Richard Hovannisian remarked:

> Following the physical destruction of a people and their material culture, memory is all is left and is targeted as the last victim. ... Falsification, deception, and half-truths reduce what was to what may have been or perhaps what was not at all.[617]

One would assume that the chronological distance of seventy years would allow a dispassionate assessment on this grim chapter of Italian history, but the legacy of recrimination shows no sign of diminishing. In public debate, there is still a strong tendency to condemn, rather than to explain, as Italian society is divided about the rendition of events. Such an attitude reveals how the country's relationship with its recent past in general, and with the *foibe* atrocities in particular, is still tainted by complex emotions: anger, pain, guilt, shame, all of which trigger deep feelings and strong opinions.

This book has attempted to cast a sober eye on past events, in such a way that adheres to facts and contextualises atrocities in the wider historical picture. The narrative did not attempt to place blame, by choosing sides in the conflict or, worse, criminalising the resistance movement to which liberty loving people owe so much. In addition, it was not an attempt of morally equating all sides, or asking whether a quantitative threshold was reached to count the *foibe* killings and deportations as democide. By placing this story within the narrative of the Second World War, this book serves to remember the victims and is a lesson in their specific tragedy - that tragedy of humanity who had lost its moral compass.

---

[617] Richard G. Hovannisian, 'Denial of the Armenian Genocide in Comparison with Holocaust Denial,' in Richard G. Hovannisian, (ed.), *Remembrance and Denial: the Case of the Armenian Genocide,* (Detroit: Wayne State University Press, 1999). p. 202.

Conclusion 251

The complex picture outlined in this book has shown that there are at least four dimensions to this story. This includes: how local civil and ethnic wars ran alongside the main war; how both Nationalists and Communists saw in brutal violence and chaos the way to carve up an alternative power; an environment of permanent and lethal brutality, almost a kind of intoxication in a period of collective wickedness; the passage from cruelty to deliberate oblivion as a way to create a sanitised narrative of the Second World War.

Due to traditional and long-standing ethnic divides, Yugoslavia was a country where resentment, bitterness, and enmity were deeply rooted. Any means were justified, not only in the fight against Italy and Germany, the arch enemies, but also in the internal fights which, between 1941 and 1945, saw the gruesome Ustaše fascist regime of Croatian Ante Pavelić torture and execute thousands of Serbs, Jews, Roma, and Communists in concentration camps. In order to create an all-Croatian state with two religions (Roman Catholicism and Islam), sadistic horror reached levels never experienced before, as Eastern Orthodox Serbs of Croatia and Bosnia-Herzegovina were slaughtered if they did not convert to Roman Catholicism.[618] As a result, the Croatian barbarity pushed Serbs into the ranks of the two groups fighting the foreign occupiers. On one side, the officers of the Yugoslav Army, who made up the core of the Chetnik resistance under the leadership of royalist Draža Mihailović, and on the other, Tito's Communist partisans, whose developed underground network would prove decisive for winning the guerrilla warfare. Whilst the war progressed and moved towards its end, Yugoslav forces combined the war of liberation with the struggle for domestic power during a very complex ethnic civil war, which took place under the shade of the Second World War. The massacres that followed in 1945 were not so much targeting withdrawing Nazi troops, but rather Slav collaborationists and Croat Ustaše. The whirlwind of cruelty in Yugoslavia was driven by revenge and by the process of structural and political change as violence served the advancement of the Communist revolution. It is estimated that the victims

---

[618] Hubert Butler, *The Invader Wore Slippers*, (London: Notting Hill Editions, 2012).

252 *Luisa Morettin*

of Tito's victorious troops counted 70,000.[619] Soon the lines between the combatants and civilians, and collaboration and counter-revolutionary actions became unclear. Scenes of horrific carnage and mass shootings have been abundantly described by surviving witnesses. One of them, Dimitrije Djordević recalled how the Communists turned over Nazi and Ustaše camps for their own use and 'both [systems] had in common the violence with which they imposed their authority.'[620] In 1947, there were so many people in Yugoslav camps and prisons that the Communist Party was forced to declare amnesty for tens of thousands.[621]

Closely connected with the domestic violence in Yugoslavia were the atrocities against Italians in Venezia Giulia. They blended with a situation of general disorder and disruption following the Armistice in 1943, and later the capitulation of the German forces in 1945. The power vacuum caused by the dissolution of normative constraints let loose the use of indiscriminate violence. The extreme empowerment given by the situation of lawlessness and the diminished accountability for violence were at the root of the crimes committed. Behind them, several motivations lay: a lethal interplay of elements given by the mutual influence and multi layered interrelation of nationalistic passions, private revenge, ethnical motives, and in large part political ideas. It is also plausible to assume that a component of the violence, which Yugoslavs unleashed, was in part due to their ingrained psychology of resentment toward the long-suffered 'superior Italian culture' and Italian middle-class city dwellers. Insecurity, subalternity, envy, and anger were directed to overthrowing political and class enemies, urbanities and western capitalism.

If it is true that only distance puts events into perspective, in the case of Tito's campaign his aims and objectives were soon clear to many of his contemporaries. The slowly corrosive psychological campaign of terror and random wholesale murder was planned and intended not only to suppress real and potential opponents to the Communist regime, but also to

---

[619] Ian Kershaw, op. cit., p. 473.
[620] Dimitrije Djordević, *Scars and Memories: Four Lives in One Lifetime*, (New York: Columbia University Press, 1994), p. 234, quoted in Misha Glenny, Op. cit., p. 531.
[621] Misha Glenny, op. cit., p. 531.

Conclusion

253

achieve territorial expansion westwards. The fact that Yugoslavia's territorial claims to Venezia Giulia were put forward to British authorities as early as 1941 explains why Tito's troops left behind some inland areas under German occupation, whilst rushing westwards towards Trieste. The expansionist element also further supports the reason behind the three waves of atrocities against Italians.

Extreme violence and the desire for destruction, nourished by hatred, took on a social awareness, becoming 'a means of inclusion and exclusion.'[622] This materialised when victims were physically beaten and within the circumstances that facilitated violence and the institutions that condoned it. The barbarisation of politics and warfare, which flared up in Venezia Giulia and Central Europe, was by no means a uniquely Fascist or Communist phenomenon. Throughout the first half of the twentieth century the whole of Europe fell, as Ian Kershaw stated, into 'a pit of barbarism.' During this period, the greatest violence was committed by the state against civilians, all the more so in comparison to the enlightened order of the Hapsburg Empire, which had ruled over the same territories and people in the previous centuries.

It is undeniable that the First World War accustomed European society to violence by unleashing the glorification of brutality and easy cruelty, however violence was already a form of social and political expression well before the beginning of the conflict. In 1909, Italy Futurism, the artistic movement launched by Filippo Tommaso Marinetti, celebrated modernity, militarism and war as 'the only true hygiene of the world.' Together with ultra-nationalists, the Futurists politically demonstrated for Italy to join the Great War, and later welcomed the rise of Fascism. The trauma of the war facilitated violence and genocidal logistics: the conflict stoked grievances and an abiding desire for revenge against those responsible for damaged national prestige, whilst nationalism was being defined by ethnicity rather than territory. Nationalist, ethnic and class hatred became the main reason behind the state inflicting violence on many

---

[622] Franziska Exeler, 'Violence et violence extreme,' in Jean-François Muracciole and Guillaume Piketty, op. cit., pp. 1381.

minorities. However, most significantly, the war blurred the distinction between combatants and civilians. Dark currents of resentment and hate ran deep beneath the social and political order of the post-war period, which was marked by the collapse of the values and institutions of Liberalism. The roots of such violence can be identified in a mix of nationalist ideology and popular sovereignty, or better the contradiction between nationhood and statehood. Further, it can be found in colonial thinking, which centred on suppressing peoples considered as inferior; and the consensus gained by Italian Socialism that, increased by the victory of the Bolsheviks in Russia in 1917, provoked the inevitable counterattack of the violent Right. Combining these elements with the experience of the Great War explains the extent of gory and gratuitous cruelty, which would characterise the rest of the century. As Lance Morrow observed, 'trench warfare prefigured the final industrialism of the Nazi death camps: there cling to the gray, corpse-littered wastelands of World War I something of the same atmosphere: individual life stripped of meaning, dignity, all life and all death rendered purposeless, and reduced to absolute metaphysical insignificance.'[623]

Whilst people felt they had lost their ideal Motherland, charismatic leaders captured the popular mood and soon identified a scapegoat, by whipping up national anger, encouraging and legitimising targeted violence against particular 'others.' A taxonomy of human and political groups was thus created and the enemy was given many vilifying names and demonised because of a blend of stereotypes and prejudices unique in the 1920s and 1930s. Social and political Darwinism helped to create an acceptance of the utility of brutal violence – killing men became natural and easy, blood appealed as a symbol of purification from the infection of the foe. As a result, it was not enough to defeat opponents: they had to be erased, belittled in their pride, humiliated in the spirit and maimed in the flesh. As the rise of fascism and the Bolshevik Revolution during the early 1920s have shown, the future belonged to those ready to engage in the political culture of the armed group. In Italy and Germany, the fear of a red

---

[623] Lance Morrow, *Evil: An Investigation*, (New York: Basic Books, 2003), p. 47.

Conclusion

255

revolution, from which Communists could emerge as victors, created the conditions for radicalised social groups to seize power under Fascist and Nazi banners. The black and brown shirt squads, with their cult of strength and sacrifice, preached how expendable human life was as long as goals were reached, and authorised violent actions by giving them a political legitimacy. The barbarisation of warfare in the Second World War would be just one-step away: the conflict was waged with unprecedented savagery, made possible by a cognitive consonance between desirability and moral admissibility of the action of elimination, and supported by the perpetrators awareness that they would be granted impunity.

Perhaps the greatest disturbing element associated with the Second World War comes from the scale and degree of violence and cruelty used against civilians not only during the war, but also in its immediate aftermath, as exemplified by the large population expulsions and the tragic settlement of accounts. It is not by chance that the 1949 Geneva Convention included the issues of the violence waged against non-combatants as an element to be internationally considered within the legal framework of conflicts.

However, as mentioned above, extreme violence was only one strand of the story: oblivion was the other. All those who survived the ethnic and political cleansing in Venezia Giulia, and decided their lives were untenable under the new Communist regime, decided to flee, thus plunging their lives into uncertainty. Leaving behind their assets and properties, they fled to Italy, mainly to Trieste and Venice from there they scattered throughout Italy: Sardinia, Lazio, Emilia Romagna, Marche, Tuscany, Veneto, Lombardia. Others left for Switzerland, the Americas, and New Zealand. Apart from having to begin their lives all over again, what all refugees had in common was being faced by a national and civic nihilism, resulting in their silence and trying to forget. What were the reasons which pushed them, who knew they had suffered a wrong, to keep silent? Why did they not fight for the recognition of what happened to them? How could the collective memory of such a violent and traumatic experience be wiped out at a national level as if it had never existed?

256   *Luisa Morettin*

The clear victory of the Allies and the Resistance gave them the power to shape the collective memory of the war. In addition, the situation of Venezia Giulia refugees brought to the surface an uncomfortable issue, which had to be quickly forgotten – the Fascist occupation of and crimes in Yugoslavia. Yugoslav silence regarding the Italian war crimes was bartered for for Italy's silence regarding the Yugoslav communist atrocities.

Several other factors played an important role in the process of 'national forgetfulness,' The precarious balance brought by post war peace and the psychological need for closure were closely connected with the desire of the Rome government to have Italy accepted back into the international community. The onset of the Cold War, with its fundamental incompatibility between the Soviet and democratic system, saw a sudden shift in East-West relations and resulted in the old allies becoming new enemies. Forgetting the *foibe* atrocities also allowed a veil to be drawn over the controversial and ambivalent role played by the PCI, *Italian Communist Party*. After the break between Tito and Stalin in June 1948, the Anglo-Americans and Italy no longer wished to antagonise Belgrade as Yugoslavia became a much needed buffer state with the Eastern block of Communist countries. This would allow Italy to ease their defence expenditure and establish mutually advantageous economic relations with her Eastern neighbouring state.[624]

Giulio Andreotti, the leader of the Christian Democrat party, who served seven terms as Prime Minister and dominated Italian politics for decades, confirmed that peace could only be found by forgetting the disputed and painful past. During a television interview, Andreotti declared: 'It was good to forget the *foibe* issue in order not to compromise relations with the PCI and our good relationship with Tito.'[625] To appreciate the disregarding of the matter as the appropriate response in the heated aftermath of the Second World War, a 2007 diplomatic incident

---

[624] Raoul Pupo, *Il lungo esodo. Istria: le persecuzioni, le foibe, l'esilio*, (Milano: BUR, 2005), pp. 18-9.
[625] Porta a Porta, RAI1, 3 February 2005.

Conclusion 257

needs to be considered.[626] In a prepared statement, during the commemoration of the *Giorno del Ricordo* on 10 February 2007, left-wing Italian President Giorgio Napolitano duly remembered the *foibe* atrocities and the ensuing migration, as custom since 2004. However, on this occasion President Napolitano added that 'the tragedy of the people from Venezia Giulia and Dalmatia was the consequence of a wave of bloody hatred and fury and of Yugoslav annexation plans that resulted in ethnical cleansing.' This speech did not sit well with Croatian President Stjepan Mesić, who retaliated, declaring himself 'dismayed' by the words used by President Napolitano, in which 'it was possible to see elements of open racism, historical revisionism and political revanschism.' Mesić continued to state that he had no intention 'to keep silent about [past] events and to allow the historical vanquished to turn into a victorious people.'[627] Later, Italian Foreign Minister Massimo D'Alema called the Croatian ambassador to a meeting to discuss the matter. The incident is a striking example of the animosity existing between the two states, over seventy years on, and the distance needed to achieve a shared moral memory based on some moral minima. It also helps to comprehend that forgetting is not healing, as historical wounds are still fresh.

The collective oblivion used to create a sanitised narrative of the world war meant thousands of uprooted Istrians and Dalmatians who fled persecution were left bitterly disappointed with the difference between the Italy they had dreamed of and the Italy they endured. They were further taken aback by the lack of compassion of their fellow nationals, especially those with left-wing inclinations, as in Italy, refugees were greeted with suspicion. If they were leaving Communist Venezia Giulia, so went the line of argumentation, then they must have been active Fascists deeply involved with the regime. The hostility shown toward them was expressed

---

[626] 'Foibe: presidente croato attacca Napolitano,' in *Il Corriere della Sera*, 13 February 2007, http://www. corriere.it/Primo_Piano/Esteri/2007/02_Febbraio/12/foibe.shtml?refresh_ce-cp, accessed 4 September 2016.

[627] 'Foibe, l'ira della Croazia contro Napolitano. D'Alema: È presidente dell'Italia antifascista,' *La Repubblica*, 12 February 2007, accessed 5 July 2018.

258   *Luisa Morettin*

in several ways and perhaps the better-known example is *il treno della vergogna* (the train of shame). On 18 February 1947, in Pola, Italian national refugees boarded a cargo train heading to the town of Ancona. When the convoy reached Bologna, they were scheduled to disembark for refreshments, as arranged by the Red Cross and the *Pontificia Opera di Assistenza*, a Vatican funded charity. However, Communist railway workers threatened to go on strike and block the important railway communication hub if the refugees disembarked. For the workers, it was 'a train full of Fascists,' against which stones and tomatoes were thrown, whilst the milk intended for children, some of whom were severely dehydrated, was deliberately spilt on the tracks. [628] The train with its human cargo was forced to continue its journey to another town. Some people on the train may have been frauds and Fascists, yet all were - at that stage – sufferers. A plaque on Platform One, at Bologna Central Station, commemorates the incident.

The incomprehension of contemporaries, who struggled to understand the circumstances that motivated thousands of Italians to leave their homeland, did not abate. The Italian Communist paper *L'Unità*, for instance, fuelled popular ignorance amongst the public as to the reasons of the voluntary exile of Venezia Giulia refugees, stirring up prejudice and rejection of the exiles at a grassroots level.[629]

Some historians, denialists and reductionists define the *foibe* atrocities as an Italian right-wing sponsored 'home-grown holocaust'[630] and therefore, they are prepared to defend and justify them in a simplistic way with using four argumentations.

In the first, they claim that the violence was mutual as it had happened within the context of international war, thus it was legitimate self-defence since Italy had invaded Yugoslavia in April 1941. If some excesses took place – so the line of thought goes - they were meant to achieve the greater good of the liberation from Axis occupation. The claim invites scrutiny of

---

[628] 'Quei profughi istriani e il Treno della Vergogna,' *Corriere della Sera*, 18 September 2015, accessed 5 July 2018.
[629] Tommaso Giglio, 'Chissà dove finirà il treno dei fascisti?,' *L'Unità*, 30 November 1946.
[630] Keith Lowe, op. cit., p. 375.

Conclusion 259

Tito's eliminationism methods, which ominously resembled fascist abuses. The argument also fails to justify that pro-Yugoslav combatants used unjust war methods (torture, random killings, rapes, kidnappings, ruthless use of prisoners' labour), and the fact that targets included illegitimate ones: defenceless civilians, prisoners of war, and Italian partisans who had helped in the anti-Fascist struggle.

In their second claim, they try to downplay events. In this respect, the quantity of the victims of pro-Tito's partisans is one of the most controversial issues in this chapter of Italian history and Italo-Yugoslav relations. There is an obsession with the statistics, which numbs the actuality of events; as if only an algebraic game could grant the killings a particular status within historical remembering. As is often the case, the disputed number of victims seems to have played a more important role in the collective imagination than the causes of such brutality. Opposing political parties have tried to manipulate numbers to their advantage: those more inclined to support the Left tend to minimise figures, whereas those inclined to support the Centre-Right have been accused of increasing them as a means of playing down the crimes for which Fascism was responsible. The Anglo-American sources, examined for this research, have shown how difficult it was to ascertain reliable figures, highlighting the exact record of victims will never be known. Difficulties in retrieving corpses from the pits, many of which remain unexplored, the inaccessibility of Yugoslav archives, the secrecy and the frantic, hasty rhythms of arrests, killings and deportations, the executioners' intention to hide proof of their crimes, the fact that abuses were carried out by several perpetrators, (i.e., partisan troops, individuals and OZNA), are all elements which make the number of people murdered in September 1943, in October 1944, and again in spring 1945, extremely hard to estimate.

In the third claim, if Italians did die, they were Fascists who deserved their end. No honest historian could deny that Fascist Italy was the aggressor and the oppressor. However barbaric and deplorable the aggression and suppression acts, the Yugoslav self-serving justification does not take into account the evident individual guilt, and deliberately condemns victims to indiscriminate punishment beyond the rule of law.

Tito's crimes cannot be explained away as a collateral damage in the course of killing the culpable, using the excuse of the 'fog of war.'

In the fourth and final argument, it is the reiterated assertion that it was the Yugoslavs who were the real victims. Listing fascist crimes allowed Belgrade to pre-empt attention to the atrocities committed by Communist partisans. Victimhood gives one a special moral and material status as reprisal strikes are easily excused and often welcomed as inevitable. However, over time, such a strategy of denial created by the Yugoslav authorities became more difficult to maintain as survivors and former prisoners of war, trickled into Udine recounting their ordeals to Allied officials. Yet, in the worldview, Tito's troops were irreprehensible heroes as having previously been victims of violence, they were viewed as morally justified and forever entitled to sympathy. As a result, the Yugoslavs never took responsibility for their actions because they used victimisation as a moral and emotional weapon.

The British and Americans appeared mainly impotent in front of Tito's ruthless determination to purge Yugoslav society of the amorphous categories of 'Fascists' and 'enemies of the people.' However, it needs to be questioned whether someone who became a Fascist Party member simply to get a job is truly a Fascist and should be punished. To note, proven Fascists, such as General Mario Roatta, the commander of the Second Italian Army, and Giacomo Zanussi, Roatta's deputy Chief of Staff, who were personally criminally responsible for many hideous atrocities in Venezia Giulia and Yugoslavia, went unpunished.

More so, it begs the question of who were the enemies of the people. The fluid designation of political or class opponents implied that anyone branded as such could not be part of Yugoslavia's future. There could be no concessions and elimination would be automatic. The victims' baleful fate was rooted in national Irredentism, shaped by two World Wars, and sealed by opposing, yet equally homicidal ideologies.

Many of the Italian refugees that the author interviewed reported how they suffered from the demeaning consequences of their label of exiles, stripped of all their assets and social distinction. They were despised and seen as inferior since they lived in makeshift accommodation or in

Conclusion

261

deportation and concentration camps, such as the San Sabba annex, near the former Nazi concentration camp in Trieste, or in Fossoli, in the province of Modena, which between 1954 and 1970 housed hundreds of families from Venezia Giulia. Some refugees lived in camps for as long as ten years and so deeply engrained were the stereotypes, that in some cases, mainland Italian families considered girls from refugee families as unsuitable fiancées.

Fellow nationals' resentment and incomprehension also stemmed from the belief that the Italian government had treated Venezia Giulia refugees favourably: farmers were given houses and fields to farm, city dwellers flats, whereas the rest of the Italian population had to fend for themselves in the hard post-war period. However, the reasons of the refugees' resettlement and the fact that they had to pay back the government for their houses, without receiving compensation for the loss of their own assets in Venezia Giulia, were hardly discussed. Authoritative journalists and writers from Venezia Giulia, such as Enzo Bettiza, Nelida Milani, and Anna Maria Mori, addressed the painful issues of displacement, uncertainty, memory and the politics of self-representation after the 'exodus,' all elements which are omitted in archival sources. A recurrent theme these writers addressed was the difficulty of being understood by those who had not been through the same experiences.

It is therefore understandable that, given the adversity they met with, refugees preferred not to speak to outsiders of their pain and suffering, although they certainly felt they were being victimised. Vicissitudes were better to be swept under the carpet. Istrians and Dalmatians knew they were different: whoever did not experience the waves of Communist terror did not know how to listen or, perhaps, did not want to listen.

Other pressing issues distracted people in Italy as in many other countries. After the Second World War, reconstruction and economic development were the priority. Everybody wanted to start afresh by putting the evil of the war behind them and look toward a brighter and better future. As a result, the *foibe* atrocities would be relegated to the sphere of local politics in the cities of Trieste and Gorizia.

The Second World War, for Venezia Giulia, ended in October 1954 with the allocation of Trieste to Italy, but for survivors and migrants from the disputed region it would never end. Although it is difficult to capture the complexities of individual lives and experiences, those of survivors of war and terror, of slave workers and of displaced persons, are not unique to Venezia Giulia. It is known that after the Second World War multitudes of ethnic Germans were expelled from Eastern Europe and many Polish Jews fled from a new wave of persecution as the Soviets wrought a terrible revenge upon anybody who had collaborated or was thought to have collaborated with the Wehrmacht. What they all had in common, regardless of their ethnic, religious and political background, was that they were traumatised victims, who for years faced the limbo of trying to build a new life in an unknown environment whilst striving for certainty and conditions which could at the least resemble normality.

As fascism, with its misrule, crimes and destruction of liberty and life, represented and still represents an 'uncomfortable past,'[631] this book provides the evidence that the *foibe* crimes assertions are justified, and yet, society is confronted with a blatant case of moral relativism or, rather, what Cushman and Meštrović call 'a frame of reference.'[632] This term implies that the ongoing atrocities in Venezia Giulia were made to fit pre-existing constructs: the Istrian community was previously associated with Italy and its very evil fascist occupation; Italians were defined as Fascists, so to many they could not be victims of the Yugoslavs, since it was impossible for Fascists to be victims.

These atrocities were not condemned, on the contrary, systematic violence continued well into 1947 under the eyes of impotent and ineffectual Allied troops. The cover-up, self-interest of and betrayal by Italian and Yugoslav authorities conspired to suppress the memory of human suffering for much longer. This showed that war was not a neat package. It was not good versus evil, as this can only be the case when

---

[631] Nicola Tranfaglia, *Un passato scomodo: fascismo e postfascismo*, (Bari: Laterza, 1996).

[632] Thomas Cushman and Stjepan G. Meštrović (ed.), *This Time We Knew. Western Responses to Genocide in Bosnia*, (New York: New York University Press, 1996), p. 28.

Conclusion 263

there are clear-cut victims and perpetrators. There was no-one who tried to understand the violence and loss suffered by the victims on both sides. Neither side openly and vocally repudiated the system of which they were a part. No retributive justice ensued as perpetrators were not punished, nor was there a revelatory justice to expose the guilty and their crimes, or at least a reconciliatory justice, which would offer heartfelt apologies for past crimes. Instead what followed was silence. A silence, which has lasted for half a century.

I continue to believe that this world does not have any ultimate purpose. But I know that something in it does have meaning, and that is man.

Albert Camus
Notebooks

BIBLIOGRAPHY

A. ARCHIVAL SOURCES

A.1 Archival Sources

ACS, Archivio Centrale dello Stato, Rome
ASMAE, Archivio Storico del Ministero degli Affari Esteri, Rome
AUSSME, Archivio dell'Ufficio Storico dello Stato Maggiore dell'Esercito, Rome
FRUS, Foreign Relations of the United States
PRO, Public Record Office, United Kingdom
 Admiralty Office Papers (ADM), ADM 1
 Foreign Office Papers (FO), FO 371
 Cabinet Office Papers (CAB), CAB 121
 Premier Office Papers (PREM), PREM 3
 War Office Papers (WO), WO 204

A.2 Printed Sources

Canavero, A., 'Le terre liberate e redente nel dibattito culturale e politico,' in *Commissione parlamentare di inchiesta sulle terre liberate e*

266   *Bibliography*

redente (luglio 1920-giugno 1922), vol. I, (Roma: Camera dei Deputati Archivio storico, 1991).

Cavallero, Ugo, *Comando Supremo. Diario 1940-43 del Capo di S.M.G.*, (Bologna: Cappelli, 1948).

Ciano, Galeazzo, *Diario 1937-1943,* (a cura di Renzo De Felice), (Milano: BUR, 2006).

Italian Genocide Policy against the Slovenes and the Croats. A Selection of Documents, (Belgrade: Institute for International Politics and Economics, 1954).

Lloyd-George, David, *War Memoirs*, 2 Vols., (London: Odhams, 1938).

Macmillan, Harold, *War Diaries. Politics and War in the Mediterranean. January 1943-May 1945*, (London: Macmillan, 1984).

Mussolini, Benito, *Opera Omnia*, (E. and D. Susmel ed.), (Firenze: Giovanni Volpe editore, 1978-1980).

Piemontese, Giuseppe, *Ventinove mesi di occupazione italiana nella provincia di Lubiana. Considerazioni e documenti*, (Lubiana: s.n., 1946).

Processo Graziani: l'Autodifesa dell'ex Maresciallo nel Resoconto Stenografico, Vol. 1, (Roma: Ruffolo, 1948).

Quaranta, Bernardo Barone (ed.), *Mussolini as Revealed in His Political Speeches. November 1914 – August 1923*, (London and Toronto: J. M. Dent, 1923).

Schramm, Percy E., *Kriegstagebuch des Oberkommandos der Wehrmacht 1940-1945 - Eine Dokumentation*, Teilband 1, (München: Weltbild, 1982).

Seton-Watson, Robert W., (ed.), *R. W. Seton-Watson and the Yugoslavs: Correspondence 1906-1941*, Vol 1, (London: British Academy, 1976).

Seymour, Charles (ed.), *The Intimate Papers of Colonel House,* (London: Houghton Mifflin, 1928), Vol 4.

Wilson, Woodrow, *Speech on the Fourteen Points Jan 8, 1918.* Accessed 25 January 2014. http://www.fordham.edu/halsall/mod/1918wilson. html.

Bibliography 267

B. SECONDARY LITERATURE

B.1 Books and Monographs

A.A. V.V., *Friuli e Venezia Giulia. Storia del '900*, (Gorizia: Libreria Editrice Goriziana, 1997).

AA.VV., *Storia contemporanea in Friuli*, (Udine: Istituto Friulano per la storia del movimento di liberazione, 2003).

Aga-Rossi, Elena and Zaslavsky, Victor, *Togliatti e Stalin. Il PCI e la politica estera staliniana negli archivi di Mosca*, (Bologna: Il Mulino, 2007).

Akhmatova, Anna, *Poems*, (New York: Alfred A. Knopf, 2006).

Albertini, Luigi, *Le origini della guerra del 1914*, (Milano: Fratelli Bocca, 1942).

Albrecht-Carrié, René, *Italy at the Paris Peace Conference*, (New York: Columbia University Press, 1938).

Anderson, Benedict, *Imagined Communities: Reflections on the Origin and Spread of Nationalism*, (London: Verso, 1983).

Apih, Elio, *Italia. Fascismo e antifascismo nella Venezia Giulia 1918-1943*, (Bari: Laterza, 1966).

———, *Le foibe giuliane*, (Gorizia: Libreria Editrice Goriziana, 2010).

Ara, Angelo and Magris, Claudio, *Trieste. Un'identità di frontiera*, (Torino: Einaudi, 1982).

Arosio, Sandra, *Scrittori di frontiera. Scipio Slataper, Giani e Carlo Stuparich*, (Milano: Guerini Editore, 1996)

Auty, Phillips and Clogg, Richard (eds.), *British Policy Towards Wartime Resistance in Yugoslavia and Greece*, (New York: Barnes and Noble, 1975).

Baerlein, Henry, *The Birth of Yugoslavia*, (London: Leonard Parsons, 1922).

Balfour, Neil and Mackay, Sally, *Paul of Yugoslavia. Britain's Maligned Friend*, (London: Hamilton, 1980).

Bambara, Gino, *Jugoslavia settebandiere. Guerra senza retrovie nella Jugoslavia occupata 1941-1943*, (Brescia Vannini, 1988).

268   *Bibliography*

———, *Non solo armistizio. Autunno 1943. Tragico sfacelo dell'Armata italiana in Jugoslavia e ai confini orientali*, (Gussago: Società Editrice Vannini, 2003).

Barker, Elisabeth, *British Policy in South-East Europe in the Second World War*, (New York: Barnes & Noble Books, 1976).

———, *Churchill and Eden at War*, (Basingstoke: Macmillan, 1978).

Battini, Michele, *Peccati di memoria. La mancata Norimberga italiana*, (Bari: Laterza 2003).

Bartolini, Stefano, *Fascismo antislavo. Il tentativo di «bonifica etnica» al confine nord orientale*, (Pistoia: I.S.R.Pt. editore, 2006).

Battaglia, Romano, *Storia della Resistenza*, (Torino: Einaudi, 1964).

Beevor, Antony, *Berlin. The Downfall 1945*, (London: Penguin, 2002).

Bettelheim, Bruno, *Surviving and Other Essays*, (London: Thames & Hudson, 1979).

———, *The Informed Heart. A Study of the Psychological Consequences of Living ender Extreme Fear and Terror*, (London: Penguin, 1986).

Boggs, S. Whittemore, *International Boundaries. A Study of Boundary Functions and Problems*, (New York: Columbia University Press, 1940).

Bosworth, Richard J. B., *Italy and the Approach of the First World War*, (London: Macmillan, 1983).

———, *Italy and the Wider World. 1860-1960*, (London and New York, Routledge, 1996).

———, *Italy the Least of Great Powers: Italian Foreign Policy before the First World War*, (Cambridge: Cambridge University Press, 1979).

———, *Mussolini*, (London: Arnold, 2002).

Burgio, Alberto, (a cura di), *Nel nome della razza: il razzismo nella storia d'Italia, 1870-1945*, (Bologna: Il Mulino, 1999).

Burgwyn, H. J., *Empire on the Adriatic. Mussolini's Conquest of Yugoslavia 1941-1943*, (New York: Enigma Books, 2005).

Butler, Hubert, *The Invader Wore Slippers*, (London: Notting Hill Editions, 2012).

Butler, L. J., *Britain and Empire. Adjusting to a Post-Imperial World*, (London and New York: I. B. Tauris, 2002).

Bibliography

269

Cambria, Adele, *Maria José*, (Milano: Longanesi, 1966).

Cannistraro, Philip, *Historical Dictionary of Fascist Italy*, (London: Greenwood Press, 1982).

Carlson, Julie A. and Weber, Elisabeth (ed.), *Speaking about Torture*, (New York: Fordham University Press, 2012).

Cattaruzza, Marina, *Italy and Its Eastern Border, 1866-2016*, (London: Routledge, 2016).

Cattaruzza, Marina, Dogo, Marco, and Pupo, Raoul (ed.), *Esodi. Trasferimenti forzati di popolazione nel Novecento europeo and Il confine orientale nel Novecento*, (Napoli: Edizioni Scientifiche Italiane, 2000).

Čermelj, Lavo, *Life-and-Death Struggle of a National Minority: the Jugoslavs in Italy*, (Ljubljana: Tiskarna Ljudske pravice, 1945).

Cervi, Mario, *The Hollow Legions. Mussolini's Blunder in Greece*. 1940-1941, (New York: Doubleday, 1971).

Cesarani, David, *Final Solution. The Fate of the Jews 1933-49*, (London: Macmillan, 2016).

Ceva, Lucio, *La condotta italiana della guerra. Cavallero e il Comando Supremo 1941-1942*, (Milano: Feltrinelli, 1975).

Chickering, Roger, *Imperial Germany and the Great War*, (Cambridge: Cambridge University Press, 1998).

Chiurco, Giorgio Alberto, *Storia della rivoluzione fascista*, Vol. 2, (Firenze: Vallecchi editore, 1929).

Churchill, Winston, *The Second World War*, Vols 1-12, (London: Cassell, 1964).

Clark, Christopher, *The Sleepwalkers. How Europe Went to War in 1914*, (London: Penguin, 2013).

Clark, Martin, *Modern Italy 1871-1982*, (London: Longman, 1984).

Clissold, Stephen, *Yugoslavia and the Soviet Union 1939-1973. A Documentary Survey*, (London: Oxford University Press, 1975).

——— , *Whirlwind. An Account of Marshal Tito's Rise to Power*, (London: Cresset Press, 1949).

Coceani, Bruno, *Trieste durante l'occupazione tedesca 1943-1945*, (Milano: La Stampa Commerciale, 1959).

Bibliography

Collotti, Enzo, *L'occupazione nazista in Europa*, (Roma: Editori Riuniti, 1964).

Cooper, Henry R., *Slavic Scriptures: The Formation of the Church Slavonic Version of the Holy Bible*, (London: Associated University Presses, 2002).

Corsellis, John and Ferrar, Marcus, *Slovenia 1945. Ricordi di morte e di sopravvivenza dopo la Seconda guerra mondiale*, (Gorizia: Libreria Editrice Goriziana, 2008).

Cox, Geoffrey, *The Race for Trieste*, (London: Kimber, 1977).

Cumin, Gustavo, *Guida della Carsia Giulia*, (Trieste: Società Alpina delle Giulie, 1929).

Cushman, Thomas and Meštrović, Stjepan G. (eds.), *This Time We Knew. Western Responses to Genocide in Bosnia*, (New York: New York University Press, 1996).

Cusin, Fabio *Antistoria d'Italia. Una demistificazione della storia ufficiale*, (Milano: Mondadori, 1972).

———, *L'italiano: realtà e illusioni*, (Roma: Atlantica, 1945).

———, *Venti secoli di bora sul Carso e sul Golfo*, (Trieste: Gabbiano, 1952).

———, *La liberazione di Trieste, contributo alla storiografia non nazionalistica di Trieste*, (Trieste: Zigiotti, 1946).

Cuzzi, Marco, *L'occupazione italiana della Slovenia (1941-1943)*, (Roma: Stato Maggiore dell'Esercito, 1998).

D'Annunzio, Gabriele, *Versi d'amore e di gloria*, (Milano Mondadori Meridiani, 2004), vol. II.

Dassovich, Mario, *Fronte jugoslavo 1943. La fase finale delle operazioni dell'esercito italiano sull'opposta sponda adriatica durante la seconda guerra mondiale*, (Udine: Del Bianco, 2000).

Dato, Gaetano, *Vergarolla 18 agosto 1946. Gli enigmi di una strage tra conflitto mondiale e guerra fredda*, (Gorizia: Libreria Editrice Goriziana, 2014).

Davies, Norman, *Europe East and West*, (London: Jonathan Cape, 2006).

Bibliography

De Castro, Diego, *Il problema di Trieste. Genesi e sviluppi della questione giuliana in relazione agli avvenimenti internazionali 1943-1952*, (Bologna: Licinio Cappelli Editore, 1953).

De Felice, Renzo, *Mussolini il Duce. Lo stato totalitario 1936-1940*, (Torino: Einaudi, 1981).

———, *Storia degli ebrei italiani sotto il fascismo*, (Torino: Einaudi, 1972).

De Grand, Alexander J., *The Italian Nationalist Association and the Rise of Fascism in Italy*, (Lincoln: University of Nebraska Press, 1978).

Dedijer, Vladimir, *The Yugoslav Auschwitz and the Vatican: The Croatian Massacre of the Serbs During World War II*, (London: Prometheus Books, 1992).

Del Boca, Angelo, *Italiani, brava gente? Un mito duro a morire,* (Vicenza: Neri Pozza Editore, 2005).

Di Nolfo, Ennio and Serra, Maurizio, *La gabbia infranta. Gli Alleati e l'Italia dal 1943 al 1945*, (Bari: Laterza, 2010).

Di Sante, Costantino, *Nei campi di Tito. Soldati, deportati e prigionieri di guerra italiani in Jugoslavia 1941-1952*, (Verona: Ombre Corte, 2007).

Dijlas, Milovan, *Conversations with Stalin*, (London: Rupert Hart-Davies, 1962).

———, *Memoir of a Revolutionary*, (New York: Harcourt Brace Jovanovich, 1973).

———, *The Unperfect Society: Beyond the New Class*, (Harcourt, Brace & World, 1969).

———, *Tito: the Story from Inside*, (London: Weidenfeld and Nicolson, 1981).

———, *Wartime*, (London: Harcourt Brace Jovanovich, 1977).

Djordević, Dimitrije, *Scars and Memories: Four Lives in One Lifetime*, (New York: Columbia University Press, 1994).

Duroselle, Jean-Baptiste, *Le Conflit de Trieste 1943-1954*, (Bruxelles: L'Institut de Sociologie de l'Université libre de Bruxelles, 1946).

Drndić, Liubo, *Le armi e la libertà dell'Istria 1941-1943*, (Fiume: Edit, 1981).

Bibliography

Duggan, Christopher, *Fascist Voices. An Intimate History of Mussolini's Italy,* (London: The Bodley Head, 2012).

———, *The Force of Destiny. A History of Italy since 1796,* (London: Penguin Books, 2007).

Ebner, Michael R., *Ordinary Violence in Mussolini's Italy,* (New York, Cambridge University Press, 2011).

Ellwood, David W., *Italy 1943-1945,* (Leicester: Leicester University Press, 1985).

———, *Rebuilding Europe: Western Europe, America and Postwar Reconstruction,* (New York: Routledge, 1992).

Fabi, Lucio, *Gente di trincea. La grande Guerra sul Carso e sull'Isonzo,* (Milano: Mursia Editore, 1994).

———, *Trieste, 1914-1918: una città in guerra,* (Trieste: MGS Press, 1996).

Fait, Francesco, (a cura di), *Scritte, lettere e voci. Tracce di vittime e superstiti della Risiera di San Sabba,* (Trieste: IRSML, 2014).

Fatutta, Fortunato, *La campagna di Jugoslavia. Aprile 1941-settembre 1943,* (Campobasso: Opportunity Books, 1996).

Ferenc, Tone, *Rab – Arbe – Arbissima. Confinamenti, rastrellamenti, internamenti nella nella Privincia di Lubiana 1941-1943,* (Ljubljana: Institut za novejso zgodovino, 2000).

Ferenc, Tone and Kodrič, Pavel, *Si ammazza troppo poco: condannati a morte, ostaggi, passati per le armi nella provincia di Lubiana 1941-1943,* (Lubiana: Società degli scrittori della storia della Lotta di Liberazione, 1999).

Finchelstein, Federico, *Transatlantic Fascism: Ideology, Violence, and the Sacred in Argentina and Italy, 1919-1945,* (Durham: Duke University Press, 2010).

Fiorentin, Graziella, *Chi ha paura dell'uomo nero?,* (Trieste: Lint, 2004).

Focardi, Filippo, *Il cattivo tedesco e il bravo italiano. La rimozione delle colpe della seconda guerra mondiale,* (Bari: Laterza, 2013).

Fogar, Galliano, *Trieste in guerra 1940-1945. Società e Resistenza,* (Trieste: ISMLFVG: 1999).

Bibliography

Foot, John, *Italy's Divided Memory*, (Basingstoke: Palgrave Macmillan, 2009).

Forcella, Enzo and Monticone, Alberto, *Plotone di esecuzione*, (Bari: Laterza, 1968).

Gabrielli, Italo, *Istria, Fiume Dalmazia. Diritti negati, genocidio programmato*, (Trieste: Associazione Culturale Giuliana, 2011).

Garde, Paul, *Vie et mort de la Yugoslavie*, (Paris: Fayard, 1992).

Gayda, Virginio, *Gli Slavi della Venezia Giulia*, (Roma: Rava & Co., 1915).

——— , *Modern Austria: Her Racial and Social Problems with a Study of Italia Irredenta*, (London: Fischer Unwin, 1915).

Glenny, Misha, *The Balkans, 1804-2012: Nationalism, War and the Great Powers*, (London: Granta, 2012).

Goldstein, Ivo, *Croatia. A History*, (London: Hurst & Co., 1999).

Gombač, Metka, Stuhlpfarrer, Karl, Mattiussi, Dario, *Als mein Vater starb: Zeichnungen und Zeugnisse von Kindern aus Konzentrationslagern der italienischen Ostgrenze (1942-1943)*, (Klagenfurt: Wieser Verlag, 2009).

Gooch, John, *Mussolini and His Generals. The Armed Forces and Fascist Foreign Policy, 1922-1940*, (Cambridge: Cambridge University Press, 2007),

Gualtieri, Roberto, *Togliatti e la politica estera italiana dalla resistenza al trattato di pace 1943-1947*, (Roma: Editori Riuniti, 1995).

Guerrazzi, Gian Francesco, *Ricordi d'Irredentismo. I primordi della Dante Alighieri* (1881-1894), (Bologna: Zanichelli, 1922).

Hametz, Maura, *Making Trieste Italian, 1918-1954*, (Woodbridge: The Boydell Press, 2005).

Hamilton, Richard F., and Herwing Holger H., *Decisions for War, 1914-1917*, (Cambridge: Cambridge University Press, 2004).

Hansen, Patrizia C. (a cura di), *Il confine orientale nel Novecento*, (Roma: Istituto della Enciclopedia Treccani, 2003).

Harris, C. R. S., *Allied Military Administration of Italy, 1943-1945*, (New York: British Information Services, 1957).

274 *Bibliography*

Heuser, Beatrice, *Western 'Containment' Policies in the Cold War: The Yugoslav Case, 1948-53,* (Abingdon: Routledge, 1989).

Hoptner, Jacob B. and Roberts, Henry L., *Yugoslavia in Crisis 1934-1941,* (New York: Columbia University Press, 1962).

Hughes-Hallett, Lucy, *The Pike. Gabriele d'Annunzio. Poet, Seducer and Preacher of War,* (London: Fourth Estate, 2013).

International Committee of the Nazi Lager of Risiera di San Sabba, *Risiera di San Sabba. History and Museum,* (Trieste: s.n., 2009).

Isnenghi, Mario (ed.), *I luoghi della memoria. Strutture ed eventi dell'Italia Unita,* (Bari: Laterza, 1997).

Jászi, Oscar, *The Dissolution of the Habsburg Monarchy,* (Chicago: University of Chicago Press, 1929).

Jovanović, Batrić, *Crna Gora, u narodnooslobodilačkom ratu i socijalističkoj revoluciji,* Vol 1, (Belgrade: Vojno delo, 1960).

Jowett, Philip, *Italian Army, 1940-1945,* Vol. 1, (Oxford: Osprey Publishing, 2000).

Judt, Tony, *When the Facts Change. Essays 1995-2010,* (London: Vintage, 2015).

Kann, Robert Adolf, *The Multinational Empire. Nationalism and National Reform in the Habsburg Monarchy, 1848-1918,* 2 vols., (New York: Columbia University Press, 1950).

Kersevan, Alessandra, *Lager italiani, Pulizia etnica e campi di concentramento fascisti per civili jugoslavi 1941-1943,* (Roma: Nutrimenti, 2008).

Kershaw, Ian, *To Hell and Back. Europe 1914-1949,* (London: Penguin Books, 2016).

Kitchen, Martin, *A World in Flames: A Short History of the Second World War in Europe and Asia, 1939–1945,* (New York: Longman, 1990).

Knox, MacGregor, *Common Destiny. Dictatorship, Foreign Policy, and War in Fascist Italy and Nazi Germany,* (Cambridge: Cambridge University Press, 2000).

—— , *Hitler's Italian Allies. Royal Armed Forces, Fascist Regime, and the War of 1940-1943,* (Cambridge: Cambridge University Press, 2000).

Bibliography

—— , *Mussolini Unleashed 1939-1941: Politics and Strategy in Fascist Italy's Last War*, (Cambridge: Cambridge University Press, 2008).

Kranjc, Gregor Joseph, *To Walk with the Devil: Slovene Collaboration and Axis Occupation, 1941-1945*, (Toronto: University of Toronto Press, 2013).

La Perna, Gaetano, *Pola-Istria-Fiume 1943-1947. L'agonia di un lembo d'Italia e la tragedia delle foibe*, (Milano: Mursia, 1993).

Lane, Ann, *Yugoslavia. When Ideals Collide*, (Basingstoke: Macmillan, 2004).

Lederer, Ivo, *Yugoslavia at the Paris Peace Conference: A Study in Frontiermaking*, (New Haven: Yale University Press, 1963).

Leschi, Vittorio, *La Resistenza italiana nella Venezia Giulia, 1943-1945: fonti archivistiche*, (Gorizia: LEG, 2007).

Lo Parco, Francesco, *Lo spirito antitedesco e l'irredentismo di Giosuè Carducci*, (Salerno: Spadafora, 1915).

Loi, Salvatore, *Le operazioni delle unità italiane in Yugoslavia (1941-1943)*, (Roma: Ufficio Storico dello Stato Maggiore dell'Esercito, 1978).

Lowe, Keith, *Savage Continent. Europe in the Aftermath of World War II*, (London: Viking, 2012).

Lyttleton, Adrian, *The Seizure of Power. Fascism in Italy 1919-1929*, (London: Weidenfield and Nicolson, 1973).

Lupo, Salvatore, Il fascismo. *La politica in un regime totalitario*, (Roma: Donzelli, 2000).

Luxardo De Franchi, Nicolò, *Dietro gli scogli di Zara*, (Gorizia: Libreria Editrice Goriziana, 2017).

Maclean, Fitzroy, *Eastern Approaches*, (London: Jonathan Cape, 1949).

Mack Smith, Denis, *Italy. A Modern History*, (Ann Harbor: University of Michigan Press, 1959).

—— , *Modern Italy. A Political History*, (New Hale and London: Yale University Press, 1997).

—— , *Mussolini's Roman Empire*, (London and New York: Longman, 1976).

276 *Bibliography*

Markham, R. H., *Tito's Imperial Communism*, (Chapel Hill: University of North Carolina, 1947.

Marrus, Michael R., *The Unwanted: European Refugees in the Twentieth Century*, (New York: Oxford University Press, 1985).

Maserati, Ennio, *L'occupazione jugoslava di Trieste, maggio-giugno 1945*, (Udine: Del Bianco, 1963).

Mason, John W., *The Dissolution of the Austro-Hungarian Empire 1867-1918*, (London and New York: Longman, 1985).

McCormick, Robert B., *Croatia Under Ante Pavelić: America, the Ustaše and Croatian Genocide*, (London: I.B. Tauris, 2014).

Mellace, Giuseppina, *Una grande tragedia dimenticata. La vera storia delle foibe*, (Roma: Newton Compton, 2018).

Mertus, Julie A., *Kosovo: How Myths and Truths Started a War*, (Berkley: University of California Press, 1999).

Mihovilović, Ive, *Trieste et son port*, (Susak: Ed. de l'Institut adriatique, 1945).

Milač, Metod, *Resistance, Imprisonment, and Forced Labor: A Slovene Student in World War II*, (Bern: Peter Lang, 2002).

Miletto, Enrico, *Con il mare negli occhi. Storie, luoghi e memorie dell'esodo istriano a Torino*, (Milano: Franco Angeli, 2005).

Montanelli, Indro, *Storia d'Italia, 1861-1919*, Vol. 6, (Milano: Rizzoli, 2003 – 1st edition 1974).

Montefiore, Simon Sebag, *Stalin: The Court of the Red Tsar*, (London: Phoenix, 2004).

Monzali, Luciano, *Italiani di Dalmazia. 1914-1924*, (Firenze: Le Lettere, 2007).

———, *Italiani di Dalmazia. Dal Risorgimento alla Grande Guerra*, (Firenze: Le Lettere, 2004).

Moodie, A. E., *The Italo-Yugoslav Boundary. A Study in Political Geography*, (London: George Philip & Son, 1945).

Morettin, Luisa, *Anatomia di un eccidio*, (Treviso: Alcione Editore, 2013).

Mori, Anna Maria and Milani, Nelida, *Bora*, (Milano: Sperling & Kupfer, 1998).

Bibliography

Morrison, Kenneth, *Montenegro. A Modern History*, (London: I.B. Tauris, 2009).

Morrow, Lance, *Evil: An Investigation*, (New York: Basic Books, 2003).

Murray, Williamson and Millet, Alan, *A War to be Won: Fighting the Second World War*, (Cambridge: Harvard University Press, 2000).

Nemec, Gloria, *Un paese perfetto. Storia e memoria di una comunità in esilio: Grisignana d'Istria 1930-1960*, (Gorizia: Libreria Editrice Goriziana, 1998).

Novak, Bogdan C., *Trieste 1941-1954. The Ethnic, Political, and Ideological Struggle*, (Chicago and London: The University of Chicago Press, 1970).

O' Brien, L. Stephen, *Traumatic Events and Mental Health*, (Cambridge: Cambridge University Press, 1998).

Oliva, Gianni, *Foibe. Le stragi negate degli italiani della Venezia Giulia e dell'Istria*, (Milano: Mondadori, 2003).

———, *L'alibi della Resistenza. Ovvero come abbiamo vinto la Seconda guerra mondiale*, (Milano: Mondadori, 2003).

———, *La resa dei conti*, (Milano: Mondadori, 1999).

Osti Guerrazzi, Amedeo, *The Italian Army in Slovenia. Strategies of Antipartisan Repression, 1941-1943*, (New York: Palgrave Macmillan, 2013).

Patterson, David, *The Shriek of Silence: A Phenomenology of the Holocaust Novel,* (Lexington: University Press of Kentucky, 1992).

Pauley, Bruce F., *The Hapsburg Legacy 1867-1939*, (New York: Holt, Rinehart and Winston, 1972).

Pavlowitch, Stevan K., *Hitler's New Disorder. The Second World War in Yugoslavia*, (London: Hurst & Company, 2008).

Pavone, Claudio, *A Civil War. A History of the Italian Resistance*, (London: Verso, 2013).

Perme, F., Zitnik, A., Nucic F., et al., *Slovenia 1941-1948-1952. Anche noi siamo morti per la patria*, (Grosuplje: Associazione per la sistemazione dei sepolcri tenuti nascosti, 2000).

Petacco, Arrigo, *L'esodo. La tragedia negata degli italiani d'Istria, Dalmazia e Venezia Giulia*, (Milano: Mondadori, 1999).

278 *Bibliography*

Pettibone, Charles D., *The Organization and Order of Battles of Militaries in World War II. Germany's and Imperial Japan Allies, Co-Belligerent, and Puppet States*, Volume VII, (Bloomington: Trafford Publishing, 2012).

Pirina, Marco, *Il confine orientale negli atti del PCI e PCJ*, (Gorizia: Edizioni ANVGD, 2009).

Pizzi, Katia, *A City in Search of an Author*, (London: Sheffield Academic Press, 2001).

Pollard, John F., *The Vatican and Italian Fascism, 1929-32: A Study in Conflict*, (New York: Cambridge University Press, 1985).

Puntoni, Paolo, *Parla Vittorio Emanuele III*, (Bologna: Il Mulino, 1993).

Pupo, Raoul, *Il lungo esodo. Istria: le persecuzioni, le foibe, l'esilio*, (Milano: BUR, 2005).

——— , *Trieste '45*, (Bari: Laterza, 2010).

Pupo, Raoul and Spazzali, Roberto, *Foibe*, (Milano: Mondadori, 2003).

Rabel, Robert, *Between East and West. Trieste, the United States and the Cold War, 1941-1954*, (Durham: Duke University Press, 1988).

Ragionieri, Ernesto, *Storia d'Italia, Vol 4:3, La storia politica e sociale*, (Torino: Einaudi, 1976).

Ragionieri, Ernesto and Valiani, Leo, *Il movimento nazionale a Trieste nella prima guerra mondiale*, (Udine: Giulio Cervani editore, 1968).

Rees, Laurence, *The Holocaust. A New History*, (London: Penguin, 2017).

Remak, Joachim, *The Origins of World War I*, (Austin: Holt, Rinehart and Winston, 1967).

Rendulić, Lothar, *Gekämpft, gesiegt, geschlagen*, (Heidelberg: Welsermühl Verlag, 1952).

Rieff, David, *In Praise of Forgetting. Historical Memory and its Ironies*, (New Haven and London: Yale University Press, 2016).

Roberts, Walter R., *Tito, Mihailović and the Allies, 1941-1945*, (New Brunswick: Rutgers University Press, 1973).

Rocchi, Flaminio, *L'esodo dei 350 mila giuliani, fiumani e dalmati*, (Roma: Edizioni Difesa Adriatica, 1971).

Rochat, Giorgio, *Le guerre italiane. 1935-1943. Dall'impero d'Etiopia alla disfatta*, (Torino: Einaudi, 2005).

Bibliography

279

Rodogno, Davide, *Fascism's European Empire. Italian Occupation during the Second World War*, (Cambridge: Cambridge University Press, 2006).

Romano, Paola, *La questione giuliana 1943-1947. La guerra e la diplomazia. Le foibe e l'esodo*, (Trieste: Lint, 1997).

Rossi, Francesco, *Mussolini e lo Stato Maggiore: avvenimenti del 1940*, (Roma: Regionale, 1951).

Rossi Kobau, Lionello, *Prigioniero di Tito 1945-1946. Un bersagliere nei campi di concentramento jugoslavi*, (Milano: Mursia, 2001).

Rusinow, Dennison I., *Italy's Austrian Heritage 1919-1946*, (Oxford: Clarendon Press, 1969).

Sachslehner, Johannes, *Zwei Millionen ham'ma erledigt: Odilo Globocnik - Hitlers Manager des Todes*, (Wien: Styria Verlag, 2014).

Sala, Teodoro, *Il fascismo italiano e gli Slavi del sud*, (Trieste: IRSML, 2008).

Salata, Francesco, *Per la storia diplomatica della questione romana*, (Milano: Treves Editore, 1929).

Salem, Richard A. (ed.), *Witness to Genocide: The Children of Rwanda. Drawings by Child Survivors of the Rwandan Genocide of 1994*, (New York: Friendship Press, 2000).

Salvatorelli, Luigi, *Pensiero e azione del Risorgimento*, (Torino: Einaudi, 1950).

Salvemini, Gaetano, *Dalla guerra mondiale alla dittatura (1916-1925)*, (Milano: Feltrinelli, 1964).

Sandonà, Augusto, *L'irredentismo nelle lotte politiche e nelle contese diplomatiche italo-austriache*, Vol 1, (Bologna: Zanichelli, 1932).

Scattolin, F., Trinca, M. and Manesso, A., *Deportati a Treviso. La repressione antislava e il campo di concentramento di Monigo (1942-1943)*, (Treviso: Istituto per la storia della Resistenza e della società contemporanea della Marca trevigiana, 2006).

Schechtman, Joseph B., *Postwar Population Transfers in Europe 1945–1955*, (Philadelphia: University of Pennsylvania Press, 1962).

280 Bibliography

Schreiber, Gerhard, *I militari italiani internati nei campi di concentramento del Terzo Reich. 1943-1945*, (Roma: Ufficio Storico SME, 1992).

Scotti, Giacomo and Viazzi, Luciano, *L'inutile vittoria. La tragica esperienza delle truppe italiane in Montenegro*, (Milano: Mursia, 1989).

Sestan, Ernesto, *Venezia Giulia. Lineamenti di storia etnica e culturale*, (Roma: Edizioni italiane, 1947).

Sestani, Armando, *Il confine orientale: una terra, molti esodi*, (Lucca: Istituto storico della Resistenza e dell'Età Contemporanea in Provincia di Lucca, 2012).

Seton-Watson, Hugh and Christopher, *The Making of Europe, R. W. Seton-Watson and the Last Years of Austria-Hungary*, (London: Methuen, 1981).

Seton-Watson, R. W., *The Southern Slav Question and the Hapsburg Monarchy*, (London: Constable & Co., 1911).

Sgorlon, Carlo, *La foiba grande*, (Milano: Mondadori, 1992).

———, *La malga di Sîr*, (Milano: Mondadori, 1996).

Sharp, Alan, *Consequences of Peace. The Versailles Settlement: Aftermath and Legacy 1919-2010*, (London: Haus Publishing, 2010).

Shephard, Ben, *A War of Nerves. Soldiers and Psychatrists 1914-1994*, (London: Pimlico, 2002).

Shores, Christopher, Cull, Brian and Malizia, Nicola, *Air War for Yugoslavia, Greece and Crete, 1940-41*, (London: Grub Street, 1987).

Sighele, Scipio, *Pagine nazionaliste,* (Milano: Treves, 1912).

———, *Il nazionalismo e i partiti politici*, (Milano: Fratelli Treves Editore, 1911).

Silvestri, Claudio, *Dalla redenzione al fascismo. Trieste 1918-1922* (Udine: Del Bianco Editore, 1959).

Singleton, Fred, *Twentieth Century Yugoslavia* (London: Macmillan, 1976).

Sluga, Glenda, *The Problem of Trieste and the Italo-Yugoslav Border. Difference, Identity, and Sovereignty in Twentieth-Century Europe*, (Albany: SUNY Press, 2001).

Bibliography

Smith, Bradley F. and Aga-Rossi, Elena, *Operation Sunrise: la resa tedesca in Italia* (Milano: Mondadori, 2005).

Snyder, Timothy, *Bloodlands. Europe between Hitler and Stalin* (London: Bodley Head, 2010).

Solzhenitsyn, Aleksandr, *The Gulag Archipelago 1918–1956,* (Boulder: Westview Press, 1997).

Sondhaus, Lawrence, *In the Service of the Emperor: Italians in the Austrian Armed Forces 1814-1918* (Scottsdale: Boulder, 1990).

Stafford, David, *Britain and European Resistance, 1940-1945. A Survey of the Special Operations Executive, with Documents* (London: Macmillan, 1980).

Starič, Peter, *My Life under Totalitarianism 1941-1991* (Augusta: Sotina Publishing, 2015).

Stefani, Giuseppe, *I fratelli Filzi,* (Roma: Problemi d'Italia, 1925).

Stoler, Mark A., *The Politics of the Second Front. American Military Planning and Diplomacy in Coalition Warfare, 1941-1943*, (Westport: Greenwood Press, 1977).

Sugar, Peter F., and Lederer, Ivo John (ed.), *Nationalism in Eastern Europe,* (Seattle and London: University of Washington Press, 1969).

Talpo, Oddone, *Dalmazia. Una cronaca per la storia*, (Roma: Ufficio Storico Stato Maggiore dell'Esercito, 1994).

Talpo, Oddone and Brcic, Sergio, *Vennero dal cielo. Zara distrutta 1943-1944*, (Campobasso: Palladino editore, 2006).

Tamaro, Attilio, *Trieste: storia di una città e di una fede,* (Milano: Istituto Editoriale Italiano, 1946).

Thayer, John A., *Italy and the Great War. Politics and Culture, 1870-1915*, (Madison and Milwaukee: University of Wisconsin Press, 1964).

Thompson, Mark, *The White War. Life and Death on the Italian Front 1915-1919*, (London: Faber and Faber, 2008).

Tomasevich, Jozo, *War and Revolution in Yugoslavia, 1941-1945. Occupation and Liberation*, (Stanford: Stanford University Press, 2001).

Tomizza, Fulvio, *La miglior vita* (Milano: Mondadori, 1977).

282 *Bibliography*

Tranfaglia, Nicola, *Un passato scomodo: fascismo e postfascismo*, (Bari: Laterza, 1996).

Trotsky, Leon, *My Life*, (London: Thornton Butterworth, 1930).

Valdevit, Giampaolo, (ed.), *Foibe, il peso del passato,* (Venezia: Marsilio Editore, 1997).

———, *La questione di Trieste 1941-1954: Politica internazionale e contesto locale*, (Milano: Angeli, 1986).

———, *Trieste. Storia di una periferia insicura*, (Milano: Mondadori, 2004).

Valiani, Leo, *La dissoluzione dell'Austria-Ungheria,* (Milano: Il Saggiatore, 1966).

Vital, David, *The Making of British Foreign Policy*, (London: George Allen and Unwin Ltd., 1968).

Vivante, Angelo, *Irredentismo Adriatico,* (Firenze: Parenti, 1912).

Von Glaise-Horstenau, Edmund, *The Collapse of the Austro-Hungarian Empire*, (London and Toronto: J. M. Dent and Sons, 1930).

Wilson, Duncan, *Tito's Yugoslavia*, (Cambridge University Press, 1979).

Winter, Jay, *Sites of Memory, Sites of Mourning. The Great War in European Cultural History*, (Cambridge: Cambridge University Press, 1998).

Wördörfer, Rudolf, *Confine orientale. Italia e Yugoslavia dal 1915 al 1955*, (Bologna: Il Mulino, 2009).

Woodward, Llewellyn, *British Foreign Policy in the Second World War*, Vols I-IV, (London: HMSO, 1971).

Žerjavić, Vladimir, *Population Losses in Yugoslavia 1941-1945*, (Zagreb: Dom & Svijet, 1997).

Zorzi, Alvise, *La Repubblica del leone,* (Milano: Bompiani, 2001).

Zuccotti, Susan, *The Italians and the Holocaust. Persecution, Rescue and Survival*, (Lincoln: University of Nebraska Press, 1996).

B.2 Chapters in Edited Volumes

Andri, Adriano, 'La scuola giuliana e friulana tra Austria e Italia,' in A.A. V.V., *Friuli e Venezia Giulia. Storia del '900*, (Gorizia: Libreria Editrice Goriziana, 1997), pp. 205-21.

Ballinger, Pamela, 'Istriani d.o.c.: silences and presences in the construction of exodus. The Istrian Esodo', in Povrzanovic, Maja and Jambresic Kirin, Renata, *War, Exile and Everyday Life*, (Zagreb: Institute of Ethnology and Folklore, 1996), pp. 117-132.

——, 'National Refugees, Displaced Persons, and the Reconstruction of Italy: the Case of Trieste,' in Reinish, Jessica and White, Elizabeth, (ed.) *The Disentanglement of Populations. Migration, Expulsion and Displacement in Post-War Europe, 1944-49*, (Basingstoke: Palgrave Macmillan, 2011), pp. 115-140.

Buzzati, Dino, 'Il crollo della baliverna,' in *Sessanta Racconti*, (Milano: Mondadori, 1958), pp. 199-205.

Carmichael, Cathie, 'Locating Trieste in the Eighteenth and Early Nineteenth Centuries', in Brumer, B. and Smitek, Z. (ed.), *Mediterranean Ethnological Summer School*, (Ljubljana: Slovene Ethnological Society, 1995), pp. 2-11.

Catalan, Tullia, 'Trieste: ritratto politico e sociale di una città borghese', in A.A.V.V., *Friuli e Venezia Giulia. Storia del '900*, (Gorizia: Libreria Editrice Goriziana, 1997), pp. 13-31.

Collotti, Enzo, 'Sul razzismo antislavo,' in Alberto Burgio (a cura di), *Nel nome della razza: il razzismo nella storia d'Italia, 1870-1945*, (Bologna: Il Mulino, 1999), pp. 201-33.

Corni, Gustavo, 'The Exodus of Italians from Istria and Dalmatia, 1945–56,' in Reinisch, Jessica and White, Elizabeth (ed.), *The Disentanglement of Populations. Migration, Expulsion and Displacement in Post-War Europe, 1944–9*, (Basingstoke: Palgrave Macmillan, 2011), pp. 71-87.

Doumanis, Nicholas, *The Italian Empire and brava gente: Oral Hisory and the Dodecanese Islands*, in Bosworth, R. J. B. and Dogliani, Patrizia

284 *Bibliography*

(ed.), *Italian Fascism. History, Memory and Representation*, (London: Macmillan, 1999), pp. 161-177.

Exeler, Franziska, 'Violence et violence extreme,' in Jean-François Muracciole and Guillaume Piketty, *Encyclopédie de la Seconde Guerre Mondiale,* (Paris: Éditions Robert Laffont pour le Ministère de la Défense, 2015), pp. 1379-1384.

Fabi, Lucio, 'La Grande Guerra,' in A.A. V.V., *Friuli e Venezia Giulia. Storia del '900,* (Gorizia: Libreria Editrice Goriziana, 1997), pp. 116-117.

Fogar, Galliano, 'Venezia Giulia 1943-1945: problemi e situazioni,' in Galliano Fogar, *Trieste 1941-1947,* (Udine: Dedolibri, 1991), pp. 57-74.

Gibianskij, Leonid, 'L'Unione Sovietica, la Jugoslavia e Trieste', in Giampaolo Valdevit (a cura di), *La crisi di Trieste. Maggio-giugno 1945. Una revisione critica,* (Trieste: IRSMLFVG, 1995), pp. 39-78.

Höbelt, Lothar, 'Well-tempered Discontent. Austrian Domestic Politics' in Mark Cornwall (ed.), *The Last Years of Austria-Hungary. A Multi-National Experiment in Early Twentieth-Century Europe,* (Exeter: University of Exeter Press, 2002), pp. 47-74.

Hovannisian, Richard G., 'Denial of the Armenian Genocide in Comparison with Holocaust Denial,' in Hovannisian, Richard G., (ed.), *Remembrance and Denial: the Case of the Armenian Genocide,* (Detroit: Wayne State University Press, 1999), pp. 201-236.

Jareb, Mario, 'The NDH's Relations with Italy and Germany,' in Sabrina P. Ramet (ed.), *The Independent State of Croatia 1941-45,* (London: Routledge, 2007), pp. 61-74.

Lebow, Richard Ned, 'The Memory of Politics in Postwar Europe', in Richard Ned Lebow, Wulf Kansteiner, Claudio Fogu (ed.), *The Memory of Politics in Postwar Europe,* (Durham: Duke University Press, 2006), pp. 1-39.

Millo, Anna, 'La società triestina agli inizi del Novecento', in A.A.V.V., *Friuli e Venezia Giulia. Storia del '900,* (Gorizia: Libreria Editrice Goriziana, 1997), pp. 47-58.

Bibliography

285

Negrelli, Giorgio, 'Trieste nel mito', in Roberto Finzi, Claudio Magris, Giovanni Miccoli (eds.), *Il Friuli e Venezia Giulia*, (Torino: Einaudi, 2002), pp. 1338-1370.

Oakey, Robin, 'Austria and the South Slavs,' in Robertson, E. and Timms, E., (eds.), *The Habsburg Legacy: National Identity in Historical Perspective*, (Edinburgh: Edinburgh University Press, 1994).

Ognjenović, Gorana and Jozelić, Jasna, (eds.), 'Introduction,' in Ognjenović, Gorana and Jozelić, Jasna, (eds.), *Revolutionary Totalitarianism, Pragmatic Socialism, Transition,* Vol. 1, (Basingstoke: Palgrave Macmilan, 2016), pp. 1-11.

Pleterski, Janko, 'The Southern Slav Question' in Mark Cornwall (ed.), *The Last Years of Austria-Hungary. A Multinational Experiment in Early Twentieth-Century Europe*, (Exeter: University of Exeter Press, 1990), pp. 119-148.

Petrovich, Michael B., 'Russia's Role in the Creation of the Yugoslav State, 1914-1918,' in Dimitrije Djordjevic (ed.), *The Creation of Yugoslavia 1914-1918*, (Oxford: Clio Books, 1980), pp. 89-101.

Pupo, Raoul, 'Violenza politica tra guerra e dopoguerra. Il caso delle foibe giuliane,' in Giampaolo Valdevit (ed.), *Foibe, il peso del passato,* (Venezia: Marsilio Editore, 1997), pp. 84-103.

Radelić, Zdenko, 'The Communist Party of Yugoslavia and the Abolition of the Multi-Party System: the Case of Croatia,' in Ognjenović, Gorana and Jozelić, Jasna, (eds.) *Revolutionary Totalitarianism, Pragmatic Socialism, Transition,* Vol. 1, (Basingstoke: Palgrave Macmilan, 2016), pp. 13-48.

Revelli, Nuto, 'La ritirata di Russia,' in Mario Isnenghi (ed.), *I luoghi della memoria. Strutture ed eventi dell'Italia Unita,* (Bari: Laterza, 1997), pp. 369-81.

Sluga, Glenda 'Italian National Memory, National Identity and Fascism', in Bosworth, R. J. B. and Dogliani, Patrizia (eds.), *Italian Fascism. History, Memory and Representation*, (London: Macmillan, 1999), pp. 178-195.

286   *Bibliography*

Vinci, Anna Maria, 'Il fascismo al confine orientale,' in *Storia d'Italia dall'Unità ad oggi. Il Friuli-Venezia Giulia, Vol.1,* (Torino: Einaudi, 2002), pp. 377-513.

——, 'Il fascismo e la società locale', in *Friuli e Venezia Giulia. Storia del '900,* (Gorizia: Libreria Editrice Goriziana, 1997, pp. 221-258.

Visintin, Angelo, 'L'assalto a «Il Piccolo»', in A.A.V.V., *Un percorso tra le violenze del Novecento nella provincia di Trieste*, (Trieste: IRSML, 2007), pp. 11-18.

Ziller, Paolo 'La Venezia Giulia dalla dissoluzione dell'Austria-Ungheria al regno d'Italia', in A.A. V.V., *Friuli e Venezia Giulia. Storia del '900,* (Gorizia: Libreria Editrice Goriziana, 1997), pp. 164-176.

B.3 Journal Articles

Ballinger, Pamela,' Imperial Nostalgia: Mythologizing Habsburg Trieste', *Journal of Modern Italian Studies*, 1 (8), 2003, pp. 84-101.

—— , 'Who defines and remembers genocide after the Cold War? Contested memories of partisan massacre in Venezia Giulia in 1943-1945,' *Journal of Genocide Research*, 2 (1), 2000, pp. 11-30.

Bakić, Dragan, 'The Italo–Yugoslav Conflict over Albania: A View from Belgrade. 1919–1939,' in *Diplomacy and Statecraft*, Vol. 25, 4, 2014, pp. 592-612.

Bartošek, Karel, 'Central and Southeastern Europe,' in Stéphane Courtois, Nicolas Werth, et al., *The Black Book of Communism. Crimes, Terror, Repression*, (Cambridge, Massachussets: Harvard University Press, 1999), pp. 394-456.

Buvoli, Stefano, 'Il fascismo nella Venezia Giulia e la persecuzione antislava,' *Storia contemporanea in Friuli*, XXVI, 27, 1996, p. 69-87.

Cobol, Giuseppe, 'Il fascismo e gli allogeni,' *Gerarchia*, VII, 9, settembre 1927, pp. 803-806.

Fatutta, Fortunato and Covelli, Franco, '1941: Attack on Yugoslavia,' *The International Magazine of Armies and Weapons*, 4 (15–17), 1975, pp. 15-7.

Bibliography

Hehn, Paul E. 'Serbia, Croatia and Germany 1941-1945: Civil War and Revolution in the Balkans,' *Canadian Slavonic Papers*, Vol. 13, No. 4 (Winter, 1971), pp. 344-373.

Keyserlingk, Robert H., 'Arnold Toynbee's Foreign Research and Press Service, 1939-43 and Its Post-War Plans for South-East Europe,' *Journal of Contemporary History*, Vol. 21, No. 4 (Oct., 1986), pp. 539-558.

Legnani, Massimo, 'Il "ginger" del generale Roatta. Le direttive della 2a armata sulla repressione antipartigiana in Slovenia e Croazia,' *Italia Contemporanea*, 209 (10), 1997, pp. 159-74.

Mantelli, Brunello, 'Gli italiani in Jugoslavia 1941-1943: occupazione militare, politiche persecutorie, crimini di guerra,' *Storia e memoria,* n. 13, 2004, pp. 23-30.

Morettin, Luisa, 'Trattati come schiavi. Intervista ad Aldo Colombai, ex-prigioniero nei campi di concentramento jugoslavi,' *Fiume Rivista di Studi Adriatici*, Jan-June 2013, Nº 27, pp. 111-18.

Nahoum-Grappe, Véronique, 'Anthropologie de la violence extreme: le crime de profanation,' in *Revue internationale des sciences sociales*, 2002/4, n° 174, pp. 601-9.

Orbanič, Srđa and Musizza Orbanič, Nataša, 'Regionalismo istriano: finzione da fine millennio,' *La Battana*, 108, (1993), pp. 55-62.

Pavlowitch, S.K., 'Momčilo Ninčić and the European Policy of the Yugoslav Government in Exile, 1941-1943,' II, *The Slavic and East European Review*, Vol. 62, No. 4 (Oct. 1984), pp. 531-533.

Patrizia Piredda, 'Interventionism in 1915 and the Man of Letters: The Ethical Commitments of Serra and the 'Armed Poet' D'Annunzio,' *Bulletin of Italian Politics*, Vol. 3, No. 2, 2011, pp. 303-317.

Schiffrer, Carlo, 'Il problema nazionale di Trieste nella storiografia austrofila e in quella irredentista,' *Trieste*, No. 40, (Nov.-Dec., 1960).

Seton-Watson, Christopher, 'Italy's Imperial Hangover,' *Journal of Contemporary History*, 15, (1980), pp. 169-170.

Stafford, David, 'SOE and the British Involvement in the Belgrade Coup d'État in March 1941,' *Slavic Review*, Vol. 36, No. 3 (Sep., 1977), pp. 399-419.

288   *Bibliography*

Tozzi, Veronica, 'The Epistemic and Moral Role of Testimony,' *History and Theory*, 51 (February 2012), pp. 1-17.

Verginella, Marta, 'Il paradigma città/campagna e la rappresentazione dualistica di uno spazio multietnico,' *Contemporanea*, 11, 4, 2008, pp. 779-792.

Verna, Frank P., 'Notes on Italian Rule under Bastianini, 1941-1943,' *International History Review*, Vol. 12, No. 3 (Aug. 1990), pp. 528-47.

Walston, James, 'History and Memory of the Italian Concentration Camps,' *The Historical Journal*, Vol. 40, No. 1 (March, 1997), pp. 169-183.

Whittam, J. R., 'Drawing the Line: Britain and the Emergence of the Trieste Question. January 1941 – May 1945,' *The English Historical Review*, Vol. 106, No 419, (April 1991), pp. 346-370.

B.4 Newspaper Articles

'Cherso, esumati i resti di 27 caduti della Seconda guerra,' *Il Piccolo*, 17 May 2019.

'Chissà dove finirà il treno dei fascisti?,' *L'Unità*, 30 November 1946.

'Foibe, l'ira della Croazia contro Napolitano. D'Alema: È presidente dell'Italia antifascista,' *La Repubblica*, 12 February 2007.

'Foibe: presidente croato attacca Napolitano,' *Corriere della Sera*, 13 February 2007.

'Foibe, si celebra il giorno del ricordo. Napolitano: mai ostaggi del passato,' *La Stampa*, 10 February 2011.

'Il Gulag senza processo,' *Avvenire*, 28 August 1996.

'Ipocriti: è stato genocidio,' *Corriere della Sera*, 18 August 1996.

'Kinder, Gentler Fascism,' *New York Times*, 28 September 2002.

'La foiba nascosta per 60 anni,' *Il Giornale*, 11 February 2018.

'Mio fratello,' *Vie Nuove*, Numero 28, 15 July 1961.

'Napolitano: Basta oblio sulle foibe,' *La Stampa*, 10 February 2010.

'Pansa. Istria e foibe: 300 mila italiani traditi dal PCI,' *Storia in rete*, 18 February 2012.

Bibliography   289

'Quei profughi istriani e il Treno della Vergogna,' *Corriere della Sera*, 18 September 2015.

'Rovigo, ANPI choc: "Le foibe sono un'invenzione storica". Salvini: "Fate schifo". I vertici nazionali si dissociano,' *Corriere del Veneto*, 10 February 2019.

'Se interviene anche l'Islam,' *Panorama*, 21 July 1991.

'Silvio Berlusconi: 10 memorable gaffes,' *The Daily Telegraph*, 7 November 2008.

'Tornano alla luce a Castua i cadaveri di italiani uccisi dagli jugoslavi,' *Il Piccolo*, 12 July 2018.

'The Southern Slav Question,' *Die Zeit,* 30 May 1903.

'The Trieste Question,' *The Spectator*, 28 June 1946.

B.5 Encyclopaedias

Colapietra, Raffaele. 'Salvatore Barzilai.' In *Dizionario Biografico degli Italiani, Vol. 7*, (Roma: Treccani, 1970). Accessed 16 November 2013. http://www.treccani.it/ enciclopedia/salvatore-barzilai_(Dizionario-Biografico).

Dean, Martin and Megargee, Geoffrey (ed.), *The United States Holocaust Memorial Museum Encyclopedia of Camps and Ghettos, 1933-1945,* Volume II, (Bloomington: Indiana University Press, 2012).

Foro, Philippe, 'L'Italie dans la seconde guerre mondiale,' Jean-François Muracciole and Guillaume Piketty (eds.), *Encyclopédie de la Seconde Guerre Mondiale*, (Paris: Éditions Robert Laffont, 2015).

Muracciole, Jean-François and Piketty, Guillaume, *Encyclopêdie de la Seconde Guerre Mondiale,* (Paris: Éditions Robert Laffont pour le Ministère de la Défense, 2015).

Plut-Pregelj, Leopoldina, Kranjc, Gregor, Lazarevic, Zarko, and Rogel, Carole, *Historical Dictionary of Slovenia*, (Lanham: Rowman & Littlefield, 2018).

290 *Bibliography*

Tamaro, Attilio. 'Irredentismo,' *Enciclopedia italiana*, (Roma: Treccani, 1933). Accessed 16 November 2013. http://www.treccani.it/enciclopedia/irredentismo_(Enciclopedia-Italiana)/.

ABOUT THE AUTHOR

Luisa Morettin, PhD
Reader in Modern History,
NCI University of London, London, UK

Luisa Morettin has a PhD in Modern History. She has held teaching and research positions at the University of Edinburgh, King's College London, and the University of Reading.

INDEX

A

Airey, Terence, 238, 248
Akhmatova, Anna, 249, 267
Alberti, Mario, 15, 27
Albertini, Luigi, 20, 24, 54, 267
Alighieri, Dante, 10, 11, 15, 16, 165, 273
Aloisi, Pompeo, 60
Ambrosio, Vittorio, 71, 79, 98, 106
Amendola, Giovanni, 21
Anfuso, Filippo, 65

B

Babler, Mr, 233, 234
Badoglio, Pietro, 45, 58, 59, 104, 106, 107
Bakumir, Milena, 87
Balbo, Italo, 33
Ballew, John W., 236
Balocco, Riccardo, 72
Barbasetti di Prun, Curio, 90
Barbera, Gaspero, 102
Barzilai, Salvatore, 11, 289
Bastianini, Giuseppe, 78, 99, 101, 104, 288
Battisti, Cesare, 11

Bauer, Otto, 17
Bergamo, Guido, 41, 122
Bettini, Salvatore, 156
Bianco, Vincenzo, 42, 226, 270, 276, 280
Billotta, Fioravante, 177
Bissolati, Leonida, 22
Boglioni, Ivo, 156
Bombelles, Josip, 65
Bombig, Giorgio, 49
Bonaparte, Napoleon, 4, 19
Bonara, Mario, 176
Bonghi, Ruggiero, 15
Bonomi, Ivanoe, 107, 207
Bowman, Alfred C., 245
Broad, Philip, 137, 241
Brown, R. A., 1, 244
Broz, Josip (see also Tito), 37, 79, 182
Budak, Mile, 60
Buson, Leone, 158
Byington Jr, Homer M., 238

C

Cadogan, Alexander, 197, 202
Cadorna, Luigi, 29
Cairoli, Benedetto, 14

294 *Index*

Camus, Albert, 263
Cannon, Cavendish W., 247
Carducci, Giosuè, 11, 22, 275
Casolari, Fedele, 118, 119
Cau, Antonio, 156
Cettini, Margherita, 177
Charles VI, Emperor, 5
Charles, Noel, 73, 210, 212, 228, 231, 233, 248, 266, 278
Chernyakhovsky, Ivan, 134
Churchill, Winston, xxxii, 135, 138, 197, 201, 204, 205, 206, 214, 215, 216, 217, 218, 268, 269
Ciano, Galeazzo, 63, 65, 66, 67, 68, 77, 83, 104, 172, 266
Cicognani, Amleto Giovanni, 94
Cifaldi, Antonio, 237
Ciuffelli, Augusto, 46, 47
Clemenceau, Georges, 36
Cobol, Giuseppe, 49, 286
Coceani, Bruno, 123, 124, 125, 126, 269
Colombai, Aldo, 161, 165, 166, 287
Colville, John R., 224, 229, 242
Corradini, Enrico, 12
Cossetto, Norma, 119
Cripps, Stafford, 193
Crispi, Francesco, 14, 15, 36
Cuneo, Ernesto, 115, 154
Cunningham, Andrew, 206

D

D'Annunzio, Gabriele, 13, 24, 35
de Beden, Riccardo, 124
De Castro, Diego, 122, 271
De Gasperi, Alcide, 184
De Giovanni, Carmine, 121
de Robespierre, Maximilien, 111
De Rubertis, Antonio, 237
Depretis, Agostino, 14
Diaz, Armando, 45

Djilas, Milovan, 86, 178, 193, 226
Djuba, Frane, 103
Duce (see also Mussolini, Benito), xxiv, 13, 58, 61, 64, 66, 67, 68, 69, 70, 83, 84, 106, 271
Durante, Nicola, 157

E

Eden, Anthony, 104, 105, 197, 200, 205, 208, 215, 268

F

Fabbri, Umberto, 84
Fantela, Nicola, 159
Federzoni, Luigi, 12
Ferrari, Giuseppe, 59
Filzi, Fabio, 11, 281
Fingerle, *don*, 159
Fogar, Luigi, 54, 123, 196, 272, 284
Franceschetti, 102
Franco, Francisco, 59, 61, 75, 276, 286
Fransoni, Francesco, 104
Franz Ferdinand, Archduke of Austria, 18, 25
Franz Josef, Emperor, 9, 11
Franz, Kurt, 18, 25, 127
Freyberg, Bernard, 135
Führer (see also Hitler, Adolf), 67, 70

G

Gaetano, Giuseppe, 22, 38, 54, 55, 102, 121, 178, 270, 275, 279
Gambara, Gastone, 113
Garibaldi, Giuseppe, 8, 10, 107, 115, 212
Garibaldi, Menotti, 10, 107, 115, 212
Gavrilovič, Milan, 193, 194
Genovesi, Marino, 158

Index

Gibbon, Francis, 7
Giglioli, Emilio, 71, 73
Giolitti, Giovanni, 9, 10, 24, 25, 48
Giunta, Francesco, 41, 47, 48, 101
Glaise von Horstenau, Edmund, 96, 114
Goblocnik, Odilo, 123, 124
Goebbels, Joseph, 226
Gramsci, Antonio, 108
Grandi, Dino, 58
Graziani, Rodolfo, 71, 266
Grazioli, Emilio, 77, 93
Grubic, Sergio, 103
Guarnaschelli, Alberto, 158

H

Halifax, Edward, 199
Hamblen, Archelaus Lewis, 242
Hankey, Henry A., 244
Harzarich, Arnaldo, 120
Hayter, William, 242
Hebrang, Andrija, 226
Herder, Johannes, 7
Hinterreger, Dr, 124
Hitler, Adolf (see also Führer), 48, 59, 61, 62, 66, 67, 69, 70, 76, 77, 106, 114, 123, 199, 204, 209, 214, 274, 277, 281
Hood, Samuel, 242
Hopkinson, Henry, 138
Horst, Adriano, 122

I

Imbriani, Matteo, 8

J

Jovanović, Slobodan, 86, 202, 274
Joyce, James, 9

K

Karađorđević, Alexander King, 60, 65
Karađorđević, Pavle Prince, 60, 65
Kardelj, Edvard, 178, 214, 226, 229
Kellett, J. A., 247
Kesselring, Albert, 108, 207
Key, David McK., 243
Kvaternik, Slavko, 78

L

Laffan, Robert, 195
Lambert, Erwin, 127
Langlechner, Stefan, 148
Leahy, William, 218
Lemnitzer, Lyman, 137
Lessing, Doris, 249
Lloyd George, David, 21, 36
Long, James E., 27, 178, 246
Lorković, Mladen, 114
Luxardo, Bianca, 275
Luxardo, Nicolò, 132, 275
Luxardo, Pietro, 132, 275

M

Macmillan, Harold, xxvii, xxxii, 26, 79, 96, 127, 201, 208, 210, 211, 212, 213, 215, 216, 218, 266, 268, 269, 273, 275, 280, 281, 283, 284, 285
Malaguti, Bruno, 115
Manganiello, Emilio, 60
Manin, Ludovico, 4
Maracchi, 64
Marchesi, Concetto, 109
Maria José of Belgium, Princess and later last Queen of Italy, 105, 269
Maria Theresa, Empress, 5
Martinello, Angelo, 121

Index

Maximilian, Archduke, 9
Mazzini, Giuseppe, 8, 23
Mazzolini, Serafino, 78, 86
Meneghello, Romano, 176
Messe, Giovanni, 106
Mestanek, Dalibor, 88
Mihailović, Draža, 79, 89, 129, 201, 204, 206, 251, 278
Milani, Nelida, 144, 146, 147, 261, 276
Mileta, Jerolim, 101
Molotov, Vyacheslav, 208, 242
Morgan, William, xv, 184, 210, 219, 225, 227, 234
Mori, Anna Maria, 144, 146, 147, 261, 276
Morra, Eugenio, 74
Mosconi, Antonio, 47, 48
Mussolini, Benito (see also Duce), xxiv, xxvii, xxviii, xxx, 11, 12, 24, 25, 27, 33, 37, 41, 42, 43, 46, 47, 48, 49, 51, 52, 54, 57, 58, 59, 60, 61, 62, 63, 65, 66, 67, 68, 69, 77, 80, 83, 84, 85, 86, 90, 99, 101, 102, 104, 105, 106, 108, 115, 123, 127, 202, 209, 227, 266, 268, 269, 271, 272, 273, 275, 279

N

Nais, Clonfeo *don*, 159
Nasci, Gabriele, 74
Nichols, Philip, 194
Nicolicchia, Luigi, 179
Nitti, Francesco Saverio, 37, 44, 47

O

Oberdan, Guglielmo (see also Oberdank, Wilhelm), 9, 11
Oberdank, Wilhelm (see also Oberdan, Guglielmo), 11
Oberhauser, Josef, 127
Orazi, Vezio, 100

Oriani, Alfredo, 12
Orlando, Vittorio Emanuele, 35, 37, 45

P

Pace, Marino, 45, 124
Padoan, Giovanni (see also Vanni), 183
Pafundi, Giovanni, 74
Pagnini, Cesare, 123, 124
Papini, Giovanni, 12
Pascoli, Giovanni, 13
Pasolini, Pier Paolo, xxi, 109
Pavelić, Ante (see also Poglavnik), 60, 61, 65, 76, 78, 95, 96, 114, 251, 276
Pecorari, Mr, 244
Pederzolli, Trifone, 53
Pejkvic, Ivan, 101
Perkan, Vittorio, 159
Petitti di Roreto, Carlo, 46
Petrarca, Francesco, 10
Petrović, Nikola I King of Montenegro, 78
Petrović-Njegoš, Mihajlo Prince of Montenegro, 78
Pettarossi, Andreina, 139, 142, 145
Pijade, Mosa, 89
Pirzio Biroli, Alessandro, 71, 74, 86, 88, 90
Pius IX, Pope, 8, 54
Pius XI, Pope, 54
Poglavnik (see also Pavelić, Ante), 76, 78
Princip, Gavrilo, 18
Prpić, Ivan, 73
Prunas, Renato, 228
Pücher, Edmondo, 25

R

Radecca, Albina, 120
Radecca, Caterina, 120
Radecca, Fosca, 120
Radeticchio, Giovanni, 150, 151, 152
Ragusin-Righi, Livio, 49

Index

Rainer, Friedrich, 9, 123, 124
Rainer, Maria Rilke, 9, 124
Ranzato, Alceo, 175, 176
Regis, James, 237
Rehbrach, Herman, 149
Rendel, George William, 198
Rendulić, Lothar, 97, 278
Renzi, Giovanni, 100
Roatta, Mario, 15, 68, 70, 72, 79, 81, 83, 92,
    98, 100, 102, 109, 112, 176, 222, 260,
    269, 270, 274, 284, 285
Robotti, Mario, 72, 79, 83, 92, 102, 112,
    113
Rokossovsky, Konstantin, 134
Roosevelt, Franklin D., 202, 204, 214, 217
Rosandic, Zorka, 103
Rose, P., 203
Rossi Kobau, Lionello, 161, 163, 164, 165,
    279
Rupnik, Leon, 116
Rusca, Luigi, 104

S

Salandra, Antonio, 25, 27
Salvemini, Gaetano, 22, 38, 54, 55, 279
Sancin, Placido, 159
Sandri, Ennio, 158
Sargent, Orme, 202
Sauro, Italo, 63
Sauro, Nazario, 11, 63
Sceck, *don*, 140, 141, 142, 143
Schranzhofer, *Herr*, 124
Scobie, Ronald M., 216
Sebastiani, Osvaldo, 64
Seldi, Salvatore, 100
Sestan, Giuseppe, 40, 180, 280
Seton-Watson, Robert, 18, 20, 21, 22, 37,
    266, 280, 287
Sforza, Carlo, 105, 199
Siccardi, Giuseppe, 154, 155

Sighele, Scipio, 14, 15, 16, 280
Silbar, Mr, 234, 235
Simović, Dušan, 69, 199
Slataper, Scipio, 39, 40, 267
Smodlaka, Josip, 20
Solzhenitsyn, Aleksandr, 163, 281
Sonnino, Sidney, 25, 35, 45
Spigo, Umberto, 114
Stalin, Joseph, 108, 119, 135, 178, 184, 193,
    200, 208, 210, 218, 226, 227, 256, 267,
    271, 276, 281
Stangl, Franz, 127
Starič, Peter, 90, 281
Stergar, Anton, 149
Stettinius, Edward, 208
Stevenson, Ralph, 229
Stojadinović, Milan, 63
Stone, Ellery W., 206, 244
Strazzeri, Gustavo, 113
Strossmayer, Josip, 144
Stuparic, Giani, 39
Sturzo, Luigi, 184
Styria, 31, 128, 279
Supilo, Frano, 20
Svevo, Italo, 9

T

Tacconi, Antonio, 119
Tardini, Domenico, 245
Tarticchio, Angelo, 159
Teissl, Hans, 114
Tiburtini, Corrado, 155
Tiengo, Romildo, 156
Tito (see also Broz, Josip), xxii, xxviii,
    xxxi, xxxii, 37, 80, 88, 91, 97, 98, 113,
    116, 117, 118, 119, 122, 129, 130, 131,
    135, 146, 147, 149, 153, 156, 157, 158,
    160, 161, 162, 164, 165, 167, 168, 169,
    170, 173, 174, 176, 177, 178, 179, 180,
    181, 182, 183, 184, 193, 201, 204, 205,

206, 207, 208, 209, 210, 211, 213, 214, 215, 216, 217, 218, 221, 222, 224, 225, 226, 227, 228, 229, 231, 233, 237, 239, 240, 241, 243, 251, 252, 256, 259, 260, 269, 271, 276, 278, 279, 282
Togliatti, Palmiro, 107, 108, 210, 226, 229, 267, 273
Tosello, Armando, 155
Toynbee, Arnold, 194, 203, 287

V

Vanni (see also Padoan, Giovanni), 183
Vecchi, Angelo, 155
Vecchi, Giovanni, 74
Venturini, Ivo, 115
Vidussoni, Aldo, 82
Viesse de Marmont, Auguste, 4
Visconti Venosta, Giovanni, 206
Vivante, Angelo, 16, 282
Volpi, Eugenio, 154

Voltaire, 221
von Ribbentrop, Joachim, 68
Vonnegut, Kurt, 57

W

Waddams, Major, 233, 236
Warner, Frederick Archibald, 243
Wickham Steed, Henry, 21
Williams, Maurice, 224
Wilson, Henry, 33, 35, 36, 37, 182, 206, 266, 282
Wirth, Christian, 127
Wolsegger, Ferdinand, 124

Z

Žerjavić, Vladimir, 95, 282
Zinger, Vladimir, 149, 150

Related Nova Publications

THE CHIEF PERIODS OF EUROPEAN HISTORY

AUTHOR: Edward A. Freeman

SERIES: Political Science and History

BOOK DESCRIPTION: The Chief Periods of European History is about the birth of modern Europe, tracing the history from the end of the Middle Ages and the Renaissance into the modern era. The book contains six lectures read in the University of Oxford in Trinity Term, 1885. It also contains the essay "Greek Cities under Roman Rule," as an appendix.

SOFTCOVER ISBN: 978-1-53615-723-9
RETAIL PRICE: $95

THE SUFFRAGETTE: THE HISTORY OF THE WOMEN'S MILITANT SUFFRAGE MOVEMENT 1905-1910

AUTHOR: E. Sylvia Pankhurst

SERIES: Political Science and History

BOOK DESCRIPTION: The History of the Women's Suffrage was written at a time when it was in the very forefront of British politics and offers an insider's perspective on the motives and ideals that inspired its leaders and followers.

HARDCOVER ISBN: 978-1-53615-517-4
RETAIL PRICE: $230

To see a complete list of Nova publications, please visit our website at www.novapublishers.com

Related Nova Publications

A SHORT HISTORY OF THE ROYAL NAVY, 1217-1815. VOLUME I

AUTHOR: David Hannay

SERIES: Political Science and History

BOOK DESCRIPTION: The book is divided into two volumes. The first volume begins with King John and ends at the Revolution of 1688. The second volume will give the history of the great struggle with France and her dependent allies, which began in 1689, and ended only when the time of great naval wars was over.

HARDCOVER ISBN: 978-1-53615-472-6
RETAIL PRICE: $310

THE AMERICAN REPUBLIC: ITS CONSTITUTION, TENDENCIES, AND DESTINY

AUTHOR: O.A. Brownson

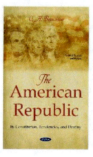

SERIES: Political Science and History

BOOK DESCRIPTION: Originally published in 1866, this book offers great historical significance of the contemporary views of the nature, necessity, extent, authority, origin, ground, and constitution of government, and the unity, nationality, constitution, tendencies, and destiny of the American Republic.

HARDCOVER ISBN: 978-1-53614-503-8
RETAIL PRICE: $230

To see a complete list of Nova publications, please visit our website at www.novapublishers.com